Empire Builder in the Texas Panhandle

NUMBER ONE:
West Texas A&M University Series
Gerald A. Craven, General Editor

William Henry Bush in the 1920s. Courtesy Bush-Emeny Trust, Amarillo

EMPIRE BUILDER
IN THE TEXAS PANHANDLE

WILLIAM HENRY BUSH

Paul H. Carlson

Texas A&M University Press
College Station

First edition

The paper used in this book meets the minimum requirements
of the American National Standard for Permanence
of Paper for Printed Library Materials, Z39.48–1984.
Binding materials have been chosen for durability.

Library of Congress Cataloging-in-Publication Data

Carlson, Paul H., 1940–
William Henry Bush : empire builder in the Texas Panhandle / by Paul H. Carlson.—(West Texas A&M University series; no. 1)
p. cm.
Includes bibliographical references and index.
ISBN 0-89096-712-1
1. Bush, William Henry, 1849–1931. 2. Businessmen—Texas—Biography. 3. Texas Panhandle (Tex.)—Economic conditions. 4. Frontier and pioneer life—Texas—Texas Panhandle. I. Title. II. Series.
HC102.5.B874C37 1996
338.092—dc20
[B] 96-10628
CIP

For Ellen

&

for Wendy Bush O'Brien Marsh

CONTENTS

ILLUSTRATIONS

Preface

Clothing wholesaler, real estate manager, cattleman, wheat grower, and philanthropist, William Henry Bush (1849–1931) amassed a large fortune through careful management of his varied enterprises. Born in upstate New York, he learned entrepreneurial skills in Chicago and used them to make significant contributions to the development of Amarillo and the Texas Panhandle. He took part in the rebuilding of downtown Chicago after the Great Fire in 1871 and participated in the Panhandle cattle industry in its pioneer stages. He contributed to Amarillo's change from a raw frontier settlement in the 1880s into a community that dominated the greater Texas Panhandle in the 1930s.

An entrepreneur in the true sense of the word, Bush was versatile, and that was a key to his success. In 1869 he went into the clothing business in Chicago and shortly afterward entered real estate and manufacturing. He next entered western ranching and took advantage of petroleum mining when natural gas was discovered on his Texas ranch. An excellent manager of employees and able to adjust to a variety of situations, he directed his investments most of the time from Chicago, but he traveled to Amarillo regularly to examine his Panhandle properties. A prudent businessman, he made a profit in nearly all of his endeavors.

Bush was not always bent over his desk and his accounting books. He played golf, as memberships in several private golf clubs testify. He traveled extensively, taking his family on tours of Europe and the United States. At his large homes in Chicago and Amarillo, he enertained well but with grace and moderation. He encouraged the development of the Art Institute of Chicago, read widely but especially in history, and became a governing annual member of the Chicago Historical Society. He endowed libraries, parks, cemeteries, schools, and scholarships, and he provided large sums of money to charitable institutions.

Amarillo benefited from his activities. Bush assisted in attracting additional railroads to the city. He helped raise funds and donated land for a badly needed hospital. He encouraged development of a modern hotel and convinced an Illinois couple to take over its management. He promoted agricultural development by advertising the region's farming potential, an activity that brought many settlers to the Panhandle. In Amarillo he was an active participant in pushing forward material improvements of all kinds. In short, he consistently engaged in enterprises that helped lay the foundation for much that came after him.

His activities in the Panhandle place Bush among the first rank of his era, but his quiet nature meant that the activities of some of his more flamboyant contemporaries were better known than his. He was a man who in 1881 cast his future and his fortune with the region, an event that profited both Bush and the Texas Panhandle.

In the 1930s, an acquaintance of Bush's, looking back over the time they had spent in the Panhandle, wrote that both had lived fifty years in Amarillo. They had looked across the plains and "reveled in their beauty." They had "endured hardships." They had "borne the burdens and carried the load," but they had "lived happily and prosperously." They had "blazed a way for the future. Now when we look back, we only dream of those old days," a time when "we were building an empire."[1]

The purpose of this work is to provide more than a biography of William H. Bush. Its broader purpose is to examine the economic growth of the Texas Panhandle, with emphasis on Amarillo, through tracing the life and work of a Chicago-based entrepreneur who played a little-known but important role in the area's history over a fifty-year period at the turn of the century. I have tried to show how a relatively unknown but large-scale Texas landowner, by adjusting to the shifting economic currents of his day, helped to influence the development of Amarillo and the greater Panhandle region.

Acknowledgments

For help in completing this book, I am indebted to many people. Professor Thomas A. Britten of Briar Cliff College in Iowa provided major assistance in the early stages of research. He pored over old newspapers, collected information, offered many helpful criticisms of an early draft of the manuscript, and in general made possible timely completion of the work. I am heavily indebted to him.

Caroline Bush Emeny, W. H. Bush's daughter, was also helpful. We corresponded and spoke by telephone, and she thoughtfully agreed to a lengthy interview at her summer home on the Frying Pan Ranch. As we talked about Bush's life and work, the magnificent view from her blufftop home provided a sweeping panorama of Frying Pan range lands. She also reviewed several portions of the manuscript and offered many useful suggestions.

Her daughter, Mary T. Emeny, who lives on the ranch, allowed me free use of the Bush-Emeny Estate's Historical Files; she proved gracious and courteous during a Bush family gathering, when, as hostess, her attention was pulled in several directions. We climbed with her over barbed-wire fences and through tangled undergrowth to get a view of Tecovas Spring, the site of the original Frying Pan headquarters. With F. G. "Butch" Collard, manager of the Frying Pan farm and ranch lands, she directed a tour of the ranch.

In New York, Gordon Allen, Herm Ortlieb, Dawn Manzer, and Donald Ingersoll furnished information, gave assistance, and showed me the places of Bush's youth. Manzer, head of the William H. Bush Memorial Library, was particularly helpful.

Barbara Blankenhorn Kerst, Anne Blocker Bush, Roger Williams, Jr., and David Bush supplied insight and information. Kerst and William S. Bush, Jr., provided pictures.

Lisa Lambert of the Panhandle-Plains Historical Museum, too, was courteous and helpful. She and her staff, especially Betty L. Bustos, contributed pictures, afforded easy access to the several collections of Bush-related materials in the museum's archives, and assisted in collecting documents of all kinds.

Staff members at the Amarillo Public Library, especially Art Bort and Rob Groman, eased the task of working through the library's extensive William H. Bush Collection, including the large and important file of Bush letters. They were patient and gracious.

David J. Murrah and his staff at Texas Tech University's fine Southwest Collection were, as usual, competent and helpful. I used their books, tape recorders, archival materials, and knowledge of West Texas history. Their cooperation proved of enormous benefit in completing the book.

The Interlibrary Loan staff at the Texas Tech University Library efficiently secured information from distant places. Like the staffs at the Center for American History at the University of Texas at Austin, the Chicago Historical Society, and Chicago's Newberry Library, they helped to ease and speed my research. Bart Rychbosch and Althea H. Huber at the Art Institute of Chicago were particularly gracious in offering assistance.

Others who offered help include Douglas Hales on the Panhandle wheat industry and Bob Burton on Amarillo railroads. Siva Chambers produced the Frying Pan map from a base map provided by Garry L. Nall. Frederick W. Rathjen of the Panhandle-Plains Historical Society and Garry L. Nall of West Texas A&M University read portions of the manuscript and offered helpful criticism. Of course, I alone accept full responsibility for any omissions or errors of fact that may exist in this book.

Nobody provided more help than Wendy Bush O'Brien Marsh and Stanley Marsh 3 of Amarillo. Indeed, they were the ones who first suggested W. H. Bush as a subject for a biography. Their thoughtful assistance in gathering material, providing pictures, and securing interviews is appreciated. Stanley Marsh also contributed financial help, without which my many trips to Amarillo, Chicago, and

Martinsburg, New York, would have been impossible. I am deeply indebted to both of them.

My wife Ellen was always patient and understanding through the long hours I spent at a task I like to think she enjoyed nearly as much as I did. Her cooperation was important.

Empire Builder
in the Texas Panhandle

CHAPTER ONE

From New York to Chicago

Shortly before nine o'clock on a dry, windy Sunday night, October 8, 1871, flames burst from the stable at Patrick O'Leary's residence on DeKoven Street in Chicago, Illinois. Within minutes, the resulting fire consumed O'Leary's barn and moved to the homes of his neighbors. By ten o'clock, the fire, propelled by violent winds, had spread across the city's West Side "in two swaths so far and wide that all [fire] engines in [Chicago] were clanging on the streets, and the court-house bell, in the downtown section, was booming wildly, unceasingly."[1]

This was no ordinary fire. Gale-force winds from the southwest blew flames, some a hundred feet or more high, through the pine shanties of the neighborhood and carried them northward and eastward toward the business district. Believing that the Chicago River would stop the spreading blaze, people poured onto downtown streets to watch the horrifying conflagration. There was no chance of that, however. At midnight, the fire, a holocaust beyond control, jumped the river and brought panic to the fire-lit downtown area. Leaving behind everything they could not carry in wagons or on their backs, people stampeded northward to escape the conflagration. Through Monday's wee hours, men, women, and children fled along North Side streets toward a cemetery near Lincoln Park. Others ran toward Lake Michigan to seek refuge along its marshy shoreline or in its icy-cold waters.

Amid the throngs of screaming people hurrying through fire-lined streets was Will Bush. A brave young clerk for a downtown merchant, Bush ran to his firm's office on Dearborn Street, broke into the burning building, grabbed a cash box and some other company material, and, with hundreds of panic-stricken people about him, raced north across the Rush Street Bridge. Bush, among the last to cross the bridge and too late to make it safely to either the lake or the cemetery, hunkered down in a boggy spot of land north of the river, where, with thousands of others who were "trying to breathe in the suffocating heat," he waited out the raging fire as it "kept to its wind-driven task of finishing the business section and the North Side."[2]

The Great Fire was a turning point—for Bush and for the city. It marked a second birth for Chicago, a city that, like the mythical phoenix, soon rose from its own ashes. It marked as well the beginning of important changes for Bush, who at considerable risk to himself had saved his employers from total disaster. The rescue of the cash box, coupled with other events associated with the fire's aftermath, set Bush apart and aided his rise to prominence in Chicago's wholesale clothing industry. Not long afterward, Bush, although a successful Chicago businessman, acquired a sprawling southwestern cattle-raising operation—the Texas Panhandle's large and celebrated Frying Pan Ranch.

William Henry Bush was from a family that traces its roots in America to the early seventeenth century. His mother's ancestors, led by William Hills, came from England in 1632. Also of English heritage, his father's ancestors, led by John Bush, arrived in Boston three years later aboard the *Lyon*, perhaps the same ship that had carried his mother's people to Massachusetts.[3]

The Hills and the Bush families were members of the Puritan church, whose leaders required that all people coming to the Massachusetts Bay Colony in the 1630s be persons of "good character." Most Puritan immigrants of the period were either middle class "husbandmen" or artisans who engaged in a skilled craft or trade, and many of them enjoyed a high level of literacy.[4]

William Hills came to America from Upminster Parish in Essex County. He stopped briefly at Roxbury, Massachusetts, before moving to Hartford, Connecticut. In the Great Migration between 1630 and 1640, more than 60 percent of the New England Puritans, such as Hills, came to Massachusetts from a small parish in one of England's eastern counties. Two hundred years later, some of the Hills descendants were among the early settlers of the Black River Valley in upstate New York.[5]

John Bush, after his arrival in Boston, went north to Maine. Because Maine was a favorite destination of Puritan emigrants from Somerset, Devonshire, and Gloucestershire counties, he may have been from England's southwestern section, perhaps the Salisbury Plain. He settled briefly near Wells and then at Casco, both in Maine's extreme southern corner. Some time later, John and his wife Grace Walker Bush, who, like many good Puritans, named their children for Biblical characters, moved to Westfield, Massachusetts, in the southwestern portion of the growing New England colony.

The family remained near Westfield through several generations. Thus, at Westfield William H. Bush traces descent from John Bush and his wife Grace Walker, through their son Samuel (1650–1733) and his wife Mary; their son Ebenezer and his wife Merriam; their son Zachariah and his wife Mary Ann Loomis; and their son Zachariah II (1742–1811) and his wife Mary Falley.[6]

Zachariah Bush II, a fourth-generation descendent of John Bush, fought in the Revolutionary War. In fact, he participated in the "Lexington Alarm," the battle on April 19, 1775, between colonial minutemen and British troops at Lexington, Massachusetts, that started the American struggle for independence. Later he received from John Hancock, the famous Boston merchant and Revolutionary leader, a commission as major in a Massachusetts militia unit. A copy of the commission hangs in the William H. Bush Memorial Library at Martinsburg, New York.

In America, many of William H. Bush's ancestors became lumbermen, builders, and cabinetmakers who also engaged in farming. As they cleared nearby forests, the families often relocated to take advantage of new opportunities in virgin timberlands. Thus, about 1799, Maj. Zachariah Bush II moved with his family (a daughter and seven surviving boys) from Westfield to Turin Township in the same Black River country of upstate New York where some of the Hills family pioneered. Although they were among the first settlers in Turin, Zachariah, his wife Mary, and at least four of their children soon afterward moved a few miles north to Houseville, a tiny hamlet in the heart of New York's scenic Lewis County.[7]

Lewis County is part of the Adirondack Upland, a roughly circular hill and mountain country in the north-central part of the state. The region's mountains are formed of hard, ancient rocks that are among the oldest in North America. Many of the mountain peaks rise above four thousand feet. Famous for its beautiful scenery, sparkling lakes, rushing streams, splashing waterfalls, and purple-topped peaks, the Adirondack Upland is cut in its western portions by the northward-flowing Black River, which empties into the eastern end of Lake Ontario near Watertown. The river divides the Tug Hill Plateau, a high, flat, rocky area with fewer lakes and smaller mountains, on the west from the impressive Adirondack Mountains on the east. Soils in the area are thin and inadequate for most agriculture; but here nonetheless, on some of the finest dairy farms in America, families raise corn, poultry, and milch and beef cattle. Other people in the region make a living at lumbering, and there is some dairying and a little mining of iron, lead, titanium, and zinc. In the second half of the twentieth century, the tourist industry assumed greater importance in the local economy.

Houseville began about 1801, when Eleazer House, an owner of extensive farmland in the area, built a hotel at the site. When the Bushes arrived, the hotel was still under construction. Located along a recently completed state road (now New York Route 26), the building was perhaps the town's main reason for existence. Described as "the best representative of the old-fashioned hotels for which [the state road] was noted," the structure, with "its ample barns, its open inviting sheds, and its watering trough, its ball-room, and its barroom," attracted many overnight travelers and community residents. Zachariah and his sons opened a sawmill on House Creek southwest of the village.[8]

Houseville remained a quiet village. With a population of about one hundred people in 1850, the community contained a Methodist church, a neatly fenced graveyard, a tavern and restaurant, a store, a blacksmith shop, a post office, and the hotel. There was in 1875 a cheese factory "some distance to the east" and "a mile east on House's creek [was] a grist-mill." Most families lived along a quarter-mile of the state road that in summer was darkened by the shade of large maple trees. The Bush home stood a block west of the main road through town.[9]

William H. Bush's grandfather, Henry Bush (1781–1837), the seventh and youngest son of Zachariah II and Mary, was about twenty years old when the family settled in Houseville. After his father's death in 1811, Henry and two of his brothers continued to run the sawmill. Meanwhile, in 1808 Henry married Clarissa House, a niece of Eleazer House. The marriage produced two daughters, the youngest just four months old when Clarissa died in 1813. Eight months later, Henry married Sarah Rockwell of Turin. They had seven children.

Bush's father, James Bush (1821–1884), was the fourth child of Henry and Sarah Rockwell Bush. James married Caroline Lucretia Hills (1823–1875), a daughter of Russell Hills, a Methodist church leader in nearby Martinsburg. After their marriage in 1845, James settled at his wife's village, a hilltop community about four miles north of Houseville.[10]

Martinsburg, founded by Gen. Walter Martin at the turn of the nineteenth century, stands hard against the Tug Hill Plateau on high ground at the western edge of the Black River Valley. From Martinsburg, the view of the surrounding country, especially towards the Black River below it on the east, is magnificent, presenting an expansive panorama across a changing tableau of graceful woodlands, well-groomed farmlands, and the green-clad Adirondacks. The first settlers—farmers, lumbermen, and businessmen—came chiefly from places near Salem, New York, and Westfield, Massachusetts. Later, Irish immigrants, having completed work on the Black River Canal and finding the land and climate to their liking, established homes through the adjoining area. Although located in a rural, sparsely populated region, Martinsburg was the seat of Lewis County until 1864, when the local railroad, wanting to avoid construction up a difficult climb to the village, built its tracks on lower ground near the river and bypassed the community.[11]

In the meantime, James Bush, upon settling in Martinsburg (a community of 210 people in 1855), opened a cabinet shop along Roaring Brook on the southwestern edge of town. Here he built cabinets and other home furnishings of wood taken from the nearby forests. He also made butter tubs and cheese boxes for dairy farmers in the area. In a two-story building that he owned on the corner of State Road (New York Route 26) and Cemetery Road, which led west to the Martinsburg Cemetery, he rented space on the ground floor to J. H.

Williams and L. M. Dunton, who operated a general merchandise store there for many years. On the second floor he may have operated, for a brief time, an "Undertaking Establishment."[12]

James and Caroline Bush resided on State Road adjacent to the store, in a home described in 1948 as "a smallish frame building with no architectural qualities."[13] In 1995, it was still occupied. Here Caroline Bush gave birth to nine children, three of whom died in infancy: James R., born February 10, 1847, died on March 30, 1848; Elizabeth, born December 6, 1851, died three days later; and Ella Amelia, born May 18, 1853, died on August 15, 1854.[14]

William H. Bush, born at his parents' home in Martinsburg on October 22, 1849, was the second of the nine children. The oldest of those who survived infancy, Will, as he was called, was four years old when his sister Emma Cornelia (the twin sister of Ella Amelia) was born in 1853. The others who reached adulthood were Harriet Northam (born in 1855), Clarissa Bell (born in 1858), Edwin Samuel (born in 1860), and Mary Katherine (born in 1866). All six of the children eventually moved west to live in Illinois, Missouri, or California.[15]

The children received what education the country school of Martinsburg offered. Will may have, in addition, briefly attended the state academy at Lowville, a few miles north of Martinsburg and after 1864 the county seat, where he was to prepare himself for college. But, according to his daughter, he received little more than "a sixth-grade education." Nonetheless, his education emphasized classical literature, writing, mathematics, geography, and spelling, with a heavy dose of western morality and virtue. It included a solid grounding in basic subjects standard at the time, and it imbued in him a love of reading "'all good books' no matter of what nature."[16]

Will's father, James Bush, described as "very tall and thin with fair skin, light brown hair and twinkling blue eyes," was popular among the Martinsburg boys. On several occasions, James took his sons and a few of their youthful companions on camping trips—"excursions" they were called—to Whetstone Gulf, a splendid camping site a few miles south of the village and near Houseville, Mr. Bush's youthful home. Perhaps the King boys (Henry, Charles, and Philo), sons of William King, who owned a hardware store in Martinsburg, went along; and perhaps James convinced his brother Henry in Houseville to bring his sons (Guilford, Stanley, Charles, and Herbert) on the trips.[17]

Called "one of the most spectacular scenic vistas east of the Rocky Mountains," Whetstone Gulf is a steep-walled, three-mile-long gorge cut by Whetstone Creek into the eastern edge of the Tug Hill Plateau. Here James Bush taught the boys to fish, trap, cook over an open fire, and handle other responsibilities of camp life. They also enjoyed swimming in the creek and hunting and hiking in the gulf. Around an evening campfire deep within the gulf's towering walls, James told stories and taught the boys songs.[18]

The popular camping place today is part of Whetstone Gulf State Park. A recreation area since the early 1800s, the State Board of Park Commissioners purchased the 522-acre site in 1928. The State Conservation Department and the federal Civilian Conservation Corps developed the park in the 1930s, planting thousands of trees, building roads, and clearing brush. Red pines, spruce, and maples make up the bulk of the park's trees. A trail, six miles in length, extends along both sides of the gulf and crosses the creek at the gulf's upper end. The view from the rim of Whetstone Gulf is one of "wild and spectacular scenery."[19]

Will Bush must have enjoyed the trips to Whetstone Gulf, for he went with his father on several of them. He participated in many other recreational activities as well, including sledding on snow in the winter, skating on frozen ponds, hunting or trapping in the woods, fishing and swimming in the lakes and rivers in the summer, and wrestling in any season of the year. When he was about eleven or twelve years old, according to his descendants, Will and an older cousin (perhaps Guilford, Stanley, or Charles, from Houseville) walked sixty miles south to Utica, sleeping in haystacks along the way, to see one of the early trains travel through upstate New York on tracks of the New York Central Railroad.[20]

Closer to home, Will Bush enjoyed outings at Whitaker Falls. A 345-acre tract of woodlands and clearings bordered by Roaring Brook (a lively stream that breaks over a series of striking, pristine waterfalls that gave the place its name), Whitaker Falls was a popular site near Martinsburg for swimming, hiking, and general community outings. Because Daniel Whitaker and his family made the place available to the public, villagers—attracted by "the natural beauty of the falls, the terraces of limestone that wall its gorges, [and] the beautiful maple grove bordering the northern rim"—used it for picnics and camping from Martinsburg's early days of settlement. Called "one of the region's hidden jewels," Whitaker Park offers its visitors one of Lewis County's best views of the sweeping Black River Valley and the majestic beauty of the Adirondack Mountains. Whitaker Falls was one of Bush's favorite places as a youth; as an adult he saw to its preservation as public park land.[21]

Like most other boys of his day, Will Bush started working while still a youth. In 1863, when he was fourteen, the Smith and Pitcher General Store in Martinsburg hired him at twelve dollars per month to clerk and handle various duties associated with a small country store. He worked there in 1863 and 1864, after which, without his father's consent, he may have left Martinsburg briefly. According to his descendants, Will ran away, hoping to become a drummer boy for a New York volunteer regiment fighting in the Civil War. An uncle—so the story goes—brought him home. In 1866 he moved to Constableville, about fourteen miles south of Martinsburg, where he worked in the mercantile firm of Seth T. Miller and Son for two hundred dollars a year plus board. He stayed there for two years, before taking a position, in September 1868, with A. H. Tyler and Co. of Lyons Falls, a few miles closer to Martinsburg.[22]

Five months later, on February 22, 1869, William H. Bush left the beautiful Black River country. Except for occasional visits to see his father and mother, or later to show the area to his own family, he seldom returned. But the region held a prominent place in his heart. In later years he subscribed to the *Lowville Journal* to keep up with news of "dear old Martinsburg," as he called it.[23] He purchased a thirty-seven-acre tract of land adjacent to Whitaker Park (to ease public access to the campgrounds) and provided funds for maintenance of the park property. He also set aside money for maintaining Martinsburg Cemetery, where his parents, a brother, and two sisters are buried; and he endowed a public library in Martinsburg, now named the William H. Bush Memorial Library. An attractive brick facility, in 1995 it contained an archive of local materials and a small museum as well as the efficient and well-kept library.

Bush headed for Chicago, no doubt attracted by the city's fabulous rise as a leading business and industrial center. Founded in 1803 and incorporated as a city in 1837, Chicago grew rapidly; by 1850 its population had reached almost thirty thousand inhabitants. Ten years later, it was the largest city in Illinois. During the 1860s, an unprecedented population boom occurred, influenced in part by the city's growth as a meat packing center following the Civil War and by an expanding market in wheat and other grains that soon allowed the Chicago Board of Trade to dominate the country's enormous grain market. Manufacturing, including heavy industry, also thrived, as Cyrus Hall McCormick and others produced much-needed machinery for the growing number of farms on the prairies and plains of the Midwest. The completion of the Union Pacific Railroad in 1869 gave Chicago a direct route to the West Coast, and by 1870 almost three hundred thousand persons lived in the city.

When he arrived in Chicago, Bush was nineteen years old. Although he had enjoyed only limited schooling, his education was firmly grounded in basic subjects, and he had several years of merchandising experience. Like his father, he was tall and thin, but with a large, round head, high forehead, and prominent nose. His dark, narrow-set eyes sparkled when he talked, and he gave off a aura of confidence and ability. Possessing a friendly, open personality, he brought with him to Chicago a "singleness of purpose," an ability to "work hard," and "the benefits of persistence." A former employer, Seth Miller, called him a "pleasant, agreeable, and attentive young man."[24]

With Chicago booming in 1869, Bush found employment without difficulty. Indeed, he may have been encouraged to go west by Henry William King, a former Martinsburg resident who operated one of the largest wholesale clothing firms in Chicago. Bush, who may have worked briefly for Henry King, soon entered the wholesale clothing business as a clerk and general helper with King Brothers and Company, founded by Charles B. and Philo R. King, Henry's brothers. He received a wage of ten dollars per week, from which he paid seven dollars a week for room and board at a rooming house near Lake Michigan, about seven blocks from his workplace. Both his responsibilities and his wages at the firm increased rapidly, however, and in 1872, just three years after beginning his work for King Brothers, Philo King (Charles had died) made him a partner.[25]

Bush's rapid climb grew from disaster. The Great Chicago Fire in 1871, which burned 17,450 structures located in a stretch of land nearly a mile wide and four miles long, destroyed the King Brothers building on Dearborn Street south of the Chicago River, in the heart of the central business district. Occurring on October 8, the fire left ninety thousand people, including Bush, homeless as winter approached, and the financial damage to King Brothers "was not less than $200,000."[26]

But, during the fire, Bush ran the seven blocks from his boarding house to the firm's office, secured a cash box and a ledger book belonging to the company, and hurried north across the Rush Street bridge over the Chicago River. His actions saved the firm from complete financial ruin. He spent a terrifying night with the cash box and ledger book among thousands of frightened people and nervous horses in a swampy stretch of land near present Washington Square, watching the fire rage out of control around him, as, wind-blown, it raced northward before burning itself out in a light rainfall near the southern and western edges of present Lincoln Park late Monday afternoon. Tired and dirty but safe, William emerged to examine the terrible devastation.[27]

Strong, single, and accountable only for himself and to his employers, W. H. Bush (as he was sometimes called), in the days and weeks that followed the tragedy, accepted responsibility for seeing to the needs of King Brothers employees, directed operations at a temporary facility out of the fire zone in West Chicago, where he now roomed, and hustled to secure merchandise from manufacturers in New York so that King Brothers could meet some of its obligations to customers. Soon wooden buildings and temporary shacks and tents were going up in the burned-over district and "stoves and bedding etc. [were] coming by thousands." The close attention to detail and the vigorous approach with which Bush assumed his new duties pushed him toward the top. Aurelia King, sister-in-law to Philo and the deceased Charles King, wrote that "the hope and cheerfulness which our business men preserve is wonderful."[28]

There followed an active period in Bush's career, perhaps the busiest of his young life. The wholesale clothing business succeeded beyond expectations, and as Bush took on greater responsibilities in its management after the 1871 fire, he put aside a good portion of his substantial earnings and invested in burned-out land on Chicago's Near North Side. The fire provided investment and other opportunities in the city's rebuilding process, and he boldly participated in the new ventures. In addition to purchases north of the river, he eventually secured, he wrote, "considerable real estate on the South and West sides" of the downtown district.[29]

Bush met and began to court Elva Frances Glidden of DeKalb, Illinois. The daughter of a local farmer and businessman, Elva was born in DeKalb on December 29, 1851. The couple met in the mid–1870s, while Bush, in his capacity as a salesman for King Brothers, visited her town. Not many months passed before Bush was making regular visits to her home, but the history of the courtship is not recorded. He was twenty-eight years old and had accumulated $28,000—a significant sum of money for that time—when he asked Elva (she was twenty-six) to be his wife. The couple married on February 1, 1877, in DeKalb, and after the marriage they returned to Chicago.[30]

Early in the courtship, Bush's mother died. Caroline was only fifty-two when she passed away in Martinsburg on January 26, 1875, and her youngest child Mary was just nine years old. Her husband buried her in the Martinsburg Cemetery on a plot of ground near the graves of her three deceased children. Although unable to attend the funeral, Bush returned to Martinsburg shortly afterward to visit his father (James) and other members of his family (Emma, Harriet, Clarissa, Edwin, and Mary) who remained in the village of his youth. He visited his mother's gravesite and walked to Whitaker Falls to see again this popular place of his youth.

Not many years after Caroline died, Bush's father married Emma Ackerman of Houseville and brought her back to Martinsburg. Tragedy ended the marriage rather quickly, however, for, on August 11, 1884, while Emma was pregnant with their only child, James Bush died at age sixty-three. Upon her husband's death, Emma moved back to Houseville, where on March 16, 1885, her son James Ackerman Bush—W. H.'s half-brother—was born.[31]

Not yet thirty-five years old, William H. Bush became head of the family. He aided his stepmother's adjustment in New York and made arrangements for his brother and sisters to come to Chicago at such time when they felt they were ready to leave Martinsburg. Over the next few years, each of them received Bush's assistance in one way or another, and each spent time at Bush's home in Chicago.[32]

As these sad events occurred in New York, Bush prospered in Chicago. He continued to invest in land on the city's Near North Side, where, after the fire, a construction boom drove up the price of downtown real estate. A year after the fire, the city's *Lakeside Monthly* reported that "land values had risen well above their prefire levels." The rising land values made housing "too expensive for most residential use." People such as Bush "who owned, managed, and financed the industrial and warehouse districts," writes William Cronon, "did much of their work in the downtown office buildings, but they too moved their homes away from city center."[33] One of the wealthiest of Chicago's housing districts stretched northward along the shore of Lake Michigan.

Here, at 606 North State Street, Bush constructed a large, comfortable home. Located near North Avenue, about two miles from his downtown business, his house was one of the first built north of Division Street. His brother Edwin and younger sisters came to Chicago at different times and lived briefly in the home with Bush and their sister-in-law before marriage or other events led them to new opportunities. Bush continued his association with the King Brothers Company, which had rebuilt its warehouse and opened offices on Monroe Street in the heart of the business district.

Meanwhile, Bush's marriage had brought him into contact with Joseph Farwell Glidden, his father-in-law, who farmed some fifteen hundred acres of rich prairie land west of Chicago.[34] Joseph F. Glidden, born in New Hampshire in 1813 but reared in New York, had worked his way west. Between 1842 and 1844, with two crude threshing machines for harvesting grain, he hired himself and the machines to farmers to use during the fall harvest seasons. At DeKalb, Illinois, he purchased a small farm and over the years added to his holdings. He served a term as sheriff of DeKalb County in 1852–53. After seeing an exhibit of barbed wire at the county fair in 1873, Glidden began tinkering with the wire and on October 27 applied for a patent on his product. Almost immediately others challenged his patent rights, and interference proceedings followed; but, a year later, on November 24, 1874, Glidden received a patent (No. 157,124) for an effective product that incorporated sharp barbs twisted into two strands of wire.[35]

Glidden in the meantime had asked Isaac L. Ellwood, a close friend and DeKalb hardware dealer, to purchase, for $265, half interest in the pending patent. When Ellwood accepted in 1874, the two men established the Barb Fence Company in DeKalb to manufacture barbed wire. Their company was an immediate success, and it struggled to keep up with the demand for its product. In the spring of 1876, Glidden, perhaps because of his advancing age, sold his share in the operation to the Washburn and Moen Manufacturing Company of Worcester, Massachusetts, for $10,000 cash and a promissory note for $50,000 at 7 percent annual interest. In addition, Glidden was to receive royalties of up to twenty-five cents per each hundred pounds of wire manufactured during the life of the patent, which expired in 1891. By 1883, Washburn and Moen, which in 1899 became the American Steel and Wire Company of New Jersey, had established a large, two-story building in DeKalb that produced about six hundred miles of barbed wire each day.[36]

Glidden had become wealthy and influential. In 1883, he helped to organize the DeKalb National Bank and became its vice-president. He bought the DeKalb Roller Grist Mill. He built and operated the Glidden Hotel, and he held interests in the *DeKalb Chronicle* and the Glidden Felt Pad Manufacturing Company. To encourage its location at DeKalb, he gave a large tract of his land to the Northern Illinois State Normal School (Northern Illinois University), established in 1895. Glidden became a director of the Chicago, Northwestern Railroad. Although he had invested heavily in ranch land in Texas, he continued to live in Illinois, running his farm in DeKalb County and participating in his DeKalb businesses. In 1889 he was worth an estimated one million dollars.[37]

Bush became a personal and professional confidante and trusted agent of his famous father-in-law. The relationship benefited both men. Bush, for example, in 1881 went to Texas to inspect Glidden's range land and to oversee the construction of a barbed-wire fence around the Glidden property. The seventy-two-year-old Glidden provided encouragement and financial backing for his son-in-law in 1885, when Bush either left King Brothers to start his own wholesale hat business or, more likely, purchased the King firm.[38]

In 1885, Bush, with his brother-in-law Francis T. Simmons (husband of Harriet), established Bush, Simmons and Company, a wholesale hat and glove dealership. The two men, with Bush serving as president and treasurer, located the firm at 241 Monroe Street in the heart of the Chicago business district; soon afterward their company, having acquired many of King Brothers' former clients, was prospering. They dealt in hats, caps, and ladies' kid gloves sold at stores throughout Chicago—which by 1890 had more than a million inhabitants and ranked second only to New York City in population—

and its expanding suburbs. The company extended its sales across Illinois; into Michigan, Indiana, Iowa, Nebraska, and Missouri; and to the Upper Midwest of Wisconsin and Minnesota.[39]

Although active with his own company, Bush continued to travel once or twice nearly every year to Glidden's ranch in the Texas Panhandle. He inspected the cattle and horse herds, met with the ranch managers, checked on the condition of the range, studied the account and ledger books, and helped in preparations for the annual cattle and horse sales. As there was no rail service to Amarillo until 1887, the trips were difficult and time-consuming affairs that kept Bush away from Chicago, his wife Elva, and his clothing business sometimes for several weeks. Each year after 1881, he took a greater interest in the Panhandle, and his letters to the ranch managers suggest not only that he represented Glidden well but also that his responsibilities for management of the ranching enterprise increased through the years.[40]

Although busy, Bush found time for other activities. He joined the Chicago Club, an organization of the city's elite businessmen and political leaders, who paid a large initiation fee and substantial annual dues. There was, nonetheless, a long waiting list of Chicago businessmen who wanted to join. In 1885 the club had five hundred members who were "largely of the firmly established in wealth." In 1892, the club purchased a building facing Lake Michigan near Michigan Avenue and Van Buren. Designed by John W. Root in Romanesque style, the structure had housed the Art Institute of Chicago. In its large clubrooms, members staged brilliant social events and entertained celebrities who visited Chicago. They also made business contacts, played whist and other card games, and discussed local politics. Bush walked to the building for lunch each business day.[41]

Bush also joined the Iroquois Club, a Democratic political body, and participated in its important functions. His association with the group brought him into close contact with John Peter Altgeld, who was the liberal Democratic governor of Illinois from 1893 to 1897. Bush used his contacts at the Iroquois Club to promote the continued development of Chicago's grand Lincoln Park, one of his favorite public activities. His leisure reading included history, and as his financial responsibilities in the Panhandle increased, he turned to books on Texas and the Southwest, collecting a large number of them.[42]

At home there were dinners and other social functions, and he and Elva drove their carriage along roads on the Lake Michigan shoreline. They joined the fashionable Fourth Presbyterian Church on Chestnut Street, where they were active members, with Bush becoming a trustee of the church. Because his marriage to Elva did not produce children, there were in his household no little ones with whom he might share his time. However, he and Elva often enjoyed the company of Harriet and Francis Simmons, a lively storyteller and amateur magician who later became prominent on the Chicago Parks Board. Harriet and Francis had a son, born in 1884 and named William Bush Simmons, and a daughter, Kathryn, born in 1892.

An uncle popular with his sister's children and intensely loyal to family and friends, Bush epitomized the proper Victorian gentleman. He seemed always to be neatly, carefully, and formally dressed. He did not smoke, and he confined his alcohol consumption to an occasional glass of fine wine. Reserved but comfortable in the company of his peers, Bush enjoyed the deep respect of his friends and business associates as well as his family. His opinions about business matters, especially real estate, received thoughtful attention.[43]

By 1892, William Henry Bush had become closely involved with activities in Texas. He and Glidden, now seventy-nine years old and more interested in his DeKalb County farm than in Texas ranch lands, had agreed in 1881 that, for his participation in developing the ranch, Bush would receive an interest in the property. Bush, as a result, had turned his attention more and more to the Southwest and to the proper management of the Texas Panhandle's Frying Pan Ranch.

CHAPTER TWO

The Frying Pan Ranch

One of the better-known institutions in the Panhandle, the Frying Pan Ranch began operations in 1881, when Henry B. Sanborn and Joseph F. Glidden entered the booming western cattle industry. The men purchased an enormous amount of territory and freely occupied adjoining land that the State of Texas had set aside for support of its schools. After it was fenced in 1882, the Frying Pan enclosed about 250,000 acres of land, most of which was located in the western half of Potter County below the Canadian River and stretching southward into the northern reaches of Randall County. Treeless (except in the creek bottoms and draws and around a few springs) and grass-covered, the range made ideal pasture for the large cattle and horse herds that cowhands drove through the new gates to begin operations on what has become one of the most celebrated ranches of the Texas Panhandle.

Potter County, home of the Frying Pan Ranch, is located on the northern edge of the Llano Estacado. At an altitude of approximately 3,600 feet and situated west of the 100th meridian, the county is part of the Western High Plains. It consists mostly of level land but contains rolling features associated with the wide Canadian River, which cuts a deep east-west trough through the county. The river and its tributary streams break the flat landscape into a series of gullies, draws, and washes. The soils are sandy, sandy loam, and clay. The summers are hot and dry, while the winters are relatively cold, with January's low temperatures averaging about twenty-four degrees. The county receives an average annual rainfall of only twenty inches.[1] Pictures of the Frying Pan Ranch dating from the 1890s are striking for their wide vistas, the absence of trees, and the general emptiness of the land.

Originally part of the huge Bexar Land District, which the state had established in 1846, Potter County with twenty-five other Panhandle counties came into existence in 1876 to provide a basis for organizing local governments. With such preparations made and Fort Elliott—established in 1875 in present Wheeler County—offering some protection and support to settlers, pioneers entered the region. Mobeetie, near Fort Elliott, and Clarendon, in Donley County, were the first towns in the eastern Panhandle to receive settlers. In the western Panhandle, Tascosa, in present Oldham County near the Canadian River and closer to Frying Pan lands, was the first substantial community.

Established by New Mexican *pastores* (sheepherders) in 1876, Tascosa was one of several Hispanic plazas that appeared along the Canadian River and its tributaries in the mid-1870s. Sheepherders from New Mexico, seeking to extend their ranges, pushed their animals eastward down the Canadian, located favorable sites at springs or along streams that provided permanent water, and set about grazing their flocks on the upland divides where grass was plentiful.[2]

One of the plazas was located at Tecovas (covering) Spring, about five miles northwest of modern Bushland, along Tecovas Creek in Potter County. The future site of the Frying Pan's headquarters, Tecovas was "a fine, bold spring of very cold water," the state geologist indicated in 1891, where "cedar in abundance grows along the bluffs of the Plains and cottonwood along the creeks." He indicated that his party had found in the "hollows a great quantity of wild grapes that were just ripening, and which were very sweet to the taste." On the plains (the Llano Estacado) south of the Canadian River breaks, he noted that "the plateau is very level and covered with a thick growth of mesquite grass."[3]

Before their confinement to reservations in New Mexico or Indian Territory (Oklahoma) after the Red River War in 1874–75, American Indians had used Tecovas Spring for generations. The spot was a favorite stopping place for Apaches, Comanches, Kiowas, and perhaps other Indian peoples before them who hunted bison, pronghorn, and other game on the Llano Estacado. A daughter of one of the early ranch managers remembered gathering arrowheads near

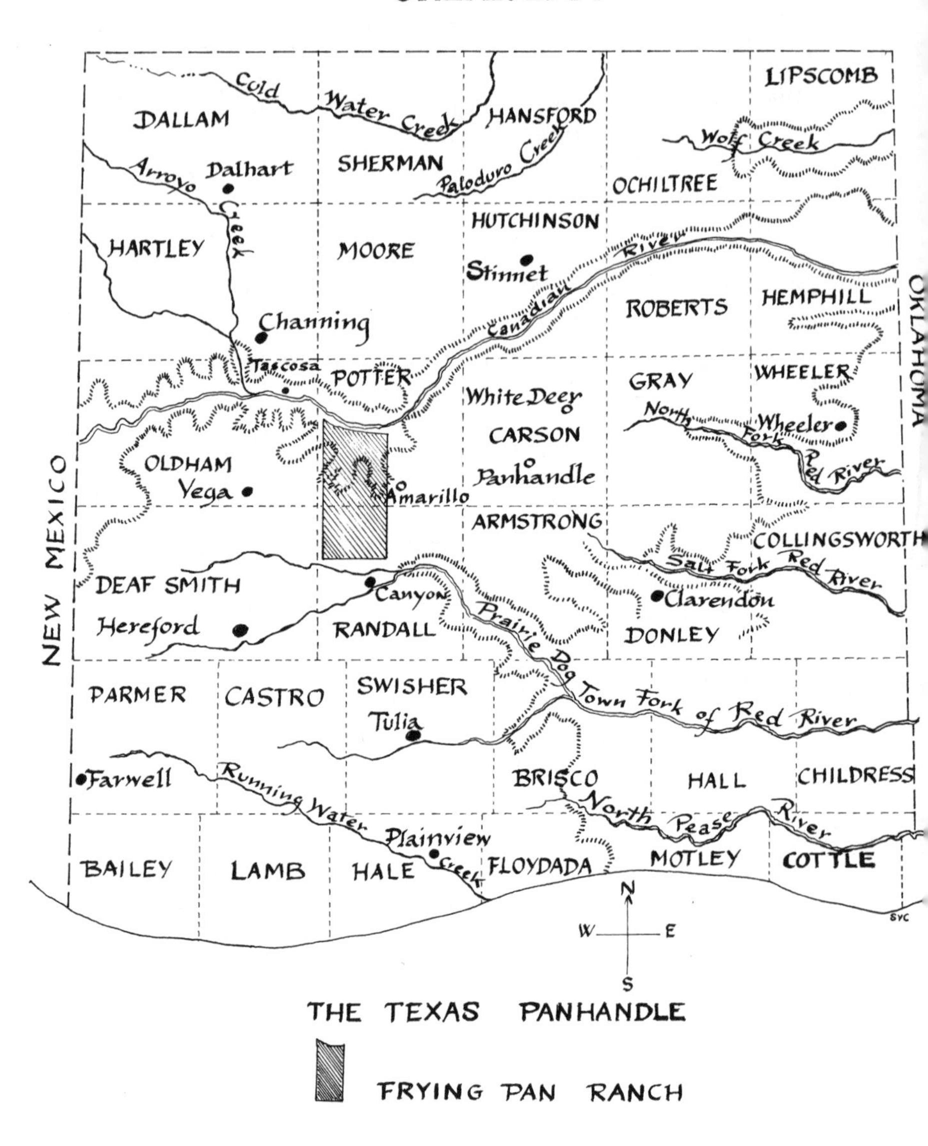

the spring. "We used to play with them all the time," she said. "There were just worlds of them out . . . there."[4]

Comancheros (traders) had also used Tecovas Spring. Mainly Pueblo Indian people and Hispanics from New Mexican villages, the *comancheros* went out to the plains to trade the agricultural and craft products of the villagers for the mules, horses, meat, and bison hides of the Plains Indians. The favorite trading sites, such as Tecovas Spring, were along river courses, at water holes, in canyons, or near lakes that Indian people for a century or more had used as camps. *Ciboleros* (bison hunters) from New Mexico likewise stopped at Tecovas Spring, and between 1875 and 1878 the place served as a watering hole for Anglo hide men during the great Southern Plains bison slaughter.

The *pastores* who had located at Tecovas Spring built a stone corral to hold their animals and an adobe structure, presumably a residence, for themselves. Their operations at the site were small, however, and never matched those at many of the other Canadian River plazas.

As Anglo cattlemen, led by the colorful Charles Goodnight, began to enter the Canadian Valley in the late 1870s, the New Mexican sheepherders found their range restricted. Not long afterward, they began to pull out of their Canadian River–based plazas, leaving behind the rock corrals and adobe structures. But for several years the sheepherders and cattlemen coexisted in the Panhandle, and Tascosa continued to survive as a colorful stage stop, supply center, and ranch-hand "watering hole." As late as 1880, there were still more sheep than cattle in the Panhandle, and "ranchmen in the region still owned only about 75,000 acres of Panhandle property."[5]

Quickly afterwards, conditions changed. Land-speculating syndicates, including one put together in New York, had entered the Panhandle soon after the creation of its twenty-six counties in 1876. The New York firm, headed by R. C. Beaty, had received land scrip in southwestern Potter and northwestern Randall counties as payment for dredging rivers in East Texas. Hoping to sell its Texas land and thus make money for its work in the state, the firm advertised its Panhandle property in newspapers and other outlets. Its patent included land that became the Frying Pan Ranch, for Glidden in DeKalb saw one of its sales notices in the *New York Times*.[6]

A Chicago group, called the Capitol Syndicate Company, between 1883 and 1888 built the new Texas State House in Austin and received land scrip as payment for the construction of the capitol. According to Seymour Connor, "It had been the original intention of the Syndicate to sell its lands to recover the cost of construction, which amounted to over three million dollars." The lack of a market, however, forced the company to utilize its land (slightly over three million acres), which stretched along the New Mexico border in the

Panhandle, as the XIT Ranch, in the hope that demand from farmer-stockmen and other settlers would improve and land prices would increase.[7]

Jot Gunter and W. B. Munson, lawyers in Sherman, in Grayson County, Texas, led another speculating company. With a contract from the state to survey Panhandle counties, later including the huge XIT grant, in exchange for land scrip, they sent to the Panhandle their surveyors John Summerfield, W. S. Mabry, and E. C. McLean, who, in about 1879 or 1880, rediscovered Tecovas Spring.

Summerfield and his employers may have been attempting to locate a good ranching site for Henry B. Sanborn, sometimes called the "Father of Amarillo," and his longtime friend and partner in Illinois, Joseph F. Glidden. Sanborn, an enormously successful salesman in Texas for Glidden's Barb Fence Company and its successor, the Washburn and Moen Manufacturing Company of Worcester, Massachusetts, had, in the fall of 1876, purchased a tract of some 2,000 acres about twelve miles west of Sherman. He continued purchasing adjacent lands until he owned 10,300 acres, on which he raised Percheron and French Coach horses, mules, improved cattle, and other livestock. Sanborn knew Gunter and Munson, and Glidden and Sanborn wanted to invest in the country's booming open-range cattle industry.[8]

The western range-cattle industry, which had experienced financial ups and downs in the 1870s, was in the early 1880s attracting unprecedented eastern and foreign investment capital. Seeking easy profits, and perhaps caught up in myths prevalent about western cattle ranching, hundreds of individuals organized land and cattle companies, bought livestock, and secured ranges, either through purchase or by free occupation of the land. In the 1880s, they established some of the largest and most colorful ranches of the American West, including the Matador Land and Cattle Company, the XIT Ranch, and the Pitchfork Land and Cattle Company. Most of the operations soon went bankrupt, but the ranches that survived the difficulties of the mid–1880s, including the Frying Pan, not only form part of America's enduring western heritage, but also continue to attract popular attention and scholarly interest.[9]

Several other factors precipitated the great western cattle boom. American Plains Indians, in 1880, were living on reservations and thus occupied smaller amounts of territory than they had previously.

Several railroads crossed the plains, and others were edging toward the region. Money was plentiful in the East, and investors were seeking outlets for it. Bison were close to extinction, and cattle prices again were rising. As a result, easterners, Englishmen, Scotsmen, Canadians, Australians, and others, wrote Walter Prescott Webb, "flocked to the Plains to become ranchers, to the amusement of the cowboys and to the disgust of the ranchmen, to whom cattle-raising was just an ordinary way of making a living."[10]

Consequently, upon locating Tecovas Spring, Summerfield as quickly as possible reached Sanborn, who, with his partner Judson P. Warner, had established a sales office in Houston, Texas. Summerfield "reported the spring's continual flow of fresh water," described the surrounding area's rich grazing potential, and encouraged Sanborn to take steps to secure the land. Convinced that the site was ideal for the ranching venture he and Glidden had in mind, Sanborn informed Glidden of Summerfield's information. When Glidden consented, the two men in 1881 completed negotiations through the Gunter and Munson law firm for the purchase of ninety-five sections of land in the area around Tecovas Spring. Soon afterward, having secured loans from Isaac L. Ellwood and P. L. Moen, they purchased an additional one hundred sections, paying less than two dollars an acre for the land.[11]

Sanborn and Glidden immediately determined to fence their range. From the Washburn and Moen Company of Worcester, Massachusetts, they secured, wrote William H. Bush, a special order for a number of train-car "loads of barb wire to be made in a special way. It was to be #9 Galvanized wire, which is about 50% heavier" than most wire used at the time, "and it was the first and only order they ever made of this heavy wire."[12] They sent Warren W. Wetzel of Grayson County, who knew and may have worked for Sanborn, to supervise construction of the fence, and William Henry Bush, representing Glidden's interests, left Chicago en route to the ranch.[13]

Wetzel, who recently had married in New York and brought his bride Katherine ("Kate") back to Sherman, arrived at the ranch first. He established a base of operations at Tecovas Spring, hired men, and located the boundaries along which to build the fence. Not long afterward, he sent for his bride. She traveled by train to Dodge City, Kansas, and from there took a stage south to Mobeetie, a distance of some two hundred miles. The passengers rode "day and night for thirty-six hours, getting their meals at the stage stands" while men exchanged the tired teams of horses for fresh ones. Wetzel met her at Mobeetie, and a hired hand drove them in a spring wagon the seventy-five miles to the Frying Pan. For a few weeks in 1881, the Wetzels lived in a tent at the Tecovas Spring while workmen dug a temporary home into the side of a hill, using rock for the front of the dugout. "This does not sound so nice," said Katherine Wetzel years afterward, "but the room was a large comfortable one, warm in winter, cool in summer."[14]

Bush took the Santa Fe Railroad to Springer, New Mexico. From there he went by stagecoach to Tascosa, and by spring wagon to Tecovas Spring, sleeping on the ground each of the four nights and five days required to make the trip. "On our way to Tascosa," Bush wrote many years later, "we met a great many covered wagons with families going back East, as they heard there had been an uprising of the Indians and several people killed." Bush and his companions "pushed right ahead and were never able to verify the rumor."[15]

On the last day of the trip, Bush and his wagon driver left Tascosa early in the morning. Night fell before they reached the ranch headquarters, and there was no moon. After several hours of travel in the dark, Bush suggested to the driver that they stop and finish the trip the next morning. The driver located a small creek, and beside it they made camp. Upon arising the next morning, they found that in fact they had arrived at their destination. The headquarters, consisting of five tents with a dugout under construction, was up the creek only a few hundred yards away.[16]

The barbed wire came by train to Dodge City, Kansas. From there teamsters hauled part of it by ox-wagon to Tascosa, about twenty-five miles northwest of Tecovas Spring, and then on to the ranch. "Our ledger and cash account," wrote Bush, "shows this 105 miles of fence cost about $39,000."[17]

When Bush arrived in the fall, Wetzel and the hired hands were already at work on the fence. Wetzel had contracted Levi McClellan, a young cowhand in the area, to provide cedar posts from Palo Duro Canyon, about forty miles away; Hispanic workmen from Tascosa and Las Vegas, New Mexico, cut posts in the Sierrita de la Cruz Creek breaks in the northwest corner of the ranch for the northern part of the fence. With two crews at work (one on the east line and one on the west), the men placed the posts in the ground two rods apart and strung four strands of wires along the line of posts, with stays halfway between each post to hold the wires in place.

When the weather permitted them to work, the men built fence through the winter and into the next spring, enclosing an area about thirty miles long (north to south) and about fifteen miles wide. They also ran an east-west fence through the middle of the property to divide the plains from the breaks of the Canadian River and enclosed a couple of small pastures near the headquarters. The Frying Pan was among the first of the western ranches entirely enclosing their property with a barbed-wire fence. "Our land comprised in this enclosure about 130,000 acres," wrote Bush, "and the alternate sections [were] 'school land' and belonged to the Government."[18]

Although Bush stayed only a few weeks, Wetzel directed the fence work through the winter. As construction progressed, five or six Hispanic workers began making large adobe bricks, four by eight by sixteen inches, for a headquarters building. From these they built a structure 20 feet wide and 180 feet long and divided into nine rooms, each 20 feet square, with no connecting interior doors. They erected a fireplace in a corner of each room and ran huge cottonwood ridgepoles down the center of the building. Willow boughs and brush covered with sod served as the roof. They placed a mortar-like substance on the floors in the kitchen and dining rooms. Plastered and whitewashed inside and out, the building, writes Laura V. Hamner, "was doubly worth the name of 'the White House.'" Located on a bluff overlooking Tecovas Spring, the headquarters could be seen for miles.[19]

As construction of the fence progressed at the ranch, Sanborn set about purchasing cattle. He secured small herds from various ranchers west of Grayson County and gathered most of the animals along the Pease River in Motley County. His cowboys held them there until they could be moved to the ranch in Potter County. He secured about fifteen thousand head.

Meanwhile, at his home near Sherman, Sanborn drew various brands in the dirt, seeking one to mark cattle at the ranch in the Panhandle. When at last he drew a circle and ran a bar out to one side of it, he determined to use it. Reportedly, he said: "That's it. That's the brand. This is the Panhandle ranch; this brand is a panhandle."[20] Because Bill Scarborough of Motley County previously had registered a similar design, Sanborn and Glidden purchased the brand from him.[21]

In the spring, about the time the fence was completed, Arch Childers (or Childs), a Sanborn employee from Grayson County, arrived to direct operations on the cattle ranges, and Wetzel assumed the position of bookkeeper and ranch manager—or superintendent, as Bush called him. Childers occupied a room at one end of the long adobe headquarters building, and Wetzel and his wife moved into the room at the other end of the structure. Soon afterward, Wetzel attached an extra room onto the side of his end of the building, giving the headquarters structure an L shape, and made the new room his office.[22]

When he returned to the Frying Pan in the spring of 1882, William H. Bush inspected the ranch. He found that Childers, with a dozen or more cowboys, had brought many of the cattle from the Pease River with him, and more arrived throughout the summer. Bush learned that the men, upon completing the fence, had enclosed within the north pasture six wild horses which "caused a great deal of trouble as they would take away our horses." The ranch hands, Bush wrote, "finally had to shoot them in order to get rid of the trouble." He discovered that the fence reached the Canadian River in the northwest but in the northeast did not include the river. The cross fence allowed the hands to "keep the cattle on the plains during the summer time, and in the breaks pasture during the winter."[23]

Bush found everyone busy. Several men from Tascosa and Las Vegas, New Mexico, were at work constructing stables and other buildings of adobe; because lumber was not available, they constructed a few corrals of the same material. The cowhands, he discovered, were shooting a large number of wolves along the breaks of the Canadian River in the north pasture and killing jackrabbits everywhere on the ranch.

Bush also discovered that his cowhands were calling the ranch the Frying Pan. In the process of rebranding the thousands of cattle that Childers and others had brought to the Panhandle, a cowboy, writes Laura Hamner, looked down at a big steer "and studied the design he had burned into the hide of the animal." The circle was on the left hip with the bar running under the tail. "Well, this ain't no Panhandle," he is reported to have said. "This is a skillet. It's a damned frying pan."[24] The name stuck, but some people called it the "Skillet Ranch," and Bush's correspondence as late as the mid–1890s continued to refer to the place as the "Pan Handle Ranch"—the name recorded in the county courthouse.[25]

As work on the stables and corrals continued, the ranch hands set about their work. The Frying Pan employed about twelve hands permanently but increased the number to twenty in the summer and forty during roundup and branding seasons. The hands broke young horses in a horse pasture of three sections (about 1,920 acres) in front of the house. They branded cattle in the south pasture on the plains and, during the winter months, moved the animals to the breaks in the north pasture where there was some protection from winter winds and cold. They castrated male calves and prepared three-year-old steers and some cows for market. Isaac L. Ellwood, Glidden's associate in the barbed-wire business, later bought many of the cattle, and Sanborn and Bush arranged to have the steers driven 225 miles to market in Dodge City.

As superintendent, Wetzel obtained most of the ranch's supplies from Springer, New Mexico. With six horses hitched to each of two or three big ranch wagons with high sideboards, he made the trip with his wife and some cowboys once or twice a year. Wetzel and Kate usually rode in a wagon fixed with a covering over the seat. "The extended body at the rear held our bedding and cooking supplies," said Kate. "We would camp in the open wherever night overtook us."[26]

The ranch received its mail at Tascosa, twenty-five miles distant and across the Canadian. Kate Wetzel remembered that she "always dreaded fording the Canadian River with its treacherous shifting quick sands." Many times when they crossed it, cowboys, she said, "would ride with us, one on either side [of the spring wagon] with a rope, one end of which was fastened securely to our [wagon] and the other" to their saddles. During such infrequent visits to Tascosa, the Wetzels and the cowboys "were often given a dance, the music was provided by one fiddle and we danced on dirt floors." After P. H. Seewald and his wife moved to Tascosa, the Wetzels "were guests in their home occasionally."[27]

As one of the first Anglo women in Potter County, Kate Wetzel added a unique touch to the Frying Pan. Ed Beard, a cowhand from the T-Anchor Ranch who had not seen a woman in some time, rode on business one afternoon to the Frying Pan headquarters. When he saw the young and beautiful Mrs. Wetzel standing in the door, "she was wearing a white apron, her hair was auburn and wavy. She looked so pretty he said he thought he was having a vision of Heaven." When J. T. Bloodworth, a Methodist circuit rider from Weatherford who visited the ranch from time to time, came to the Frying Pan, Kate held prayer services with all the cowhands and led them in singing old, familiar hymns until late in the evening. When she got homesick for New York, she pretended that her husband's desk was a piano and she would "play and sing [her] homesickness away."[28]

Kate said in an interview that she "looked after the health of the cowboys, but [she] never prescribed any toddies." She said that "hot ginger tea was my remedy and I never lost a patient." In turn, the hands treated her with genteel respect. "The cowboys," she remembered, "always stood until I was seated at the table," and they never uttered "a disrespectful word . . . in my presence."[29]

Mrs. Wetzel also assisted the gardener, Santiago ("Jim") García, in his chores. García, who enjoyed a reputation as a "wonderful" gardener, grew melons, beans, onions, "and all sorts of tempting food, in a land where vegetables were a rarity."[30] There was plenty of water available at Tecovas Spring, and the soil along the creek bottom proved ideal for growing vegetables.

In 1883, cowboys in the Texas Panhandle went on strike. Led by Tom Harris, the respected wagon boss of the LS Ranch, perhaps one hundred or more cowhands struck five ranches, including the LIT, T-Anchor, LE, LS, and LX. The ranches, which surrounded the Frying Pan, were largely open-range operations with only a few drift fences to restrain their cattle, and the hands, wanting higher wages, struck just before the important spring roundup. They were unsuccessful, however, for the owners hired replacements; and the strikers, many of whom drifted into Tascosa, where they spent what little income they had saved for the strike, soon ran short of money. The Frying Pan, because it needed no "line riders" to prevent cattle from drifting to other ranges, employed fewer cowhands, and those few Frying Pan cowboys did not join the strike.[31] However, among the twenty-four men who signed the original strike notice was one J. L. Grissom. If he was the same John Grissom who worked on the Frying Pan, the records do not reveal the fact.

The cowboy strike affected the Frying Pan. Cowhands from the ranch normally participated in both April and September roundups to return cattle that had slipped through fences, to brand calves, and to organize herds for market. As word of the strike spread, Wetzel and Childers consulted with neighboring ranch managers on what course of action to take; sent word to Bush, Glidden, and Sanborn; and encouraged state officials to send Texas Rangers to the Panhandle. Frying Pan hands, as usual, joined the April roundup; and the strike, which lasted two and a half months, fizzled. There was no violence, and very few cowboys received pay increases.

Not long afterward, Wetzel found that a custom had developed in which each Panhandle ranch was expected from time to time to give a big party—a "blow out," it was called. Held once a year, these were polite but fancy affairs. When the LIT held its party, for example, the manager, "knowing the neatness of cowboys generally, required each boy to walk across the floor in front of him and unless he could put his feet on the line drawn, he was not permitted to dance that night." Ranch managers wanted any of their employees who attended to be sober and well-dressed. They usually were.[32]

The Frying Pan held its first "blow out" early in January, 1884. Because it was to be a large and elaborate affair, Kate Wetzel and the ranch cook, William Trescott, worked for a week to bake, cook, and prepare for it. Warren Wetzel ordered oysters from Dodge City. Packed in a tin box and covered with ice, the oysters, delivered on the stagecoach, were still frozen when they reached the ranch. Guests "came from a distance of eighty miles or more." About seventy-five people attended, only twenty of whom were women. As people arrived in the afternoon, the Frying Pan hosts offered the guests hot coffee, sandwiches, and doughnuts. They served supper about nightfall, and afterward "we danced all night," with the waltz, polka, and schottische among the more popular dances. At midnight the Wetzels brought out the oysters, a surprising and delightful treat that was one of the highlights of the party. At dawn Trescott and his helpers prepared breakfast for everyone, after which the Frying Pan cowboys bid their tired guests a safe journey home.[33]

During the spring roundup in April, Trescott, or one of the other cooks, gave Kate Wetzel "a fright." Indicating that all the cowboys would be in soon for supper, Kate asked the cook to have a good meal for the hands, "for a change from their regular camp food." He became sullen, went to his room, and returned with a loaded gun, which he placed in a corner of the kitchen. Suspecting that he intended trouble, Kate "ordered him to the door with his gun, told him to point it up and to shoot it empty." She later recalled that "he did as I commanded. I have often wondered what I should have done had he refused."[34]

In July, Bush and Glidden visited the ranch. Although Sanborn came regularly to the Frying Pan and Bush made his usual one or two appearances a year, the 1884 visit was Joseph Glidden's first trip to the Panhandle. It was memorable. The two men went by train to Dodge City and, writes Bush, on July 4 "started for the ranch by stage . . . to Tascosa." We had as our "fellow companion all the way a celebrated gambler by the name of Tom Emery. He had the most beautiful revolver with handle of pearl that I have ever seen." During the entire trip, Emery insisted on sitting on Bush's left in the stagecoach "for the reason that if he happened to meet any cowboys he never allowed any of them to 'Get the Drop' on him."[35]

Before they arrived, "the whole ranch was alert," writes Laura V. Hamner. "Everybody wanted [Glidden] to like the ranch and the country." Soon after his arrival, Kate Wetzel asked him what he thought of the land. According to Hamner, the seventy-one-year-old Glidden snorted, looked with scorn at a stretch of dried, brown pasture, and replied that "the country is all right, but there's not enough grass to feed a goose." Kate countered politely that the grass, even in its dormant stage, remained nutritious; and, writes Hamner, "she called his attention to his cattle, rolling fat, that grazed on the grass he had maligned."[36]

About that time, Kate later remembered, a gust of wind blew Glidden's hat off, sending the large black derby rolling over the prairie. A cowhand, when he saw the hat speeding away, mounted his horse, "got his rope undone, rode to and lassoed the hat and brought it back to Mr. Glidden."[37]

The Frying Pan changed range managers in 1884. Childers left to return to Sherman in Grayson County. The owners hired Bob Bassett to replace him. Bassett came from the SE Ranch in New Mexico, but for unknown reasons "he and Sanborn could not get along, and after two or three months he resigned." Sanborn then promoted John Grissom to range manager. Grissom had come from Grayson County in 1882 with one of the first herds brought to the

Frying Pan. He stayed until 1888 or 1889, when Charlie Gillespie, who had worked on the ranch for several years, took his place.[38]

Meanwhile, in 1885 the Frying Pan, much to its owners' surprise, found itself involved in a lawsuit. Two years earlier, in 1883, the state legislature had passed a law providing for competitive leasing of its school lands—the alternate sections it had reserved for support of education—at not less than four cents an acre. Many cattlemen, including Glidden and Sanborn, either had fenced in the school lands as part of their pastures or had occupied them as part of their open-range operations. Now they were to offer the state four cents an acre each year for use of the land. Although they objected, they paid the minimum lease fee, but when the State Land Office, which had been created by the same legislative act, asked for eight cents per acre, many Panhandle operators rebelled and refused to pay the larger amount.

In response, John D. Templeton, the Texas attorney general, instructed W. H. Woodman, the district attorney in Clarendon, to bring charges against the Panhandle ranches, including the Frying Pan, for illegal enclosure of the school lands. Woodman called the grand jury into session. Charles Goodnight of the JA Ranch and many of the cattlemen in question served on the jury, with Goodnight as foreman. The grand jury, after considering the evidence, indicted its foreman Goodnight, several of its own members, and many other Panhandle ranchers (fifty-two in all), including Glidden and Sanborn, for "unlawfully fencing and herding on public school lands."

At the subsequent trial in Clarendon, District Judge Frank Willis presided. The jurors included Panhandle cowboys who worked for the men being tried. During the proceedings, the cattlemen admitted that they had fenced the alternate school lands, and the state admitted that the defendants had made legal tender bids of four cents an acre on the lands, but not the eight cents the Land Office wanted. Judge Willis instructed the jury that, if it believed the defense's claim that the cattlemen had made their four-cent bids yearly to the state, it was to find a verdict of not guilty.[39]

Quickly the jury found the cattlemen innocent of any wrongdoing. In fact, Glidden and Sanborn did not know that they had been indicted until after word reached them that they had been acquitted.

Soon afterward, wrote Sanborn, they "leased for six years," at four cents an acre, some 120,000 acres of school land that was enclosed within their fences.[40]

In the meanwhile, the state impeached Willis for allowing cowboys who worked for the defendants to serve on the jury. But, when his defense attorneys pointed out that the population of the Panhandle was sparse enough that there was no other choice, Willis won acquittal of the charges.[41]

During the first three years of its operation, the Frying Pan Ranch enjoyed substantial profits. Ranch expenses, Sanborn noted, reached about $20,000 annually, but receipts "from the regular crop of matured beeves has averaged at least $40,000 annually." The ranch in 1885 held twenty thousand cattle, the largest number the Frying Pan would graze in any one year. That year, however, national cattle prices, which had been exceptionally high, broke downward, and the ranch found itself in a price crunch. Sanborn wrote in December, 1886, that receipts totaled less than $30,000 for the year, but he believed that soon "we shall be in position to realize annually about double the amount we are now."[42]

Sanborn was wrong. Because cattle ranges in the United States were heavily overstocked, prices continued down, and the breathtaking expansion of the western cattle industry collapsed.

Bad weather also contributed to the decline. Severe weather in the Panhandle began when a great blizzard hit Texas on New Year's Eve, 1885. Christmas week had been clear and pleasant until late on the last day of the year, when a huge cloud bank reared up to the north. Quickly the blizzard struck, with a roaring sheet of dry sleet. By daybreak on New Year's Day, 1886, the wind had become a tearing, grinding monster that neither man nor animal could face. The icy blast pushed frightened cattle southward until the animals blindly bumped into the fences, where, pressed together and covered with snow and ice, they suffocated and died. As the snow continued to whirl and blow, the first waves of livestock pushed against the fences and piled up to form bridges over which succeeding animals crossed to continue their flight. LX and LS cattle crossed the Canadian and mixed with Frying Pan animals in the Canadian River breaks, where finally they received some protection from the storm.

Early on the morning of the tenth day, the blizzard blew out. When he rode out to survey the damage, John Grissom, in charge of the Frying Pan ranges, found cattle that bore the brands of neighboring ranches to the north mixed with his own herds and dead animals along all the fences. His cowboys salvaged some of the hides and burned some of the dead animals, but, with little heart for the job, they left most of the corpses to wolves, coyotes, and buzzards.

Late in the month, another blizzard howled across the Panhandle. On the heels of the storm came a numbing cold that drove temperatures below zero. For several days no one ventured out, and cattle gathered in bunches against fences and froze to death. Della Tyler Key, a regional historian, writes that it was "one of the worst disasters ever to hit" Potter County and the Texas Panhandle.[43]

In the spring, there was little rain, and the summer of 1886 turned hot and dry, withering ranch pasturage and drying up the streams. Although most of the springs on the Frying Pan continued to flow, the water quickly disappeared in the deep sands of the creek beds. As the drought continued into the fall, range conditions worsened, and cattle could not find enough grass on which to feed. The drought killed thousands of cattle and left "annual calf crops short by as much as twenty percent on many ranches."[44] When large destructive prairie fires swept the ranges, ranchers began to dump their livestock on the market, further depressing prices.

Another difficult winter followed the drought. Although not as rough as the previous one in the Panhandle, the winter of 1886–87 proved disastrous over the larger Great Plains. On the northern plains, in November snow blanketed the country deep enough that cattle, starving after the long drought, could not scrape with their hooves down to the grass. There was little the ranchers and cowhands could do but huddle about their shelters and worry about their herds. When the weather improved and they could go in search of their animals, ranchers and cowboys all across the plains, writes one chronicler, "saw a sight they spent the rest of their lives trying to forget." They found carcasses heaped upon one another in every ravine, gaunt animals staggering along on frozen feet, and piles of dead cattle along the fences.[45]

The vicious weather cycle and overstocked ranges ended the open-range era of ranching. Coupled with declining prices, these conditions also forced many cattlemen into bankruptcy and sent the whole western Cattle Kingdom (as it was called) toppling. The men who survived the troubles of the mid–1880s turned what had been a glorious adventure into a profit-making, market-oriented business. The Frying Pan survived, but the scorching drought in the summer of 1886, sandwiched between two ruinous winters, placed heavy pressure on the ranch's ability to make a profit.[46]

In the spring of 1887, the Frying Pan and some neighboring ranches held one of the largest roundups in the Panhandle. Cattle, scattered by the winter storms, had drifted across ranges from Oklahoma to New Mexico, and the pressures of declining prices, coupled with poor range conditions, created panic in the Panhandle cattle industry and encouraged ranchers to sort through and divide their animals more thoroughly than in previous cooperative roundups. They began this one on May 30 at the eastern edge of the LX and moved westward from there, working the plains, canyons, and breaks of the LX, LIT, LS, XIT, LE, T-Anchor, and Frying Pan ranches. Cowhands from each ranch participated. They separated the cattle according to brands, cut out calves for branding, and herded each animal to its home range. In all, they covered four million acres of land and worked some two hundred thousand head of livestock, on some days branding as many as five hundred calves.[47]

Later that summer, the long drought, which had started in 1885, broke. Heavy rains, according to the *Tascosa Pioneer*, "flooded the country on August 31." Until then, Panhandle grasses were "generally very short and pretty well dried up," and area cattlemen were worried about the conditions of their pastures.[48] With fewer cattle on the land and an end to the drought, range conditions on the Frying Pan began to improve, and Wetzel and Grissom, with Bush's consent, considered erecting windmills and putting in stock tanks.

Before work could begin, however, the Fort Worth and Denver City Railroad cut a wide swath through the Frying Pan Ranch. In the spring of 1887, a construction camp, called "Ragtown" because of the large number of tents at the place, had been established along Amarillo Creek on the edge of Frying Pan property. Graders worked across Frying Pan lands between Amarillo Creek and the Canadian River near Tascosa in Oldham County; before the year ended, workers, advancing about one and a half miles a day, laid track through southern Potter County and northwestward toward Tascosa. Not long afterward, the railroad fenced its right of way, cutting the Frying Pan into east and west pastures.

William H. Bush visited the Frying Pan during the railroad-building project. Representing Glidden's interests, he observed the construction work and reported to Glidden and Sanborn on its progress. Because the state could not provide clear title to all the land over which the railroad passed, the Fort Worth and Denver purchased some of its right of way from the Frying Pan owners. The income for Glidden and Sanborn, while not large, helped save the ranch during the period of low cattle prices in the late 1880s.

As the Fort Worth and Denver extended its lines through the ranch, the Frying Pan owners could look back over a half-dozen years of halting prosperity. Their ranch was one of the first large cattle operations completely enclosing their range with barbed-wire fencing. They had survived the price panic of the mid–1880s, fierce blizzards and killing drought, and the end of open-range ranching. But, with the coming of the railroad in 1887, they could look forward to whatever significant benefits the Fort Worth and Denver City Railroad might provide.

Many of the benefits, as it turned out, would be related to the appearance of a struggling new community on the eastern edge of the Frying Pan. As a result, Sanborn, Glidden, Bush, and the Frying Pan Ranch all played important roles in the early development of Amarillo, a city sometimes called "the Princess of the Panhandle."

CHAPTER THREE

The Frying Pan and Early Amarillo

The city of Amarillo traces its origins to a railroad construction camp along the upper reaches of Amarillo Creek in southern Potter County and on the eastern edge of the Frying Pan Ranch. After some difficulties over a favorable site, Henry B. Sanborn of the Frying Pan convinced local citizens to reestablish the town on a tract of land that he and Joseph F. Glidden owned about three miles east of their large ranch. From a humble beginning in 1887, Amarillo by 1910 had grown into the dominant city in the Panhandle.

The story is complicated. In 1887, several developments, occurring simultaneously, brought the Fort Worth and Denver City Railroad through Frying Pan pastures, created the town of Amarillo, and stimulated the organization of Potter County.

Chartered in 1873, the Fort Worth and Denver, because of economic difficulties related to a national financial panic in the 1870s, did not lay its first rails until early 1882. Its track moved west from Fort Worth at a steady pace until 1885, when financial trouble and disputes with the construction company again slowed its progress. Work began in earnest in 1886, with plans to complete the line through Panhandle City in Carson County. There its tracks would intersect with the Southern Kansas Railroad, later to become a branch line of the Atchison, Topeka and Santa Fe. Sanborn, however, deeply in debt and pressured by creditors, helped company engineers convince Grenville Dodge of the Fort Worth and Denver to redirect its line some twenty-five miles south, through Washburn in Armstrong County and from there along a path that took the railroad northwestward through the Frying Pan Ranch. Given such a result, Sanborn wrote, "we cannot but anticipate a large enhancement of value in our realty."[1]

Thus, in the summer of 1887, Potter County enjoyed a population boom of sorts. Railroad surveyors had marked a route across the Frying Pan that kept clear of the Canadian River breaks and avoided the treacherous quicksand of the wide stream, but as a result the railroad also had avoided Tascosa, the leading town in the western Panhandle. In Armstrong County, track crews were laying rails and advancing northwestward toward the ranch at approximately one and a half miles a day. Ahead of them, graders were working through Frying Pan pastures, and they had established a construction camp, "Ragtown," along Amarillo Creek. Within a couple of months, there may have been as many as five hundred people—including railroad workers, hangers-on, cowboys who had just completed the big 1887 roundup, and settlers—living at or near Ragtown.[2]

Some trouble accompanied the boom. In July, John Grissom, the Frying Pan's range manager, and two of his top hands, Charles Gillespie and Charles Wood, perhaps having had too much alcohol to drink, fired their guns in Ragtown, threatening its inhabitants and creating a nuisance. Charged with disturbing the peace, Grissom and Gillespie received fines of ten dollars each, but the judge acquitted Wood. Other trouble, relating to public drunkenness and fighting, caused the sheriff from Tascosa, J. M. Robinson, to employ James R. Gober, a young cowhand from the LX Ranch, as deputy at the tent city. Gober, who began his work on August 1, created a "jail" by placing a chain around two cottonwood trees and tying suspects to the chain.

The events at Ragtown encouraged several speculators to establish a permanent town and organize Potter County. Believing that the intersection of the Southern Kansas railway and the Fort Worth and Denver line would be near Amarillo Creek, rival promoters quickly began spirited competition for a favorable townsite—all on or near Frying Pan pastures. Jesse R. Jenkins of Tascosa, a rancher and saloon operator with a bar in Ragtown, filed claim to the Ragtown site about a mile southeast of where the railroad crossed Amarillo Creek. W. B. Plemons, a lawyer who later was elected county judge, filed on a site about two miles southeast of the bridge and close to the spring at the head of Amarillo Creek. Col. James C. Berry, an enterprising real estate dealer and cattleman, led a small group who claimed a site south of the railroad grade, just below Wild Horse Lake and about four miles southeast of the bridge. Berry's group paid the state $1,280 for their section (640 acres) of school land.[3]

As a result of all this activity, William Henry Bush hurried to Texas in early August. He followed his usual route, going by train to Dodge City and from there by stagecoach to Tascosa and on to the ranch. He examined the railroad work, inspected the town sites, and reported to Glidden and Sanborn on conditions in the Panhandle. He complained later that settlers living in wagons, tents, and dugouts illegally were occupying school lands along the stagecoach line that operated between Ragtown and Tascosa.[4]

Although there seemed little that he could do, Bush was not completely disappointed. He understood that the Frying Pan might benefit from population growth along its eastern pastures and that the railroad would cut the cost of moving cattle to market. Because of an abundance of water nearby, many people, including Bush, saw the area "as a likely site for [a] new cattle shipping point," particularly if a second rail line intersected the Fort Worth and Denver in the vicinity of Amarillo Creek. Indeed, many of the settlers who arrived in the summer and fall of 1887 had come to take advantage of such hoped-for prosperity.[5]

Town building was not the only political activity. Warren Wetzel, the Frying Pan superintendent who had encouraged Bush to visit, led a delegation of citizens to Tascosa to seek "home rule" for Potter County. On August 6, the representatives supposedly presented a petition, claiming 164 voting citizens and seeking organization of their county, to the Oldham County Commissioners Court, which had political jurisdiction over Potter and several other western Panhandle counties. To the surprise of many Tascosans, the Oldham County officials accepted the document (which cannot be found in either Oldham County or Potter County records) and ordered an election for a county seat, as well as for county officials, to take place on Tuesday, August 30, 1887.

Immediately townsite promoters intensified their efforts. Berry's group, which included a number of prominent citizens from Abilene, Texas, brought W. B. Plemons into its circle (probably in exchange for supporting his candidacy for county judge) and activities promoting a town at Plemons' site were abandoned. Warren Wetzel was among those associated with Berry and Plemons, and, at Wetzel's suggestion, Berry chose the name *Oneida* for the town. Jesse Jenkins, who dominated the Ragtown site, chose *Odessa*, or *Adessa*, as the name of his village. Entering the race late, Frank Lester, perhaps in association with Henry Sanborn, claimed a section of school land about two miles east of the Berry site and named his projected townsite *Plains City*. As early as August 13, however, the editor of the *Tascosa Pioneer* was calling the whole area *Amarillo*.[6]

Sanborn, after huddling with railroad executives in Fort Worth, had gone to Houston on other business. After receiving word from Bush about all the activity on and near the Frying Pan Ranch, he telegraphed Glidden in DeKalb, Illinois. In response, Glidden, although seventy-four years old, went by train to Houston, and from there the two men hurried to the Frying Pan Ranch, arriving in time to witness the spirited townsite promotions. They spent a week in the Panhandle, but departed on August 29, 1887, the day before the elections, with Sanborn determined to get involved in the local process of town building.[7]

The elections came off on schedule. Officials divided the county into four voting precincts: one at the LX Ranch, one at Berry's site, one at a placed called McKinney's Store, and one at the Frying Pan Ranch. This last, precinct three, had B. E. Green, a lawyer and surveyor from Montague County, as presiding officer. At least three of the election officials—John Grissom, Charles Gillespie, and John Arnot—were ranch employees. They received two dollars each for their services. Kate Wetzel, in whose dining room at the ranch headquarters the elections occurred, was in the room with the election board. She watched as the board recorded fifteen votes from the ranch: seven for Oneida (which the editor of the *Tascosa Pioneer* on August 20 was now calling "Amarillo City"), five for Odessa, and three for Plains City. Voters at the ranch elected Charles Gillespie, a popular Frying Pan cowhand, as commissioner of precinct three.[8]

Berry's Oneida won the vote for county seat. It won in part because Berry, to ensure its victory, had offered "LS Ranch cowboys, who comprised the majority of the electorate, two town lots each in exchange for their support."[9] The site, which centered along the right-of-way of the Fort Worth and Denver City Railroad and today is known as "Old Town" Amarillo, was situated on school land about two miles east of the Frying Pan Ranch. It was low-lying, well-watered prairie land with Wild Horse Lake—which served as a watering place for cattle herds that drovers moved northward through the Panhandle—located on the northwestern quarter of the section. About the time of the election, the railroad reached Oneida, and almost immediately the place became known as "Amarillo."

As the community grew, Henry H. Luckett, a surveyor and land speculator from Abilene, laid out the new town. He made the east-west streets, which began south of the tracks, eighty feet wide; they intersected with avenues that Berry named for friends and local residents. Luckett marked out lots in each of the gridlike blocks, and Berry made plans to sell or otherwise dispose of them as he had promised. People from Ragtown, Tascosa, Mobeetie, and elsewhere arrived to open a business or find work. Several people came from Colorado City, some 250 miles away.[10]

While Luckett laid out the town, the Potter County commissioners held their first meeting, on September 26, 1887. Judge W. B. Plemons, who had won the August election easily, presided; Charles Gillespie of the Frying Pan Ranch represented precinct three. The commissioners determined that, until a temporary courthouse could be built, the county clerk, W. D. Laird, should work in a tent. The sheriff, young James R. Gober, was to use "a flimsy wooden jail."[11]

James T. Berry, in the meantime, completed arrangements with officials of the Fort Worth and Denver City Railroad for a right-of-way through the townsite and for construction of a passenger station and freight depot. Work on the building began a few months later. In addition, as railroad building in the area ended and construction crews headquartered at Ragtown moved away, several of the people associated with the old "tent city" relocated in Amarillo. In November, the town received a post office. Thus, through the fall of 1887 and into the next spring, Berry's site was a busy place, attracting many residents.

Among those who moved to Amarillo was Warren W. Wetzel, the Frying Pan bookkeeper and superintendent. Having received a one-eighth interest in Berry's townsite, Wetzel gave up his position at the Frying Pan to engage in lot sales and other business in Amarillo. His wife and two young children, who had gone to New York on an extended visit, returned in 1888 to find that they now were living in Amarillo. In a related move, John Grissom left the Frying Pan. Charles Gillespie took Grissom's place as range manager, a position he held until 1891, when he also moved to Amarillo to open a livery stable.[12]

Meanwhile, because a range fire had burned large sections of Frying Pan grazing lands, Glidden and Sanborn sought fresh grass to get their cattle through the winter. Late in the fall of 1887, they leased from the State of Texas seventy sections of school land near White Deer in Carson County, about thirty miles from the ranch. They decided to move seven thousand cattle to the place and hold them there through the winter. In December, Frying Pan cowboys trailed about three thousand head to the new pasture, consisting of school sections that alternated with sections claimed by the Francklyn Land and Cattle Company.

Trouble followed. First, Francklyn managers saw the intrusion as trespassing and immediately met with Sanborn in Dallas to discuss the matter. They wanted the Frying Pan cattle out of what they considered their range. Sanborn offered to pay two hundred dollars per month for use of the Francklyn sections but insisted on his right to the alternate school lands. They parted without settling the matter, but Sanborn was satisfied with delay, for he wanted to keep the cattle on the leased property only a few months.

Then an early winter storm wrought havoc. The storm, which struck much of the Panhandle on December 19, mixed the Frying Pan cattle with those of the Francklyn Land and Cattle Company. Cowhands from both ranches cooperated in separating the animals and subsequently in keeping the herds apart, but they had to remain at the difficult task all winter. Moreover, the storm scattered through several ranges the four thousand Frying Pan animals still en route from Potter County, and Frying Pan cowboys could not collect them until spring, when Panhandle ranchers would hold their annual cooperative roundup. During the subsequent roundup, ranch hands located most of the scattered animals. Sanborn ordered his cowboys to return both them and the three thousand cattle still held in Carson County to the ranch near Amarillo.[13]

By this time, in the spring of 1888, Amarillo was becoming an important cattle-shipping point. For some years, ranchers had moved their animals by way of Wild Horse Lake to Dodge City, Kansas, located on the Santa Fe line some 225 miles farther north. The lake and the east branch of Amarillo Creek provided water and a good stopping place for cattle drovers from the south and southeast. Now Texas cattlemen could load their animals at Amarillo, from whence the railroad would carry them either east to the large market in Fort Worth or north to Denver, where agents might sell them to ranchers with livestock operations located on the plains north and east of there.

Because there were neither corrals nor loading chutes at the place, shipping from Amarillo at first proved difficult. The railroad built a temporary chute west of Wild Horse Lake, but most drovers pushed their herds through the little village and on to Dodge City. A few men turned their animals toward Panhandle City, the point at which the Fort Worth and Denver originally had been expected to intersect the Southern Kansas Railroad (Santa Fe). There they hoped to sell the cattle to commission agents from the Kansas City stockyards. They were disappointed. The Southern Kansas had not reached the place yet, and drovers moved their cattle to Dodge City.

Over the winter of 1887–88, Fort Worth and Denver City Railroad officials decided to locate permanent stock pens at Amarillo. "Realizing that water is the greatest factor in the shipping of cattle," wrote H. H. Brooks on May 17, 1888, in the initial issue of his *Amarillo Champion* (the town's first newspaper), the railway would "move their immense stock pens to a point one mile west of Amarillo." The site, Brooks boasted inaccurately, would "place them within one or two miles of a hundred springs in East and West Amarillo. If 200,000 cattle drank at this unlimited supply each day, the streams would not be perceptibly lower."[14]

The company selected a site on the north heights at Wild Horse Lake. Here, east of the tracks and on approximately twenty acres of land, it built huge corrals, numerous pens, and enough chutes to load four railroad cars at once. Even as construction moved forward in the spring of 1888, writes Della Tyler Key, "thousands of cattle were held around the town awaiting cars," and several livestock commission buyers, with C. W. Merchant the chief agent in Amarillo, negotiated the purchase of West Texas and Panhandle cattle.[15]

Brooks, the newspaper editor, noted that the Fort Worth and Denver already was negotiating "for the extension of the Santa Fe Railroad from its temporary terminus at Panhandle City." When the extension was completed, he concluded, "we are persuaded that this city is to be the great cattle shipping point in Northwest Texas." Stockmen, he predicted, would "ship 200,000 head of cattle from Amarillo in the next two years."[16]

Although six years passed before the numbers fulfilled Brooks' dizzy prediction, thousands of animals left Amarillo by train. A shortage of cattle cars slowed delivery. Indeed, according to Key, "there was much bickering between the railroad and the cattlemen over the lack of cattle cars." Each side blamed the other for the shortage. But, as a result of the insufficient number of cars, cattlemen held thousands of animals around Amarillo, sometimes waiting up to two weeks before shipment.[17]

In response, drovers completed arrangements to use range land around Amarillo as a holding ground for livestock awaiting shipment. Cowhands held some herds for several days, and "for several months of the year, the prairies on all sides of Amarillo were covered with large herds [waiting] their turn to be loaded into cars." Duncan Kersey, sometimes called Amarillo's "first native," remembered that "frequently there would be a hundred thousand cattle, or more, pastured close to town, from twenty or more ranches, each with fifteen or twenty men to the herd."[18]

The Frying Pan Ranch provided "twelve or more sections of land" along Amarillo Creek for such cattle, and huge herds grazed continuously on its pastures northwest of the city. The daughter of a Frying Pan manager remembered that "there would be herds that looked like a thousand cattle on the hills—[well,] not much of a hill anyway." To prevent the cattle from stampeding, cowhands guarded them day and night.[19]

Along Palo Duro Creek in Randall County, about eight miles southeast of Amarillo, drovers established a second holding ground. Even larger herds grazed here. Mrs. Davis Tudor remembered that, when she was a child, her father said that he wanted "everyone of you to come with me to see a sight you'll never see again" and took the family to inspect the herds near their home. They saw a solid mass of cattle, "by count fifty thousand of them," spreading in all directions nearly as far as they could see. As the sun set on that quiet, autumn evening, they watched "the cattle as they milled about, bawling softly" and observed "the smoke that spiraled upward from the many campfires, all forming a charming scene never to be forgotten."[20]

Meanwhile, in early summer, 1888, when Grenville Dodge completed a rail line (the Panhandle Railway Company) between Washburn and Panhandle City, a second railroad reached Amarillo. The new track connected the Southern Kansas (Santa Fe) at Panhandle City with the Fort Worth and Denver at Washburn; from there, Santa Fe trains used Fort Worth and Denver tracks to reach Amarillo. With direct access to the Midwest through Panhandle City, Wichita, and Kansas City, Amarillo's future was secure.

Three months later, according to B. Byron Price and Frederick W. Rathjen, Amarillo "boasted eleven stores, several saloons, a hotel [the Tremont], a restaurant, two lawyers, two real estate offices, two cattle brokers, and a population of 200." The main business district, they indicate, was near Third Avenue and Parker Street, but "much of the commercial activity centered on the stockyards northwest of town," where the Fort Worth and Denver had its corrals and stock pens.[21] Lunch counters, saloons, brothels, and similar businesses accounted for some of the activity, but a boot shop and other stores catered to the cowboy trade.

By this time, Henry Sanborn, unhappy at his failure to obtain an interest in the Berry townsite, had determined to build a new town. Short of cash as usual, Sanborn secured financial backing from his partner, Joseph Glidden, and from Glidden's son-in-law, William H. Bush. Calling attention to Amarillo's location in a draw that would flood after heavy rains, Sanborn "vowed that he would spend $100,000 to put the town where it belonged."[22] In June, 1888, he acquired a section of land—the present Glidden and Sanborn Addition—bordering the Berry site on the east, plus two additional sections of land, paying six thousand dollars for the property. Shortly afterward, he obtained additional land to the south.

On September 8, 1888, the editor of the *Tascosa Pioneer* indicated that "Sanborn is platting the section for the purpose of putting hundreds of lots on the market forthwith." Sanborn, the editor wrote, was determined to build a large hotel and hoped to construct whole rows of business houses for renting. "Lots," the paper noted, "will be given away free."[23]

Although in fact he provided some lots at no cost to new settlers,

Sanborn sold the majority of those his surveyor laid out. Indeed, with Joseph Glidden, lumberman M.T. Jones, and G.A.F. Parker, he formed the Panhandle Loan Association to provide credit for lot buyers and home builders. The company's headquarters was at Sanborn's office in Houston, but it maintained a "branch office" in Amarillo, where Parker was the sales agent. The company, with a capital stock of fifty thousand dollars, opened in early 1889 and held exclusive rights to sell lots in the Glidden and Sanborn Addition.

Upon forming the Panhandle Loan Association, Sanborn initiated a vigorous lot sale. Backed by the financial resources of Glidden and the loan company, he offered easy terms for purchase and immediate access to the lots. A Potter County historian indicated that the lots sold for prices ranging from seventy-five to two hundred dollars, "usually with cash payment down and three notes of equal value to be paid in three years." Town planners located most of the residential lots near Third Avenue along Fillmore, Pierce, and Buchanan streets, whose presidential names Bush may have suggested to Glidden. Wood-frame buildings, some of which Glidden and Sanborn built, occupied Polk Street south of the railroad, where a depot would be located, and north of Sanborn's hotel.[24]

The hotel was a magnificent structure. Located at Third Avenue and Polk Street and costing more than forty thousand dollars to erect, it was a large, two-story frame building of some forty rooms. Painted yellow and named the Amarillo Hotel, it contained common baths and outdoor toilets. Sanborn drilled a well and put up a windmill in the back of the hotel. He hired W. P. Hardwick to manage the facility. Called "the finest hotel in the Panhandle," it opened in April, 1889. Promptly afterward, "ranchers and cattle buyers . . . made the place their headquarters when in town," and owners of cattle herds awaiting shipment stayed there until their animals could be moved out by rail.[25]

Although they labored desperately to prevent a mass exodus of their citizens to Sanborn's site, promoters of Berry's "Old Town" Amarillo were unsuccessful. The final blow fell when unusually heavy spring rains in 1889 flooded Berry's low-lying townsite, inundating the streets and buildings that existed near the bottom of the draw. Now convinced that "New Town" was a better choice, many people placed their homes and businesses on skids and moved them to Sanborn's site on higher, drier ground. Even Col. James T. Berry and his fellow promoters moved. By August, the recently completed brick courthouse, an imposing two-and-one-half-story building, was the sole large structure remaining in "Old Town." Price and Rathjen write that it "stood like a lone sentinel on the prairie."[26]

Included in the move was the Tremont Hotel. Sanborn purchased the large building and went to great trouble to move it to his addition. Severe winter weather delayed the move, but, in the spring of 1890, he placed it near his own Amarillo Hotel, renamed it "the Annex," used it to supplement the rooms in his original hotel, and created a small park between the buildings. Some early residents remember that they "used to have some real nice parties there in the park. It was the only place we had to go."[27]

In the meantime, several men, Henry Sanborn among them, had established the First National Bank. It opened for business in December, 1889, in a frame building on Polk Street. Three years later, the Amarillo National Bank opened. It occupied a room at the Amarillo Hotel before moving to a two-story building on Polk Street.

Amarillo grew. By the summer of 1890, its population had reached 482, more than half of Potter County's inhabitants. The main business section centered along three blocks of Polk Street, and the majority of residences spread eastward from there. By 1900, the population had nearly tripled, with 1,442 people.[28]

Clearly, the Frying Pan's Henry Sanborn deserves the title "Father of Amarillo." Although he was described as haughty and somewhat aloof, "a very precise gentlemen [who] you would . . . think was an Englishman from the way he talked," Sanborn had laid out the town, bought out his rivals, and convinced people from Berry's townsite to move onto land that he and Joseph Glidden owned. Glidden and Sanborn often financed the moves, and Sanborn played a leading role in establishing many of the key businesses in early Amarillo.[29]

There were hazards associated with Sanborn's town-building activities. For William H. Bush, the most important ones related to Sanborn's growing neglect of the Frying Pan Ranch. Like most ranches in the Panhandle, the Frying Pan had suffered during the price panic and severe weather of 1885–87. Sanborn increasingly focused on Amarillo, his ranch in Grayson County, a ranch he had purchased recently in Clay County, and his enterprises in Houston, where he maintained an office for his barbed-wire business. The Frying Pan did not recover fully from the events of the mid–1880s, and Sanborn's inattention aggravated the problems.

Bush visited Amarillo and the ranch early in 1889, about the time when Charles Gillespie became manager. Concerned about the large amount of money Sanborn was pouring into the new town, Bush inspected the activities in Amarillo and conferred with Gillespie about events on the ranch. With the trusted Wetzel gone, Bush also was anxious to keep in touch with conditions on the range, including all the work associated with cattle ranching. Wetzel, who remained Bush's friend for many years, had been judicious in his letter writing, reporting regularly and faithfully on ranch employees and on activities associated with the calving, branding, and selling of cattle.[30]

Bush toured the ranch, checking the pastures and inspecting the railroad right-of-way. Because the Fort Worth and Denver had constructed three railroad sidings on its tracks through the Frying Pan, Bush worried that farmer-settlers might take up residence on school land nearby. Sidings existed at modern Cliffside (Sanborn Siding), Gentry (Field Siding), and Ady (Amy Siding), and these exerted a powerful attraction for farmer-stockmen coming to Potter County as Amarillo grew. Bush also worried about people, such as Jesse Jenkins, who had obtained title to school lands that once had formed part of the Frying Pan's pastures.[31]

Bush and Gillespie discussed the construction of wells on the ranch, planning to place them in pastures on the Llano Estacado south of the Canadian River breaks. After a meeting with Sanborn, Bush directed the ranch manager to contract for the drilling of wells and the erection of windmills. Strong prairie winds on the Llano Estacado would allow the mills to run nearly around the clock almost all year. With a low-lying wooden trough or tank placed near the windmill, water would be available for the cattle even in drought years. Bush did not want a repetition of the conditions of 1886, when the cattle had had to be moved to already overgrazed pastures in the Canadian River breaks.[32]

Wells with windmills also appeared in town. Some people drilled wells in their yards and placed windmills over the wells; from these, the mills drew water from about 170 feet and emptied it into wooden tanks. More common, however, was the appearance of water wagons. John Murphy, who had come from Brownwood in 1887, may have been the first person to haul water in a wagon to city residences. Residents placed the water in barrels, from which they scooped the water as they needed it. The daughters of Henry Beverley remembered that "we got a barrel once a week. . . . It got full of paper and trash of every description. We would just take the dipper and dip off the trash and drink the water."[33]

An effective water system also appeared. Sanborn and Glidden in 1889 established the Glidden and Sanborn Water Works Company. From headquarters at a site bounded by Fifth and Sixth avenues and Buchanan and Lincoln streets, the company installed several miles of pipes to deliver water to hydrants around town. Residents then took water from the hydrants. Soon additional wells, powered by windmills, were in service; and eventually pumping stations appeared. In 1892, the company expanded its operation by placing ten-inch mains to the increasing number of residents in Amarillo.[34]

Excited by Amarillo's prospects, Bush secured an interest in property on Polk Street. Sometime later, he erected the Bush Building at 520 Polk Street. At first he rented office space there, but later the building served a variety of purposes. At one time it was known as the Bush Racket store; then it became a boarding house. In 1898, a newspaper advertisement for the Bush Building announced that furnished rooms were available: "Brand new mattresses, and everything clean, orderly and restful. . . . We have a large room with two beds and stove for families. Special care taken of children. Lodging twenty-five cents."[35] When a fire swept through portions of the business district in 1901, the Bush Building burned to the ground. Although insured for one thousand dollars, it was not rebuilt; Bush found other uses for the lot.[36]

Bush worried more about the ranch. As late as the mid–1890s, his letters reflect his concern for the condition of range grasses. Pleased that the long drought had broken with a heavy rain in late August, 1887 (the day after the voting to establish a county seat in Amarillo), Bush regularly inquired about rainfall amounts and the quality of the pastures. Good rainfalls continued into the next year; and in May, 1888, a rain poured "down in torrents and streaks."[37] The resulting runoff weakened the underpinnings of the railway bridge across Amarillo Creek on Frying Pan pastures. Sometime after the sudden downpour, a Fort Worth and Denver freight train, attempting to cross the bridge as it headed northwest to Denver, wrecked. The local newspaper reported that "engineer King was instantly killed, and the fireman and brakeman badly used up. The sad calamity was due to a washout."[38]

Bush's worry about the ranch was well founded. Sanborn, realizing that greater profits could be made in town building, focused his attention elsewhere. The number of cattle on the Frying Pan had declined to less than 8,100 head, and cattle prices remained very low in the period after the price panic of the mid–1880s. Purebred Hereford bulls, needed to upgrade the rangy Frying Pan cattle, were expensive and, in Bush's view, did not represent a sound investment while beef prices remained low. Cattle sales at the time did not cover the cost of operating the ranch.

Wolves and other predators remained problems. The large gray or timber wolf, *Canis lupus*, called the lobo wolf in the Panhandle, was the most dangerous predator. As early settlers destroyed their main prey (deer and pronghorns), the wolves turned on the domesticated cattle, particularly young calves. The county offered bounties on wolf pelts, and cattlemen organized hunting drives to rid the region of the animals. Hiding in the Canadian River breaks and hunting in packs, the wolves continued to be a problem for the Frying Pan until near the turn of the century. In his letters to the ranch managers, Bush frequently inquired about calf losses to wolves.[39]

The coyote, *Canis latrans*, was another predator. While their main diet was rats, gophers, rabbits, and dead animals, coyotes upon occasion also attacked calves, and farmers and ranchers in the Panhandle, with mixed results, have hunted them for more than a century. They were not as troublesome to Frying Pan herds as wolves, however, and Bush made no mention of them in his extant letters.

But an old problem reappeared. Shortly after Bush left the Panhandle to return home to Chicago, a heavy rainfall (the one in April, 1889, which flooded J. T. Berry's "Old Town") marked an end to the short "wet cycle" of 1887–89, which had given Bush some hope of profits to rival those of the 1884–85. Instead, another long period of drought, extending into 1893, hit the Panhandle and the Frying Pan Ranch. Of major proportions, the drought dried up water holes and charred prairie grass, causing the Frying Pan further to reduce the number of cattle grazing on its extensive pastures.[40]

During the drought of 1889–93, management of the Frying Pan gradually shifted to Bush. Glidden, now nearly eighty years old, wanted to tend his farm in DeKalb, and in fact he had turned over most of his various businesses to Bush, requesting that his son-in-law find a buyer for several of them. Sanborn, who now was more interested in town building, held land in several scattered Texas counties, and he was under pressure from his creditors for payment on the land and cattle he owned around the state. Stretched thin, his attention turned away from the ranch.[41]

As a result, in 1891, when Charles Gillespie left the ranch to open a livery stable in Amarillo, Bush encouraged Sanborn to hire Harry M. Beverley as the Frying Pan manager. Beverley, a rancher near San Antonio, had driven cattle over the old Chisholm Trail to Abilene; for a brief period, with his parents, he had operated a famous general store (Wright, Beverley & Company) in Dodge City. With his wife and three children, Beverley settled easily into the old headquarters building at Tecovas Spring.[42]

Bush and Beverley got along well. With Glidden losing interest in the ranch and Sanborn preoccupied with Amarillo's development and his mounting fiscal problems, Beverley increasingly looked to Bush for instructions. They corresponded often and respected each other's opinions. Faced with the ranch's declining profitability, Bush, upon gaining the new manager's confidence, moved to take charge of what remained a cattle empire in the Texas Panhandle.

CHAPTER FOUR

An Empire of Cattle

Between 1889 and 1892, the Frying Pan Ranch, suffering from drought and depressed livestock prices, struggled to make a profit. During this period, with Henry B. Sanborn appearing overextended and his father-in-law, Joseph F. Glidden, more interested in his Illinois farm, William Henry Bush gradually assumed a larger responsibility for affairs on the sprawling ranch. Finally, with Glidden's concurrence, Bush determined to end the Glidden-Sanborn partnership and take control of the faltering 250,000- acre cattle operation.

One of Bush's important early steps was hiring Harry Mason Beverley as the Frying Pan manager. When Charles Gillespie decided to move to Amarillo, Bush urged Sanborn to replace the manager with Beverley, an experienced cattleman from San Antonio. Born in Goliad County, Beverley had farmed and raised cattle at Falls City in Karnes County and near San Antonio. As we have seen, he had trailed cattle to Dodge City, where his father operated a prominent business, before coming to the Frying Pan in 1890. In 1891, he became the ranch manager.[1]

Beverley brought his wife and three children to the Frying Pan in 1891, when he moved with them into the headquarters building. His family went back to San Antonio the following year but returned to Amarillo in 1893. With no school nearby, Mrs. Beverley taught reading and writing to her son and two daughters during the 1891–92 winter that they were at the ranch. In the summer, the children played along Tecovas Creek, watched the cowboys break horses in the pasture near the headquarters, and enjoyed other activities associated with the ranch. They gathered arrow points from pastures near the spring, crafted "stick horses" from willows growing along the creek, and, when assisted by the cowboys or their father, rode ponies around the headquarters buildings.[2]

The children remembered the white adobe ranch house. It was located on a bluff above Tecovas Spring. The ranch hands, said one of Beverley's daughters, "had to go down there and bring up all the water that was used in buckets from that spring. It was a marvelous spring; it just came gushing out of the rock. It was warm in the winter and cold in the summer."[3]

In addition to being an important water source, the spring was a busy place for other reasons. Frying Pan cowhands had built a rock house to shelter it and erected a barbed-wire fence to keep cattle away. Inside the tiny building, a trough, "through which water ran from the spring," kept milk, vegetables, and other food items cool in the summer heat.

While Beverley managed the ranch, Mrs. C. L. Mitchell was the ranch cook. She and her husband, who also was a Frying Pan employee, had a son and daughter, and one of the boy's duties was to take "the milk down there." One of Beverley's daughters explained: "You know they said in those days that they never had any milk, but we did and [Mrs. Mitchell] took care of that milk."[4]

During Beverley's management, the Frying Pan employed several interesting cowhands. One of them, Mel Armstrong, was just thirteen years old when he went to work for Beverley. The two remained close friends for many years. In 1898, Armstrong married Clishie Mitchell, daughter of the former Frying Pan cook. George Hayden, for whose family Hayden Street in Amarillo was named, worked on the ranch for a brief time. Sam Dunn, a loquacious cowhand who "would talk your arm off," became the target of a famous bunkhouse prank when a fellow employee found a bleached human skull on the Frying Pan range. When no one else was there, the cowhand placed the skull in a prominent place in the bunkhouse and with pen and ink printed on the skull: "Talked to death by Sam Dunn."[5]

Another employee was a "bronc buster" whom the cowhands nicknamed Billy the Kid—not the infamous William Bonney, of course, but a "peaceful gentleman" from Tascosa. The Kid, remembered one of Beverley's daughters, "could ride a horse!" The Kid and Pat Poteet, another bronc buster, broke horses near the headquarters as the Beverley and Mitchell children watched. Cora Green, Harry Beverley's daughter, remembered that it was one of their favorite activities. "We always had a ringside seat," she said, "and whenever we see these broncs that they are riding now for money, they don't compare at all with those fellows that broke those broncs." The cowboys considered that being thrown from a horse was a disgrace, and Green indicated that she never saw a cowboy "pitched off."[6]

When he was quite a young man, Guy Culp of Amarillo went to work at the Frying Pan. He had not planned it that way, however. As Roy Riddle said Culp told him, Culp and a companion, Guy Williams, the son of an Amarillo constable, in 1891 decided to run away from home. They caught an old stray mule in an alley, gathered a few provisions, mounted the animal, and set out. They did not get far before they decided that the bony old mule's back was not fit for bareback riders. Discouraged, they returned to Amarillo and, after "considerable maneuvering," acquired some harness and an old water sled. After hitching the mule to the sled and throwing in their provisions, they took their seats and once more set out from home.

Near Amarillo Creek on Frying Pan pastures, "Skillety Bill" Johnson, the Frying Pan wagon boss, saw the boys and rode up to investigate. Intrigued by the mule, Johnson asked them a few questions: "Where did they get him? . . . Didn't they know that was stealing? . . . And wasn't there a law in this country which with dispatch and efficiency took care of horse thieves?" Culp and Williams answered each question with "serious and profuse explanations," but to little avail. The wagon boss apparently decided to teach the boys a lesson and scare them into returning home to Amarillo.[7]

Johnson roped the mule and led it, with the sled and the boys, to a nearby Frying Pan camp where his men were working a large cattle herd. Recruiting his cowboys into the ruse, Johnson and a couple of others tied Culp and Williams to the end of the sled with trace chains from the mule. With the boys accused of horse stealing, several cowhands demanded an immediate trial and summary justice. When others agreed, the cowboys appointed a judge. Skillety Bill volunteered to defend the boys, and "Dwarf" Peppers, a carnival little person turned cowhand, became the prosecutor.

Riddle writes that "the trial waxed hot." Peppers "said pretty bad things about horse thieves in general" and about the young defendants in particular. Guy Williams began to break down, but the feisty Culp got angry enough at Peppers' mean-spirited charges that, "forgetting the imminent danger of hanging, . . . [he] offered to whip the prosecutor, who seemed just about his size—maybe a little smaller." About this time, Williams burst into tears, and the trial quickly ended in acquittal. The men set the captives free, and Williams headed on foot for home. Culp "decided to stick around and partake of the chuck that was about ready." That got him a job following the chuck wagon. Ten days later, when Dwarf Peppers left to take a job with a carnival, the Frying Pan boss promoted Culp to cowboy. Guy Culp was twelve years old, a "cowboy" indeed.[8]

In 1891, when Culp joined the Frying Pan as a cowboy, wolves still ravaged the herds. Cora Green, the manager's daughter, remembered that "we had lobo wolves and coyotes. . . . Those wolves were awful mean, and we had some wildcats." William Bush wrote frequently of his concern about the damage wolves inflicted upon range cattle, especially in the spring, when newborn calves were particularly susceptible to attack. In September, 1892, however, Bush wrote to Beverley that he was glad to hear that damage to calves from wolves had not been "so great this season as in the past."[9]

The eradication of wolves was a concern for stockmen from the time they first moved into the Panhandle country. Identified as an enemy that slaughtered livestock, lobo wolves presented "a grave problem." Cattlemen with their cowboys organized drives "to run down and destroy them." They set out poison and encouraged county officials to establish rewards ranging from five to fifty dollars for wolves' scalps.[10]

Records of the Potter County Commissioners Court for 1891 and 1892 reveal that the court paid "bounty after bounty . . . for lobo scalps." Della Tyler Key writes that Nelson Curtis, on August 10, 1891, received twenty dollars for the scalps of three wolves and a mountain lion. R. E. Paine got a similar amount for four wolves, and on the next day Charlie G. Landis accepted seven dollars for two wolf scalps. In November, Paine received nearly fifty dollars "for eight [wolf] scalps, two wildcats and two small wolves killed."[11]

Frying Pan employees also collected bounties. Commissioners Court records for February, 1892, indicate that George S. Hayden earned six dollars for scalps and John Arnot got sixteen dollars. Ranch manager H. M. Beverley received sixteen dollars for scalps during the month. When bounty payments continued high, the court, in August, 1892, abandoned such payments. Nonetheless, drives to eliminate wolves, jackrabbits, and prairie dogs (a sturdy little animal that eats grasses and roots and was a serious ranch pest) continued until at least the turn of the century.[12]

Prairie fires were of equal concern. During the long period of drought between 1889 and 1893, fires roared across large portions of the Panhandle, including Frying Pan property, turning the grasses into charred acres of black dust. "We had prairie fires all the time," remembered the daughter of H. M. Beverley. "It wasn't anything to have your pasture burned off . . . just ever so often."[13] There were some benefits. The fires killed noxious weeds and prevented mesquite and cedar trees from intruding on the range lands; when it came back, the prairie grass "was greener than ever." The fires also killed grass-eating prairie dogs and grasshoppers—"we didn't have many grasshoppers in those days . . . not so many flies either."[14]

In 1892 and 1893, fires were likewise destructive. High winds associated with the level and treeless Llano Estacado carried fires quickly across the drought-devastated range, driving prairie dogs, grasshoppers, pronghorns, wolves, coyotes, snakes, and other animals before them. Cowboys got out with water barrels, gunnysacks, and other crude equipment to battle the flames, but often the best they could do was to save buildings and windmills.[15]

Perhaps the worst drought year was 1892. The playa lakes went dry first, and before June the range grasses were already brown and increasingly sparse. Then many of the Frying Pan wells on the high plains went dry, and cowboys at the headquarters needed to haul water in buckets from Tecovas Spring to provide for their animals in the area—"every bit of water that was used had to be carried up. There wasn't a bit of water in the wells."[16] With little grass left on which the cattle could graze, Frying Pan cowboys in July moved their range herds northward into the Canadian River breaks, but the region provided scant relief.

Relief finally came in late August. Heavy rains fell across the Panhandle, filling the playas, restoring water to some of the wells, and providing moisture to the parched prairie grasses. On September 22, Bush wrote to Beverley, indicating that he was pleased with Beverley's recent letter which noted that "lots of rain" had fallen and that the pastures were recovering. Beverley had indicated, too, that his cowboys had branded 1,769 calves, with about 40 to 45 calves left to brand. In addition, the horse herd had produced 21 new colts, but as yet they had not been branded.[17]

In the same letter, Bush worried about nesters. "I am informed," he wrote, "that there is a movement on foot by some parties to endeavor to get West of the Pan Handle quarters and prepare to capture a considerable [part] of our cross fence." He noted that the settlers would be entitled to the land "unless we had taken it up before they made their application." He warned Beverley to take possession of the property and to "occupy the sections in question." Finally, he indicated that he planned to visit the Frying Pan between December, 1892, and February, 1893.[18]

As these developments occurred in Texas, Bush was busy in Chicago. "Everybody in Chicago," he wrote, "is head over heels getting ready for the World's Fair." He was writing, of course, of the World Columbian Exposition that Chicago would host in the summer and fall of 1893. But there were other activities. "Elva gives a party Saturday night," he wrote to an uncle, "and a dinner tonight—so you well know she is pretty [tired]." The Sanborns also spent a few days visiting the Bushes in Chicago, and Bush was engaged with I. L. Ellwood, Glidden's close friend in Illinois, in endeavoring to get a railroad built west from Chicago to DeKalb.[19]

His most important activities, however, were associated with the ranch. Sanborn's attention to the Frying Pan had been slipping over the past year or two, and Glidden, now seventy-nine years old, was interested in liquidating much of his property. As a result, ranch operations increasingly had become Bush's responsibility. Moreover, Sanborn's contract with Washburn and Moen Manufacturing Company for exclusive rights to sell Glidden barbed wire in Texas ended in 1891, and Sanborn was looking for new enterprises on which to use his enormous energies. Then, in January, 1892, Sanborn purchased the Hutchins House in Houston. Hoping to make it one of the principal hotels in the city, he planned to spend some $45,000 to repair the building. With good reason, Glidden and Bush were concerned that Sanborn's interest in their Panhandle ranch would continue to diminish. Thus, beginning in the spring and continuing into the summer of 1892, Bush and Glidden entered into negotiations with Sanborn for disposition of the Frying Pan Ranch.

Because selling the ranch would be difficult and probably unprofitable during a time of drought and low cattle prices, Glidden and Sanborn negotiated a unique settlement. Having agreed "to pay all liens or whatever there might be against the land prior to the time of the sale," Glidden on August 8, 1892, transferred his lots and other interests in Amarillo to Sanborn. In turn, Sanborn, in exchange for a large cash payment from his partner, "transferred his interests in the [ranch], with the exception of about 10,000 acres [in Randall County], to Mr. Glidden." The two men further agreed jointly to hold the cattle, on which there remained a debt of $150,000 owed to Isaac L. Ellwood, for two years, at which time they would sell the animals and pay out what might remain of their financial obligations to Glidden's longtime friend. Sanborn consented to operate the ranch until they sold the livestock, including both cattle and horses. Immediately after the deal was closed, Glidden transferred his ownership of the ranch, about 120,000 acres of land plus range rights to the leased school sections, to his daughter Elva and her husband William H. Bush.[20]

Thus, on August 8, 1892, the Bushes became owners of the Frying Pan Ranch. "We have down there 15 x 30 miles enclosed by a No. 9 wire fence," Bush wrote a business associate in Chicago. "All told," he reported, "[we have] 250,000 acres of land, with two cross fences," a ranch house, corrals, and wells, plus a large herd of cattle and some eighty horses. There is "a mortgage . . . against the cattle, nothing against the land," he concluded.[21]

Although they owned a veritable empire of land, the Bushes were in an awkward situation. Sanborn was to operate their ranch, or at least manage the cattle herds, for two years; but Sanborn, who owned ranch property throughout Texas, was, it seemed to Bush, always short of cash and heavily in debt to a number of creditors—including Bush and Glidden, to whom he owed several thousand dollars. As a result of his cash-flow problems, Sanborn, who according to the August 8 agreement was supposed to have paid tax assessments on the Frying Pan lands, did not pay the county taxes. Bush's complaints to Sanborn got no results, and in December Bush himself paid assessments on over 154 sections of land in Potter and Randall counties.[22]

In addition, Sanborn left Amarillo, the place from which Bush and Glidden had expected him to run the Frying Pan. He went to Houston—former site of his sales office for Glidden barbed wire, the place where he had established headquarters for the Panhandle Loan Association (the company he had organized to provide credit for people wanting to buy lots in the Glidden-Sanborn Addition in Amarillo), and the location of his recently purchased Hutchins House Hotel. Next he traveled to his ranch at the fork of the Little Wichita and Red rivers in Clay County, and from there left for his favorite ranch in Grayson County. In any case, Sanborn was not in Amarillo to oversee operations on the Frying Pan.

Beverley consequently continued writing to Bush for directions concerning ranch operations. Following Bush's instructions, he filed on some of the school sections on the ranch, and Bush sent him money to purchase the land. Beverley arranged the sale of some two-year-old heifers and some bulls to O. H. Nelson, a prominent Panhandle cattleman with a large ranch northeast of the Frying Pan, receiving only $18.50 per head for the 540 animals. "I suppose they were not quite as good as they should be," Bush wrote. In addition, he sent Beverley money to pay "the boys," as he called the ranch hands.[23]

The two men continued to worry about nesters. Beverley, after filing on some school sections in September, reported that additional settlers were occupying dugouts on some of the other sections within Frying Pan fences. In November, Bush wrote: "About those three sections you speak about, having dugouts. You know first about this." Bush wanted his manager to file on the land before the nesters claimed it and to place Frying Pan cowboys on the property. The scheme worked in some places, but with Amarillo's growth pressing on the eastern edge of the ranch, settlers could and did take possession of school lands along the Fort Worth and Denver tracks, especially near the sidings, and on eastern portions of the ranch.[24]

Becoming frustrated with the prospects of making a profit in ranching, Bush began to look for a buyer for the ranch. He wrote to George H. Bowen, a cattleman in Leavenworth, Kansas, offering 155 sections and asking, "What would be your charges for the same?" When Bowen showed no interest, Bush dropped the matter temporarily, but, not many months later, he again sought buyers for his Panhandle property. He was unsuccessful.[25]

The unsuccessful attempts to sell the ranch worried Beverley, who now wondered about his future with the Frying Pan. Bush wrote to him: "Now in regard to the matter that you wrote me about in regard to your future prospects, etc. All I can say is that I know of no one that would suit me any better than yourself, but you understand Mr. Sanborn has the management of the affair and the cattle for 23 months longer." Bush indicated, however, that "it is our intention to run the cattle on the pasture the same in the future as in the past, possibly a stock company and possibly individual."[26]

There matters stood until mid-February, 1893, when William and Elva Bush visited the Panhandle. They reached the area by railroad, going first to Denver and, with rail passes, taking a Fort Worth and Denver train from there to Amarillo. They stayed in Sanborn's Amarillo Hotel, which was still under the management of W. P. and Ellen Hardwick, and a cowhand drove them in a buggy to the ranch. While they were at the ranch, a heavy rain fell nearly continuously for three days. It flooded the Canadian River and caused the roof of one of the adobe buildings at the headquarters to buckle. The collapsed roof pinned some cowhands in the building, but it did not injure them. It also, wrote John L. McCarty, "threw several large snakes into the room, much to the disgust of W. H. Bush."[27]

Bush met with Beverley. The men spoke of the bad winter weather, which had left a "short crop of grass," the condition of the herds, the nesters, and other topics related to the ranch. Bush complained of "unusually high" taxes and wondered if Beverley might be interested in trying his hand at farming portions of the ranch. Although his response is not on record, Beverley, a cattleman, was probably not keen on the idea of farming, but, as he stayed with the ranch for two more years, he must have humored his boss.

Bush also consulted his Amarillo lawyer, W. F. McGowan. He wanted McGowan to see what he could do about saving some of the school sections on the ranch by having Beverley or the cowhands live on them. In addition, he asked his lawyer to talk with some of the area land owners about experimenting on their property with raising various fruits and vegetables. He wanted to know what crops might work best on what Bush called his "flat lands."[28]

During the two weeks that the Bushes stayed in Amarillo, they visited in the home of Warren and Kate Wetzel, the former Frying Pan superintendent and his wife. Wetzel, who served as the embattled mayor of Amarillo from 1892 to 1894, was a businessman in the city. Wetzel suggested that he and Bush enter into an agreement on raising cattle on the Frying Pan. The Wetzels would live in the headquarters building on the ranch, he suggested, and run the operation in the Panhandle, leaving Bush free to continue his business in

Chicago. Although he considered it, Bush did not commit himself on the Wetzel proposition.

No doubt others in the city entertained the Bushes. The couple owned one of the larger ranches in the Panhandle, and Amarillo was one of the largest cattle-shipping points in the country. Many cattlemen who shipped their animals from the city stayed at the same Amarillo Hotel and held their livestock on Frying Pan lands while they waited for their cattle to be loaded onto train cars at the chutes above Wild Horse Lake.

Upon his return to Chicago, Bush, reinvigorated concerning the prospects for his Frying Pan Ranch, followed up on his plans for farming in the Panhandle. He wrote to McGowan about claiming another section of school land by having Beverley live on it and suggested that perhaps McGowan should encourage the ranch manager to consider planting fruit trees from California. Accepting a belief common among early settlers on the Great Plains, he reasoned that the presence of trees "in time would increase the rainfall." Bush wanted to start with eucalyptus trees and add cherry and peach trees afterward. "Talk this over with some of the people there," he told McGowan, "and see if they do not want to experiment the same as we are trying to do."[29]

On the same day that he wrote to McGowan, March 22, 1893, Bush sent a letter to Beverley. He indicated that he had just returned from a business trip in the East and that he had sent to the ranch a Plymouth Rock rooster and a couple of hens. He wanted the manager to use the chickens to begin a small flock on the ranch. Having already ordered eucalyptus trees for the ranch from California, he asked Beverley if the shipment had arrived. Two weeks later, he sent a check to pay freight on the fruit and eucalyptus trees and wrote, "I hope you can fix up a little ground where they can be irrigated at least once a month and made to grow and see if there is anything in them for us."[30]

Bush had other plans for Beverley and the ranch. Noting that wild grapes grew abundantly in the Sierrita de la Cruz breaks, he spoke of raising domestic grapes on the ranch. He wanted to plant some varieties he had examined on his recent trip to New York. "I am confident that our country will do for those eastern grapes," he informed his manager, but he also wanted to get some western grapes to the ranch. In a letter to Beverley, he asked about the chickens: "I hope that you can soon raise a large amount of chickens which can be made profitable in many ways." Beverley was not enthusiastic, however, and the chickens, trees, and grapes never were successful.[31]

Before his own enthusiasm waned, Bush continued searching for ways to make the ranch profitable. When he heard that the St. Louis and San Francisco (Frisco) Railroad was contemplating a line through the Southwest, he wrote to its officers. "We are the owners of a large amount of land in Potter County," he indicated, "and would like to have your people cross the land, and would make favorable terms." The railroad did not respond, but Bush asked McGowan, his Amarillo lawyer, to look into the prospects.[32]

Still trying to hold onto the school sections within the Frying Pan pastures, Bush considered buying out nesters. He instructed McGowan to check into the matter. Two months later, after McGowan had reported back to him, Bush wrote to James Holland and John H. Wills, land agents in Amarillo, requesting a list of people who had filed on the alternate school sections in Randall County. The process moved slowly, however, and before he could carry out his plans, other events overtook Bush, causing him to let the matter drop.[33]

One of Bush's problems was a national economic depression in 1893. This severe downturn in the economy slowed business activity and forced many firms into bankruptcy. In Chicago, Chemical National Bank, of which Bush was an important officer, suffered through a shortage of cash reserves. A branch of the bank was located on the grounds of the World Columbian Exposition, and it had accepted deposits from exhibitors, including many foreigners. Shortly after the fair opened, the downtown bank failed, and the branch closed. In trying to save the faltering institution and guarantee foreign deposits, Bush and others sought out new large customers and tried to rally officers to shore up the bank. Although enough money was raised to cover foreign deposits at the branch bank, efforts to save Chemical National failed, and Bush watched it struggle through reorganization under new management.[34]

With the bank struggling and his plans for the Frying Pan getting little support in Amarillo, Bush began to lose his enthusiasm for turning the ranch into a diversified agricultural enterprise. In addition, Isaac L. Ellwood, who held a mortgage on the Frying Pan cattle, was beginning to press Glidden and Sanborn for payment on his loan. At the end of September, 1893, Bush wrote to Sanborn. Because of difficulties with one of his creditors, Sanborn had traded his favorite Grayson County ranch and other considerations for an expensive home in Kansas City (called "one of the finest residences in the city") and now was living in Missouri. Bush indicated that Ellwood was "anxious for his money" and suggested that Sanborn sell some of the Frying Pan cattle to pay off the lienholder.[35]

Sanborn, attending to other affairs, was too busy to run the Frying Pan as his August, 1892, agreement with Glidden and Bush had stipulated he would do. He was not too busy, however, to take his wife to Chicago, stay with the Bushes, and attend the World Columbian Exposition with them. Undoubtedly Sanborn and Bush discussed the condition of the debt to Ellwood, for, just a few weeks later, Bush wrote again to Sanborn, indicating this time that Ellwood was going to the Panhandle to inspect the Frying Pan herds and that "Ellwood is ready to foreclose." Bush was polite but firm in his insistence that Sanborn pay Ellwood.[36]

Finally, Sanborn acted. In a letter to Bush, he outlined what he had proposed to Ellwood: deliver the three-year-old steers to Ellwood in payment of the loan. Bush wrote back to Sanborn: "Your plan seems to be a good one and I hope you will be able to effect a trade with Mr. Ellwood on the basis you have named to him." The same day, Bush sent a letter to Ellwood, in which he discussed Sanborn's scheme and expressed his hope that Ellwood "would agree to taking three-year-old steers to pay off the mortgage."[37]

Bush, however, clearly was upset. Sanborn had sold and shipped some cattle, but he had not provided Bush with an accounting of the transaction. Moreover, Sanborn had sold some "other old cattle," and Bush had expected him to use income from the second sale to "pay interest money [to Ellwood] and leave money for other expenses." Bush, who had not received Glidden's share of the receipts from either sale, informed Sanborn that now was the time to have "this matter settled with [Ellwood] one way or the other." He indicated that Ellwood would be in Amarillo in November, and Bush told Sanborn to meet the mortgage holder there.[38]

Sanborn agreed and, in November, 1893, met Ellwood in Amarillo. When they toured the ranch and examined the cattle, they found that there were not enough steers to pay the entire mortgage, but, as part payment on the Glidden-Sanborn debt, Ellwood agreed to take about twelve hundred of the Frying Pan's three-year-old steers and extend the mortgage for a year.

Led by Frank Norfleet, wagon boss, and D. N. Arnett, manager, cowboys of Ellwood's Spade Ranch near Lubbock had driven a herd of cattle to Amarillo for rail shipment from there to the Kansas City market. Upon their return to Lubbock, they prepared to drive the Frying Pan steers back to the Spade Ranch.

As explained by John Arnot, a Frying Pan cowhand, "it did not take us but about four days to work [the herds in the south pasture] and get enough cattle to fill the contract." They collected the steers at Adobe Creek windmill, about eight miles west of Amarillo. "We were to hold the cattle there that night," wrote Arnot, "as it was close to the road to Canyon, and the Spade outfit could come past there, receive the steers, and be on their way in a short time." The roundup went smoothly, and, on the last night, the Frying Pan hands with three men on "first guard" bedded down the cattle beneath a shining moon.[39]

Then came trouble. A dark bank of clouds had risen in the north when, about eleven o'clock, Arnot and two other others went on "second guard." Shortly afterward, Arnot remembered, "a breeze blew up from the north bringing with it clouds that soon obscured the moon." Ten minutes later came a cold wind. "Anticipating what was on the way, I ran my horse to camp and called for all hands to get up and come to the herd with all possible speed." The wind had become a howling gale of stinging snow and ice. The cattle drifted with the storm, and only with considerable good luck were the men able to hold the drifting animals.[40]

"By daylight the storm had abated," Arnot wrote, and some of the hands went to the chuckwagon for breakfast. Because the wind was still too high for cooking, the hungry cowboys stretched a wagon sheet as a windbreak and got a fire going for a big pot of coffee, "which put new life and heat into a bunch of cold, exhausted, and disheartened cowpunchers."[41]

Because sleet and snow had begun falling again, the Frying Pan's manager, H. M. Beverley, did not anticipate delivering the cattle that day. Expecting to hold them another night and thinking that there were not enough steers to meet the contract, he ordered Arnot and four others to ride to the west end of the pasture, about nine miles from the wagon, and secure about two hundred more animals. As the men worked through herds in some small canyons and collected the required number, the winds died down and the snow ceased. When they got the animals back to the wagon about three o'clock, the men found that the Spade outfit had already taken what steers had been collected and started south.

Arnot and his four cowhands also found that the cook had a good, hot meal ready for them. Having been in the saddle nearly twenty hours, the men were a dirty, tired, hungry bunch. Blowing snow and dust had encrusted their faces with a layer of mud and dirt, and their "eyelids were almost swollen shut by the wind whipping dust and sand into [their] eyes." Three, having lost their hats, had substituted "bandanna handkerchiefs for headgear."[42]

With Ellwood having accepted the steers and extended the mortgage for twelve months, Bush moved to take charge of the Frying Pan. In December, he sent a check to Beverley to pay the year's taxes and asked him for the ranch's tax lists. He requested a listing of all cattle on the ranch: the number of "1-year olds, 2-year olds, and 3-year olds." He wanted as well a list of "those cattle sold and those on hand" and encouraged his manager to keep cowboys on the school lands.[43]

In Chicago, he met with John Wills, his Amarillo land agent, requesting that Wills's firm work up a new and complete financial assessment of the ranch property. Also he wanted Wills and his partner, James Holland, to seek a renter for the ranch. When they completed their work in early January, 1894, Holland and Wills reported an "assessment on Frying Pan property of $136,420." Bush, after he examined their report, indicated that some of the ranch property was not listed and asked about the discrepancies. When they reported back a week later, Bush was satisfied.[44]

With the information he wanted at hand, Bush resumed his efforts to sell the ranch. In March, he wrote again to Sanborn in Kansas City about the need to settle their obligations with Ellwood and requested that Sanborn, who had friends who wanted to buy or rent Frying Pan pastures, seek a buyer. He wrote also to Beverley, asking him if he had "any friends there . . . who have money enough to buy the ranch and the cattle?" In Chicago, he reported to a business associate, Bushrod E. Hoppin, that he was looking for a partner to help him buy out Sanborn's interest in the cattle.[45]

Bush's efforts got no response, but Sanborn, growing testy over

Bush's inquiries about cattle receipts, tax lists, the unpaid Ellwood loan, and other matters relating to the Frying Pan Ranch, asked Bush to buy out his (Sanborn's) share in the cattle. Bush responded that he was trying to do just that, "but Friend Sanborn," he wrote, "it is very doubtful whether I can raise the money to buy the cattle, or whether we can agree on a price that will be satisfactory to the people that are associated with me in the matter."[46]

Increasingly frustrated by his activities associated with the Frying Pan Ranch, Bush, acting as an agent for his father-in-law, Joseph Glidden, moved to dissolve the Glidden-Sanborn partnership on the cattle and take complete control of operations on the range. He knew that Beverley, former managers Charles Gillespie and Warren Wetzel, Amarillo banker-rancher Benjamin T. Ware, and others were interested in either leasing pastures on the ranch or joining him in a cattle operation on the property, and he wanted Sanborn out of the picture so that he might move on such propositions. Sanborn, as usual, put off taking action that might free Bush to enter into new arrangements.

The biggest hurdle remained the costly loan from Ellwood. Sanborn, Glidden, and Bush were paying Ellwood interest on the loan at between 6 and 8 percent annually. Boston and Chicago investors who wanted to join Bush in a cattle venture were not willing to pay more than the 1893 depression rate of 2.75 percent on loans that they would need to enter the business. In addition, Bush noted, the "Boston people want plenty of security."[47]

Sanborn, apparently interested in keeping his hand in the Frying Pan Ranch, suggested in August, 1894, that he and Bush keep the livestock and continue their association in the cattle business. Bush rejected Sanborn's offer. "Our family," he wrote to Sanborn, "all are anxious . . . to secure the release of the mortgage . . . and have Ellwood paid off. . . . You can make your own deal with Ellwood after he is paid." Bush indicated that he would meet with Sanborn to discuss final disposition of the Frying Pan's range cattle and the Ellwood loan: "I'll see you in Kansas City."[48]

When their meeting came off on schedule in mid-September, 1894, Bush and Glidden at last reached an accord. They agreed to meet with Ellwood in November at the Frying Pan Ranch. There, at Bush's insistence, they would sell all the remaining cattle, pay off the mortgage, and end the faltering Sanborn connection.

In the meantime, Bush signed an agreement with Harry Beverley that allowed his ranch manager to lease several sections in the south pasture. Beverley would pay five cents an acre annually to secure use of the land for three years, at the end of which time the two men would decide whether or not to renew the contract for an additional three years.

Bush considered some other lease agreements as well, including one with Warren Wetzel. When Wetzel asked about renting the ranch headquarters, Bush indicated that the building would take a little fixing, but that he would rent it and some adjoining sections in the north pasture if Wetzel paid for the repairs. The former superintendent, who had made application for the school land around the headquarters, was slow to accept the offer, and Bush made other arrangements for the headquarters property. Nonetheless, Bush indicated that he was pleased with Wetzel's plans, "as we do not want any sheep men getting in there."[49]

Through the last half of October, 1894, Bush was busy. He tended to his wholesale hat business in Chicago even as he conferred with Ellwood in DeKalb and corresponded with Sanborn in Kansas City about closing the Panhandle cattle affair. Two days after meeting with Ellwood, he wrote to the lienholder: "I wish that we might arrange to turn you over all of the cattle. . . . I'll take care of my half of it, for Mrs. Bush's part." But he indicated that "Sanborn is expecting to make some arrangements with you, should the cattle fall off, to take care of his half of the money." To Sanborn he wrote that Ellwood would "be in Amarillo between the first and tenth of November. He wants to buy all of the cattle, to liquidate the mortgage, or in other words he wants his pay." He instructed Sanborn to meet him in Amarillo.[50]

Bush arrived in Amarillo on November 10, 1894. Over the following two weeks, he, Sanborn, Ellwood, and their cowhands rounded up, sorted, bought, and sold all cattle on the Frying Pan Ranch. A half-dozen cowboys drove the 1,192 three-year-old steers south to Ellwood's Spade Ranch near Lubbock. Others moved the remainder of the herd, numbering about 3,200 head, to Frying Pan lands that Ellwood leased from Bush near the Fort Worth and Denver stock pens. From there Ellwood planned to ship the animals to market in the spring.[51]

Ellwood paid nearly $80,400 for the cattle, including steers, cows, bulls, yearlings, and any stray animals they might later find in the Canadian River breaks. He also bought a wagon for fifty dollars and the right to use the Frying Pan brand on the strays. Because there still remained a debt to Ellwood of some $60,000, Bush, with his wife's consent, agreed to mortgage the headquarters property and some pasture land until Glidden and Sanborn could pull together a final payment.[52]

Glidden paid quickly. To close his half of the large debt, Glidden in December sold his 250 shares in the Superior Barbed Wire Company, valued at nearly $40,000, to Ellwood, who refunded the extra money to his old friend and former partner.[53]

To pay his portion, Sanborn resorted to complicated maneuvers. Short of cash, he asked Bush to pay his $30,000 share of the Ellwood debt, offering Bush the nearly eleven thousand acres of Frying Pan land he had retained from the 1892 deal. Bush preferred that Sanborn "mortgage his property to Ellwood or somebody to pay his share," but Ellwood was not interested. Moreover, Sanborn had mortgaged some Glidden-Sanborn cattle to the Kansas City Cattle Company, a livestock commission firm, for $6,000, and he was about $4,500 "overdrawn on [his Frying Pan] books." All told, Sanborn owed Bush, Glidden, and Ellwood about $41,000. Bush persuaded Ellwood to accept Sanborn's note on the cattle mortgaged to the Kansas City firm, and to square Sanborn's remaining $35,000 debt, he wrote to Glidden that "it is my opinion that we can get a mortgage on the 11,000 [acres], then he has three or four odd sections near [Amarillo], besides the townsite and possibly his house in Kansas City, that I presume we could get our money back on." Sanborn, although unwilling as yet to give up his Kansas City home, on November 28, 1894, accepted a settlement (a deed of trust "intended as a mortgage") along the lines Bush outlined to Glidden, and Ellwood was paid.[54]

Thus, in early 1895, Bush, now clearly in control of Frying Pan operations, could look forward to directing the ranch in ways more in accord with his own inclinations. He and Elva owned over 100,000 acres free of debt, with seventy horses on the range, and held a deed of trust, or "mortgage," on Sanborn's property in Amarillo and his ranch land in both Potter and Randall counties. The old No. 9 barbed wire still enclosed 250,000 acres of grazing land, and with scores of cowboys on their property guarding tens of thousands of animals awaiting shipment at Amarillo, the ranch continued to hold an empire of cattle in the Panhandle. In a letter to his stepmother, Bush indicated that he had "great expectations for the future of the country."[55] First, however, he needed to tend to his Chicago business.

The original Frying Pan Ranch house and staff, circa 1884. Courtesy Prints and Photographs Collection, Center for American History, University of Texas at Austin

Views of original Amarillo Stock Yards near Wild Horse Lake in 1890s. Courtesy Southwest Collection, Texas Tech University, Lubbock

William H. Bush, center, his half-brother James Bush, right, and unidentified companion during trip to Europe in 1906. Courtesy William S. Bush, Jr.

Henry B. Sanborn, often called the Father of Amarillo. Courtesy Panhandle-Plains Historical Museum, Canyon, Texas

State Street in Chicago, circa 1905, looking north from Madison Street. Courtesy Chicago Historical Society. Photo by Barnes-Crosby

Downtown Amarillo, circa 1908. Courtesy Panhandle-Plains Historical Museum, Canyon, Texas

Bush home at Frying Pan Ranch, circa 1918. Courtesy of William S. Bush, Jr.

Wheat threshing operation on Frying Pan farm lands, circa 1920. Courtesy William S. Bush, Jr.

From left to right: Ruth Bush, daughters Caroline and Emeline, and William H. Bush, at their Chicago home, circa 1925. William H. Bush Collection. Courtesy Panhandle-Plains Historical Museum, Canyon, Texas

Saint Anthony's Sanatorium. The section to the left was the original hospital that William H. Bush helped to establish. Courtesy Panhandle-Plains Historical Museum, Canyon, Texas

The Bush Library housed in the old Hazen home, before the modern building was constructed in 1980. Courtesy William H. Bush Memorial Library, Martinsburg, New York

Formerly the Bush home on the Frying Pan Ranch, Toad Hall is the current residence of Wendy and Stanley Marsh 3. The trees surrounding the house were planted by Ruth Bush prior to 1920. Courtesy the Marsh family

CHAPTER FIVE

Building a Chicago Business

In the early 1890s, the national economic depression that weakened the Panhandle cattle industry also disrupted Chicago business activity. Banks failed, businesses faltered, investments slowed, and soup kitchens appeared. The economic downturn affected William Henry Bush, but careful management of his many real estate holdings; delay in undertaking risky new ventures; reorganization of Bush, Simmons and Company, his flagship operation; and settlement of the Frying Pan Ranch indebtedness got him through the brief but difficult depression in sound financial shape. Indeed, because he carefully built his Chicago business, his net worth was greater after the depression than before it.

The real estate holdings were many and varied. Bush leased commercial buildings and lots in downtown Chicago. He owned and rented homes in Chicago's residential districts, including the North Side; and in rural areas of Illinois, Texas, Kansas, and Iowa he held title to land that he rented to farmers and stockmen. Through the worst months of the depression in 1893, he bought, sold, or leased property, making a profit on nearly every transaction.

Between September, 1892, and May, 1893, Bush completed several real estate transactions. He told his uncle, Miles Willis, that he would accept some unspecified agreements on the transfer of property in Kansas and accept the deal. To Andrew Peterson, Bush sold two lots he owned in the Abram Ellwood subdivision in DeKalb. He informed E. B. Woolworth of Clinton, New York, concerning some property Bush owned on Clark Street in Chicago: "Since it backs up against a railroad it will not do so much for a residence." He negotiated the lease of commercial property on Center Avenue in Cicero, Illinois, to G. W. McLester and Company. He agreed to sell to Henry L. Turner and Company "property on South Dearborn Street fronting East between 29th and 30th streets." For $1,500 a year, he rented property at 323 Chicago Avenue to Brockhausen, Fischer and Company. And, in a letter to William Mulvery, he indicated that he had sold a house at 27 Kendall Street for $3,500 and stated that he would consider trading for a lot called "the Sheridan" property "if the Sheridan property is not too high."[1]

Concomitantly, Bush served as an agent for Joseph Glidden. He bought, sold, and leased lots and buildings in Chicago for him. In one such instance, he indicated that he could rent out a store that Glidden owned for fifty-five dollars a month if Glidden would fix the floor and widen the shelves. Suggesting that the proposition was a good investment, he recommended in January, 1893, that his father-in-law go ahead with the repairs.[2]

During the period in which he completed such transactions, Bush turned down several other opportunities. After returning from a trip to Kansas City in March, 1893, he rejected a proposal to join a business venture in Kansas, presumably a livestock commission company. When James C. Talmage, a railroad executive in Denver, Colorado, asked him in April, 1893, to participate in a large land and cattle operation in Wyoming, Bush declined the offer, saying that he was too busy at the time "to consider such a large undertaking."[3]

With his father-in-law and Isaac Ellwood, Bush sought to get the Chicago, Burlington and Quincy Railroad to build a rail line between Chicago and DeKalb. Several things precipitated the move. The three men believed that significant sums of money could be made from a railroad that connected Chicago with growing communities on the western prairies. They also wanted a railroad in DeKalb. All three owned land and businesses in the city, and they believed the railroad would enhance the value of their properties. Moreover, Bush, who had plans to open a facility to manufacture clothing in DeKalb, wanted the rail line for easy access between the projected plant and his Chicago wholesale operations.

Bush took the leading role in the venture. His plan was to get a number of DeKalb and Chicago businessmen to join Glidden, Ellwood, and himself in providing some of the money that would be needed. In October, 1892, he wrote to S. C. Lott of DeKalb: "I am of the opinion now that we are on the right track with regard to the railroad. . . . We put up half and the people on the road put up half." In November, Bush, having secured commitments from several investors, was optimistic about the line's future, but, only six months later, he wrote to Ellwood that the "railroad is being delayed."[4]

In fact, the venture got nowhere. The nationwide economic downturn in 1893 not only discouraged railway construction, but also caused a number of large railroad companies to fail or at least enter into receivership. Bush may have been lucky, for, in this case at least, he and the other would-be railroaders did not lose their money. The railroad came to DeKalb later.

Although the DeKalb railroad scheme foundered, Bush's clothing business in Chicago boomed. Anticipating increased business during the World Columbian Exposition (the "World Fair," as he called it), Bush expanded his retail clothing operation at 241 Monroe Street, and he encouraged Glidden to rent out an empty store building his father-in-law owned. In April, 1893, Bush noted that business was brisk enough "so that we hardly know which way to turn," and in June he complained to the Frying Pan Ranch superintendent that, because of the activity at the store, there "is no time for meals."[5]

Business continued brisk into the next year. In June, 1894, Bush noted that "we are very busy in our store with the straw goods trade," but he also indicated that there was some "problem clearing $44,000 from inventory." When his brother-in-law and partner, Francis T. Simmons, went to Europe for a few months, Bush's work load increased, and he wrote to Seth Miller, the son of his former employer in Constableville, New York, that "with business being rather close," he was very busy at the store. Two months later, he informed Isaac Ellwood: "I have an unusual amount of business on hand at the present."[6]

At the same time, Bush attended to his larger wholesale trade. In October of each year, his firm—Bush, Simmons and Company—prepared for the approaching Christmas season; sales then were crucial to the success of the business. He and Simmons called in the salesmen, showed them the new merchandise lines, and planned and organized the seasonal sales push. The partners were always busy at this time of year, Bush noted, "as we are getting our travelling men off."[7]

With both the retail and wholesale ends of the business going well, Bush moved to add a manufacturing arm to the company's operations. Joined by his brother Edwin and his partner Francis T. Simmons, he determined to buy the Glidden Felt Pad Manufacturing Company, a firm that made slippers, men's hats, and felt goods. Owned by his father-in-law but operated by Glidden's relatives, the company had experienced financial difficulties during the business downturn in the 1890s, a time when Glidden sought to liquidate many of his businesses.

Bush, who was an officer in the firm, moved quickly. In the spring of 1893, he lined up a few Illinois investors in Chicago and DeKalb; went to Fredonia, New York, where the company maintained a manufacturing plant; and sought information on business records and receipts. Then, in July, he organized a shareholders' meeting at his offices in Chicago. By the end of the month, he owned the Glidden Felt Pad Manufacturing Company. Bush, his brother Edwin, and Francis T. Simmons were the new "commissioners," as Bush called the principal officers; and Bush and Bush, Simmons and Company were the leading stockholders. When the reorganization was complete, the firm, with a capital investment of $35,000, had no indebtedness.[8]

Immediately afterward, Bush relocated at least one division of the company to DeKalb. Upon placing Chase Glidden, who ran the plant in New York, in charge of removing equipment and machinery to Illinois, Bush instructed Will Glidden, who oversaw a company office in DeKalb, to prepare "receipts on a day to day basis" and to send money to Fredonia so that Chase might continue to ship machinery to Illinois.[9]

Thus, in the summer of 1893, during some of the worst months of the national depression of the 1890s, Bush reorganized his clothing business. He now could manufacture many of the hats, gloves, slippers, and other goods that he distributed through his extensive wholesale trade. Meanwhile, the Chicago's World Fair, whose grounds were at Jackson Park on the Lake Michigan shoreline a few miles south of downtown, stimulated a boom at the retail operation that Bush maintained at 241 Monroe Street in downtown Chicago.[10]

Bush, it seems clear, was a remarkable businessman. Not counting general drygoods stores, in the mid–1880s there had been in Chicago 235 retailers of hats and gloves. A decade later there were many more, and the value of their trade reached at least eight million dollars. Among these, in the mid–1890s, Bush, Simmons and Company was one of the two largest of seventeen wholesalers of hats and gloves in the city, and now Bush and his partners had direct access to manufacturing and retailing. Both the manufacturing and retailing branches of the business remained tiny in comparison to the wholesale trade, which stretched through Illinois and much of the Midwest. The company maintained sales representatives in Indiana, Iowa, Kansas, Michigan, Minnesota, Missouri, Nebraska, and Wisconsin. In March, 1894, writing that "we are well equipped in the boot line," Bush asked a Mr. Prendergast of Hastings, Michigan, to join the Glidden Felt Pad Manufacturing Company, buy an interest in it, and manage and run the boot line.[11]

Not all went well. Tariffs on imported hats and wool, imposed by the McKinley Tariff of 1890, increased the cost of doing business for both the manufacturing and the wholesale operations. Bush, whose manufacturing company imported half of all the wool and mohair it used, wanted the duties on foreign wool lowered. Likewise, as his wholesale company imported most of its hats and gloves from makers in Europe, he sought to eliminate, or at least lower, the duties on imported hats.

Bush's position on tariff rates was complicated, however, for the Glidden Felt Pad Company made men's hats. Thus, lowering the schedules on imported hats would have a negative impact on his manufacturing company. Moreover, although his company also manufactured some of its felt goods from imported material, Bush desired higher tariffs on imported felt. Apparently he believed that, with lower rates on wool and hats, his firm could compete more successfully against the larger hat and boot makers who imported most of the felt they used in the manufacturing process.[12]

Bush received little of what he wanted. The United States Congress had been debating a new import bill for several months, when Bush, in February, 1894, wrote to the chairman of the Senate's Finance Committee outlining his company's needs. But, to Bush's chagrin, when the Wilson-Gorman Tariff was enacted, it generally provided for high duties on imported goods, including hats. The new tariff also allowed all grades of wool, including felt goods, to enter the country duty-free, meaning that, of those import taxes he sought, Bush got only the wool schedules, which, under the older McKinley Tariff, already were quite low.[13]

A more personal disappointment related to his cousin, Charles Bush, of Earlville, Iowa, about thirty miles west of Dubuque. Charles, with his father Henry and brothers Guilford and Herbert, had migrated to the Midwest. He raised enormous numbers of chickens for eggs and collected additional eggs—apparently hundreds of cases of them—from area farmers to sell to wholesalers in midwestern towns and cities, including Chicago. The firm, Bush and Company, also ran a creamery and a store. W. H. Bush had loaned money to his cousin's firm, but in financial trouble related to the national economic depression of the 1890s, Charles, by late 1893, had fallen behind in his payments not only to Bush but also to an Earlville bank and at least five other creditors.[14]

In February, 1894, Bush wrote to his cousin requesting payment on the loan. In response, Charles sent about $255, but W. H. again complained, noting that payment on several large shipments of eggs was to have been made directly to him in Chicago, rather than to the company in Earlville. Bush further suggested that Charles contact the creditors, explain the company's financial situation, and make arrangements to meet the debt obligations. He indicated that he was not going to loan any more money, and two months later, writing that "we are very short up just now ourselves," he again refused to loan money to "Charlie." Four days later, he reconsidered and sent five hundred dollars to Charles' wife, Augusta.[15]

Then, in late June, a fire destroyed the Bush and Company "plant," as well as a hotel, in Earlville. Although there was insurance on the property, Charles had no easy time collecting the money. W. H. Bush, as a mortgage holder on the egg operation, then requested that the insurance company send him payment on the company's loss, but it delayed. He complained to Charles that "I have heard no more from those bankers. . . . I think they are trying to play a bluff on me, I wonder if they think I am nothing but a school boy."[16] When he threatened a lawsuit against the firm, Bush and the insurance company reached a settlement.

The fire brought the Bushes together. W. H. and Elva agreed to have Charles and Augusta's nineteen-year-old son Fred spend the summer with them in Chicago. "We will be glad to have him come," Bush wrote to Charles, "and will try to take good care of him, until it is time for him to go to school." Bush, with the concurrence of both Charles and Fred, then made arrangements to send Fred to a boarding school in Orchard Lake, Michigan, the Michigan Military Academy, where Bush had sponsored other young people. He paid the tuition, and to provide Fred with proper school dress, he borrowed an old Orchard Lake military uniform from his neighbor and benefactor, former Martinsburg resident Henry W. King.[17]

Other family events kept Bush occupied through the spring and summer of 1894. In May, he took his mother-in-law, Lucinda Glidden, to Athica, Indiana, to receive special medical treatment for an ailment that had been bothering her for some time. With his ten-year-old nephew, William Simmons, he continued on to New York, where he visited his stepmother Emma and his half-brother James in Houseville. It was, he wrote, "a very nice trip." Upon returning to Chicago, he discovered that his nephew had left behind a "pocketbook with $7.50 in it." Bush suggested that Emma give the pocketbook and money to James. While Mrs. Glidden was in Athica, W. H. and Elva visited Joseph Glidden in DeKalb. Your husband "is looking after the farm," Bush wrote to Mrs. Glidden, especially the "oats, corn, potatoes, and hay. . . . We are anxious that you should get a good deal of relief."[18]

When his sister Harriet (or "Hattie," as he called her) and her husband Francis T. Simmons went to Europe, the Bushes and W. H.'s youngest sister Mary took care of Hattie's children, William and two-year-old Kathryn. Bush wrote that Hattie and Francis were "having a pretty nice time, etc.," in Europe and that the two children "seem to be doing finely."[19] In August, he and Elva took the children with them for a week's vacation on Mackinac Island, and, early in September, he and Elva visited Philo King, his old partner in King Brothers and Company, at King's vacation home on Delavan Lake in Wisconsin.[20]

On October 22, 1894, Bush, as was his custom, arose early and ate breakfast with Elva. It was his birthday. Then, from his North Side home, he walked two blocks west on North Avenue to catch one of the new electric cable cars that rumbled south down Clark Street. With Bush on board, the streetcar turned east on Division and south again on State before crossing the Chicago River. Once inside the

Loop, in Chicago's downtown business district, Bush got off the car at Monroe Street and walked to his office at 241 Monroe. At noon, promptly, he walked to the Chicago Club for lunch; at two o'clock he was back at work. At six o'clock he boarded a streetcar for home, where, with Elva and their current family guests, he enjoyed a large dinner and afterward a leisurely evening filled mainly with reading and conversation.[21]

William H. Bush was forty-five years old. A tall man with a large head that sat on broad shoulders, he had dark hair, a straight nose, and a slight cleft in his chin. He wore a huge, thick mustache but otherwise was clean-shaven. He was in good health and was well-to-do, if not wealthy. He had no children. Relatives described him as an "imposing" man of "personal fortitude," with an "ordered and questioning mind." He was a careful reader of history, biography, and philosophy, one who took a serious interest in subjects ranging from Thomas Edison to François Voltaire. A staunch Presbyterian who accepted Christian ideas of an omnipotent Almighty, he did not understand how anyone, such as Voltaire, could be an agnostic.[22]

In 1894, Bush was one of the minor capitalists of Chicago. On an economic rung below such men as Marshall Field, Philip Armour, and George Pullman, members of Bush's group, who also belonged to the influential Chicago Club, were less competitors than partners. They were shrewd enough to reinvest much of their income and to serve on the boards of directors of each other's companies. According to Susan E. Hirsch and Robert I. Goler, many of them, including Bush, "led large and far-flung empires" and had a financial interest in firms or banks other than those which "bore their names." Wealthy men of Chicago in the 1890s typically were self-made. Their "ideas and business acumen," say Hirsch and Goler, had lifted them "from modest circumstances to positions of . . . wealth. They trusted their own judgment and took large financial risks willingly." As their companies grew, they "often retained the outlook of small businessmen who believed that they, and they alone, should make decisions."[23]

Families of the Bush group formed a social elite ranking just below that of the Pullmans and Potter Palmers. They traveled around Chicago in fine horse-drawn carriages and journeyed to New York, London, and Paris, places they considered the great cities. They enjoyed "a structured round of parties, dinners, and debuts," write

Chicago historians, and "they could afford the finest entertainments—theater and concerts—that the city provided."[24]

Bush and Elva lived in a fine, comfortable home at 606 North State Street, where they employed a maid and a part-time driver-stablehand. Large without being ostentatious, the house was located near North Avenue and across from Lincoln Park, in Chicago's affluent Gold Coast section—a neighborhood second only, perhaps, to the Prairie Avenue region, where Chicago's wealthiest millionaires erected miniature castles and chateaux. The Bush home stood three-quarters of a mile north of the fashionable Fourth Presbyterian Church, on the southern edge of the Gold Coast. As with most other homes in the neighborhood, a black wrought-iron fence and entrance gate enclosed the driveway and a small, orderly garden. Their neighbors included some of Chicago's most successful businessmen, and across the street was the residence of the Catholic Archbishop, Patrick Feehan.[25]

As described by Bush's daughter, the narrow brownstone house contained three floors plus an attic. At the front, on the first floor, were a living room and a library, separated by large double doors. The living room contained a sweeping, curved bay window and a fireplace. A sliding door led to the dining room, and from there swinging doors led through a wide pantry to the kitchen, behind which was a smaller kitchen pantry. To protect their fine china from chipping during washing, the Bushes installed a kitchen sink of soft lead. Below the sink they placed a series of pipes to warm the china plates before using. Rooms on the first floor were trimmed with golden oak and contained ceilings at least nine feet high. On the second and third floors were the bedrooms and other living spaces.[26]

Behind the house, the Bushes had a stable large enough for four horses and two carriages. The stable opened onto the alley. It contained a contraption resembling an elevator so that, during cold-weather months, the summer carriage could be raised out of the way and the winter carriage lowered in its place. On the second floor was a small living space for their stableman, containing a washstand and other conveniences.[27]

As informal head of an extended family, Bush cared deeply for his relatives. He kept in touch with them through letters and personal visits and, to the extent that he could manage it, he took care of some of their financial concerns. For example, he brought his brother Edwin into the wholesale hat business and with him bought farmland in Illinois. He gave his sister Emma a quitclaim deed to some property in Willow Springs, Illinois, southwest of Chicago, near where he and Edwin owned a 120-acre farm. He regularly sent money to his stepmother in New York and watched the progress of her son James, his half-brother. In a letter to his stepmother, he wrote: "We were very glad to receive the letter from James. We think he does remarkably well. From his letter writing, he must be getting on very nice. We hope he keeps well all the while, as well as you all."[28]

In a more serious matter, Bush aided Mary E. Weber, a Glidden relative and a good friend of the Bush family. Mary's husband, Chester M. Weber, who lived in Milwaukee, died in 1894. Bush was executor of Weber's small estate, and now he became guardian of Mary's daughter Helen. When Mary moved back to Brookline, Massachusetts, Bush handled legal matters in Chicago and Milwaukee, paid funeral expenses and court costs, and, from resources of the estate, arranged a banking account upon which Mary could draw to support herself and her child.[29]

Late in the fall of 1894, Bush turned his attention again to his various business enterprises. He complained to R. E. Hurlbut in Brownwood, Texas, that his firm, Hurlbut and Harden, were two months behind in their lease payments on Frying Pan lands. He wrote to Hurlbut that the latter owed "two payments of $192 each. Pay Amarillo National Bank" or send "the money to [me] in Chicago."[30] He cleaned up a few matters regarding Chicago real estate, particularly on South Dearborn Avenue, where he and an adjoining landowner built a fence to separate their properties, and he saw to organizing his salesmen for the annual Christmas season.

In addition, Bush made plans to move his store to a corner location across Monroe Street. The task was a major one. He purchased a site at 220 and 222 Monroe, cleaned out the place, reorganized the floorspace with new partitions, and brought in carpenters, painters, and plumbers to remodel the new location. In mid-January, the men completed the work, and Bush's firm moved its merchandise across the street. "We have just moved into our new store," he wrote to M. B. Sylvester of Martinsburg, New York, "and it is a great improvement on our old one."[31]

Although occupied with the store, Bush was not too busy to keep in touch with his stepmother. In November, 1894, enclosing a check to cover expenses, he asked her to send a few bushels of butternuts to his North State Street home. Apparently he wanted them for Christmas. He also noted that he was "very glad to hear that Jamie is doing so well at school" and indicated that his sister Emma "is expecting to go to Europe about the eighth of December."[32]

In the same letter, Bush, indicating that he and Elva had finally taken control of the Frying Pan Ranch, outlined his plans for the future of their Texas Panhandle property. Within our pastures, he noted, the school land without access to water is selling for two dollars an acre and three dollars with water. Where there is no water, a buyer can drill a well and put up a windmill at very small expense. We can rent one or two sections of our property to the buyer of adjoining school "land at 5 [cents] an acre, and this would take care of about 64 head of cattle very nicely." With over 100,000 acres, free of debt, to rent annually at five cents per acre, he held "great expectations" for Amarillo and the Panhandle country.[33]

In fact, before Christmas 1894, Bush controlled much more in Texas than the Frying Pan Ranch. As part of the final settlement with Isaac Ellwood on Frying Pan cattle, he had received a 160-acre farm near Wichita Falls, Texas, and a deed of trust (but recorded "intended as a mortgage") to much of Henry B. Sanborn's property in Amarillo. The property included the Amarillo Hotel and Annex; several pieces of land in the East Amarillo and Ridgemere additions; block sixty, an empty piece of land bordered by Taylor, Fillmore, and Fifth and Sixth avenues, in the Glidden and Sanborn Addition; other considerations in Amarillo; and twenty-one sections of range land in Potter and Randall counties. In exchange for the deed of trust, or "mortgage," Bush, with Glidden's help, had paid Sanborn's share of the remaining debt to Ellwood on Frying Pan cattle.[34]

With the ranch situation cleared, Bush and Elva took some time to relax. They went by train to New York City, where they stayed at the Holland House, and here they spent the Christmas holidays. They invited Chester A. Snider and his wife, of Kansas City, to join them in New York. Upon returning to Chicago on December 27, they made plans for a grand celebration at their home early in January, inviting relatives from Earlville, DeKalb, and Chicago to the event.[35]

Bush and Elva also developed a livelier social life. Bush joined the Art Institute of Chicago, paying one hundred dollars for a life membership in the growing organization. He took an active role in the Chicago Historical Society, whose offices were not far from his North Side home. He attended its meetings and represented the society at various functions in the city. Already an avid book collector, he became a serious bibliophile. He and Elva participated in evening events staged at the Chicago Club, and more often than in the past they attended local concerts and evening lectures.[36]

Not all was pleasant. Joseph Glidden, nearly eighty-three years old, in March, 1895, suffered a "very bad smash up" near the fairgrounds on the western edge of DeKalb. Glidden's horses bolted, and "he was run away with." A second wagon crashed into Glidden's out-of-control buggy, Bush indicated, and "the horses on the other wagon, killed the woman, who was driving." Glidden, who was "badly hurt on one side," spent more than a week in bed, attended by Elva and Mrs. Glidden. He soon recovered from his physical injuries, but getting over the woman's death took longer.[37]

In the summer, with Glidden recovering, the Bushes went to Europe. They traveled with W. B. Thom and his wife, of New York, and Charles S. Givens and a friend, of San Francisco. They left New York City on May 16 on board the *Augusta Victoria* and landed a week later at Le Havre on the French coast. They spent a couple of weeks in Paris and then toured France, Switzerland, and parts of Italy before returning to Paris. When news that Lucinda Glidden was ill reached them in July, they cut short their lengthy vacation, left behind at the customs office a number of items they had purchased for their home, and took the first available ship, *The City of Paris*, home.[38]

The illness was cancer. Mrs. Glidden needed an operation to remove a growth on her left side under her arm. Hospitalized in Chicago, she underwent the operation on August 1. Mrs. Bush and Hattie Simmons were with her during the operation, which was a success; after spending two weeks or more in the hospital, she went to the Bush home, where Elva could care for her. At the end of August, 1895, Bush wrote to his sister Mary that Mrs. Glidden was "doing as well as could be expected."[39]

In the letter to his sister, who was in Europe at the time, Bush asked Mary to pick up the curtains and "other stuff" that he had left at the customs office in Paris. He further indicated that their brother "Ed has been down to New York City and Oil City [in Pennsylvania] for a few days and is now at home. Stella and Rachel [Edwin's wife and daughter] are all very well, also the others here."[40]

The hat business also prospered. Early in March, 1895, Bush indicated to Henry Sanborn that "we have been so busy here in the store, that we find [time] for nothing else. We shipped last month more than five times the amount we did last February." To W. B. Thom, he wrote on March 16: "Last Thursday we shipped $6,100 [worth of drygoods], so you see we are working very hard."[41] The wholesale trade, which had weathered the 1893–94 depression in sound financial shape, now entered a period of striking growth.

Bush's real estate ventures, however, still suffered. In a letter to Mary E. Weber, the wife of a deceased business associate, Bush complained that he had "had to reduce the rent on [a house on Chicago Avenue] last year from $75.00 to $50.00, and we have now had to rent it for another year for $50.00." She could see, he wrote, "that rents are very low, especially with houses that I have to rent."[42]

He also complained about his investment in Chicago's Globe National Bank. Bush, in the spring of 1895, owned fifty shares of stock in the bank and, remembering the Chemical Bank debacle two years earlier, he wondered if he should sell out. "I would rather pocket the loss now than later," he indicated to the bank's comptroller. "I have no stock in any company that has paid me so little in the last three years as this one."[43]

Despite the banking and rental situations, Bush was well off financially, and his growing wealth allowed him to take a more active role in public life. Interested in quality education, he began to press state legislators for a teacher-training, or normal, school in northern Illinois. To State Sen. D. D. Hunt, he indicated on January 12, 1895, that he would be willing lead a campaign among "the merchants in this section" for such a school. Five days later, after hearing from Hunt, he told the senator that he wanted "to launch a letter writing campaign in favor of DeKalb." He suggested to Hunt that "it might be that I could bring some influence to bear in this matter."[44]

Indeed, he could. Bush convinced Joseph Glidden to donate sixty-three acres of land on the western edge of DeKalb, at the old county fairgrounds (the same grounds at which Glidden in 1873 had first seen samples of barbed wire), for the institution; and he joined with Isaac Ellwood in heading up a campaign to promote DeKalb as the best site for the school. Ellwood went to Springfield, the state capital, to lobby for the institution, and Bush pushed his letter-writing project. He collected 152 letters in support of a DeKalb location for the school, wrote an introduction to the collection, gathered endorsements from leading citizens in Chicago and other cities in northern Illinois, and sent copies of the letters, endorsements, and introduction to each member of the state legislature. Among the endorsements was one from Charles B. Farwell of Chicago's Capitol Land Syndicate, owners of the huge XIT Ranch in the Texas Panhandle.[45]

The work paid off. In the summer of 1895, the state legislature established Northern Illinois State Normal School on Glidden's land at DeKalb. A two-year college designed to train teachers, the school in 1899 offered its first post-secondary instruction; in 1921, upon changing its name to Northern Illinois State Teachers College, it became a four-year institution. In 1955, it changed its name again, to Northern Illinois State College, and two years later adopted its present name, Northern Illinois University.

Bush also urged state and city officials to expand and develop Lincoln Park northward along Lake Michigan. With its roads and its blend of landscaping and pine forests that sloped up from the shore, the place was an attractive spot for Chicago residents. Bush lived across North Avenue from the park, and he and Elva in summer often walked along its paths or drove their carriage along its shoreline roads. He knew that land values were increasing in the area, and he believed that the city ought to purchase additional acreage before land prices became prohibitive for park development.[46]

Concerned about the financial status of his relatives in Earlville, Iowa, Bush moved to help them out. To his cousin Charles he wrote: "In regard to the thousand dollars to Augusta, I can let you have it, any time." He suggested that, "in regard to Fred, it seems to me that if he is going to take up a profession, he should begin at it at once, in some shape." He indicated: "I have tried to figure out some plan by which [Fred] could get started in here, early this fall." He asked Charles, who with his brother Herbert wanted to relocate in DeKalb, to consider taking over the Glidden Roller Grist Mill in the town, but, in the meantime, "What would you think of taking the South room on the 1st floor [of the Glidden Felt Pad factory], which is right up to the RR track." Charles might "use this part to handle eggs and other stuff there, until such time as I could do something better for you."[47]

Bush, in fact, did "something better." He provided Charles and his son Guilford with enough money to enable them to purchase the grist mill. Located on a quarter of a block of land "right in the center of the town," it was, Bush estimated, valued at "twenty-two or twenty-five thousand dollars . . . , including the machinery and other things." Indicating that Glidden might sell it for seven or eight thousand dollars, with one thousand down and the balance at 6 percent interest, he arranged for Charles to acquire the property.[48]

In Texas, meanwhile, Bush had begun renting portions of the Frying Pan Ranch to cattlemen and farmer-stockmen. He leased several sections to his manager Harry Beverley; a few sections to Warren Wetzel; and smaller tracts to R. R. and J. R. Wheatley, J. D. Roach, W. O. Jones, Tom Lawrence, and others. In addition, Ellwood held a lease on the headquarters and several sections in the pasture east and north of there. The real estate firm of Holland and Wills handled most of the transactions.[49]

Beverley assumed responsibility for the nearly seventy horses, two mules, and personal property that remained on the ranch and in Bush's possession. Beverley moved the horses and mules to his range, placed the wagons under sheds at the headquarters, and stored with the wagons such equipment as plows, hayforks, and harnesses. Cooking utensils and furniture pertaining to the ranch he put in one of the rooms at the headquarters building that Ellwood's men did not use, but he kept the beds, stoves, and chairs available for the new cowhands. Then, in preparation for a sale at some later date, he made out a list of all the equipment and sent the list to Bush.[50]

Several months later, Bush, with Ellwood's concurrence, leased the headquarters and some forty thousand adjoining acres to Charles N. Whitman, one of the owners of the Lee-Scott (LS) Cattle Company. Ellwood was by that time "glad to give up his lease," and the LS outfit was a reliable old neighbor of the Frying Pan Ranch.[51]

During negotiations concerning the LS lease, Bush sold the household property that remained at the headquarters. He also got rid of some of the ranching equipment and made arrangements with Beverley to sell at a 10 percent commission all the wagons, buckboards, machines, and other equipment that remained at the ranch. He sold all but eighteen horses and two mules to the XIT Ranch, and he asked Warren Wetzel what he would "take on the eighteen horses and two mules," but Wetzel was not interested.[52]

While they are not clear, extant records suggest that, in mid–1895, Beverley stepped aside as Frying Pan manager. He and Bush had a falling out over disposition of property on the ranch. They disagreed about the buckboard, harnesses, and household utensils at the headquarters buildings and about the horse herd, which had increased to thirty-five head. Although he continued to sell the horses at a 10 percent commission and to lease pasture land from Bush, Beverley no longer served as manager, and not long afterward he moved to Amarillo.[53]

Thus, in mid–1895, with his trusted manager gone, Bush was out of cattle ranching. Except to raise some Guernsey milch cows for a brief time after his retirement, he did not again raise cattle. He kept the ranch, however, from time to time selling some of the eastern sections when property values there increased as Amarillo's population grew. Some of the land he gave to relatives. Most of the land he leased to ranchers and farmer-stockmen, and, as investments, he continued to purchase some of the school land located within his fences.[54]

Although out of cattle ranching, William Henry Bush remained determined to make his Texas Panhandle lands turn a profit. As a result, he and the Frying Pan Ranch continued to play vital roles in the building of Amarillo.

CHAPTER SIX

Building Amarillo

With a population of nearly one thousand inhabitants, Amarillo in the late 1890s was the railroad and commercial center of the Texas Panhandle. During the following decade, the city entered something of a boom period, as additional railroads extended lines through the city, as settlers staked out claims to local farmland, and as people such as William Henry Bush pushed urban improvements and the continued building of Amarillo.

The city, however, only stumbled toward its boom. Amarillo had incorporated in early 1892, and on April 2 of that year, its citizens elected as mayor Warren W. Wetzel, the former Frying Pan superintendent. Shortly afterward, Wetzel and the city council established a municipal government and set about organizing its administration and arranging its finances. Then came trouble. Two members of the city council, not satisfied with the direction of local government, resigned in June, and, although their places quickly were filled, at the end of July several people, objecting both to the city's legal boundaries (which extended well beyond the limits of town settlement) and to city tax assessments on property essentially in rural areas, filed an injunction against Wetzel and the council members. The injunction, aimed at preventing the collection of city taxes, sought to restrain the council from performing its civil functions.

There followed a series of lawsuits, court actions, and town surveys. Additional city officers resigned their positions, and the city council, because of injunctions against it, met sporadically. When, after its January 17, 1894, meeting, the courts upheld a third injunction against it, the city government dissolved, and the county commissioners again administered Amarillo's affairs.[1]

Partly as a result of this brouhaha, urban improvements slowed. There was no city drainage system, writes Della Tyler Key, and the streets remained ungraded. In wet weather, "the streets were deep with mud . . . and water stood on Polk Street." In dry weather, the streets were filled with dust and dirt. Wood-frame buildings, "creating fire hazards, lined Polk Street," and "sidewalks consisted of wooden porches." Utility construction and other city services received little attention.[2]

Nonetheless, some progress was made. In 1893, county citizens voted to move the county seat to the Glidden and Sanborn Addition and, after nearly three years of debate over location, built a new, one-story courthouse at Fifth and Taylor. A stage line with daily service opened to Canyon, and mail service to distant communities improved. Some men cut a road southwestward through Frying Pan pastures to Roswell, New Mexico, and a volunteer fire department was created. Moreover, in 1895, wrote James Cox, Amarillo remained "the largest cattle shipping station for stock in the United States. The cattle shipment from Amarillo has reached between 2,500 and 3,700 cars annually during the past four years."[3]

One of the most important improvements was the acquisition of a third railroad. Henry Sanborn and W. H. Fuqua, president of First National Bank, upon hearing that the Pecos Valley Railroad was planning to place a line northeastward from Roswell to the Panhandle, in 1895 moved to convince officials of the railway to run their line to Amarillo. An attorney, Squire H. Madden, went to Chicago, met with the Frying Pan's William H. Bush, and together the men lobbied Santa Fe railroad officials to connect in Amarillo with the Pecos Valley line. The Santa Fe agreed, but only after citizens in Amarillo, led by Sanborn, offered to finance a joint terminal for the railroads. The Pecos Valley line reached the city in March, 1899.[4]

In another improvement, the city again organized its government. Amarillo voters, in March, 1899, passed a second incorporation measure and chose R. L. Stringfellow as mayor. Byron Price and Frederick Rathjen write that the new city "council moved more cautiously than had its [1892] predecessor and established town boundaries comprising only two square miles." The new city limits included only "parts of the Glidden-Sanborn, Plemons, Mirror, and Holland additions." This time the city government faced no challenges to its right to exist.[5]

Meanwhile, William H. Bush had purchased most of Sanborn's property in Amarillo. Needing funds to help underwrite the projected Pecos Valley–Santa Fe terminal, Sanborn, on February 5, 1898, in exchange for over ten thousand dollars in cash and other considerations, granted Bush a warranty deed to his real estate in Amarillo. Since the 1894 sale of Frying Pan cattle to Isaac Ellwood, Bush had owned a deed of trust ("intended as a mortgage") on the property. Now he held legal title to it. The property included all of Sanborn's interest in the Glidden-Sanborn Addition; all of the Plemons, Mirror, and Holland additions; land in what now forms part of the East Amarillo and Ridgemere additions; and some eighteen sections of land in Potter and Randall counties that had been part of the Frying Pan Ranch. It also included the Amarillo Hotel and Annex.[6]

The transaction was unusual, as Bush already held a mortgage on the property, and it would not mature for another eighteen months. But Sanborn needed the additional funds, and Bush, although he was not interested in owning the Amarillo land or operating a hotel, advanced the cash and accepted the warranty deed. A short time after delivery of the deed, Sanborn, at no cost to Bush, agreed to help him sell the property, but in exchange Bush allowed Sanborn to use the former Frying Pan sections and keep profits from the hotel for two years, or until February 1, 1900.[7]

G. H. Sutherland operated the hotel. Its fourth manager, Sutherland had replaced J. M. Kindred, who had followed Warren Wetzel. Wetzel had taken over the hotel from W. T. Hardwick in 1894, or about the time Bush acquired the deed of trust ("intended as a mortgage"). Under Sutherland, the hotel continued to attract ranchers and cattle buyers, but in 1898, many of its customers were tourists and prospective settlers who were in Amarillo to examine farmland. Sutherland encouraged a local livery stable to run a bus service from the hotel to the falls of Palo Duro Canyon "for the accommodation of tourists, sightseers and pleasure parties"—a practice that had started when Hardwick was manager. Although in need of some repairs, the structure was still "the finest hotel in the Panhandle."[8]

Bush wanted to sell his new property in Amarillo, but he was disappointed. Perhaps because of depressed cattle prices, sales were slow in 1898; only with difficulty was he able, over the next year or two, to dispose of a couple of farming sections and a few choice lots in town. Sanborn, still living in Kansas City, was no help.[9]

Some of the land Bush gave away, donating it for a hospital. His interest in a medical facility stemmed in part from a terrible accident that had befallen a neighbor's cowhand while Bush was on one of his yearly inspections of the Frying Pan Ranch. There was no place at which the man could get adequate treatment for his badly injured leg, and Bush became convinced that Amarillo needed a hospital. About the same time, physician David R. Fly, businessman James D. Hamlin, and a few other city leaders were actively seeking to establish a "sanitarium," as they called the facility. A correspondent for the *Evening News* asked, "Have we not philanthropists in our midst who will donate a plot of ground for the proposed Sanitarium; thus handing down their name to posterity as public benefactors?"[10]

According to his daughter, Bush visited San Antonio to ask the Sisters of Charity of the Order of Incarnate Word of Saint Anthony to provide the hospital staff. For this "most Presbyterian of Presbyterians," seeking aid from women of the Catholic Church was a personally difficult task, but Bush made his pitch. Local papers also pushed the hospital. The *Amarillo Weekly News* suggested in August, 1899, that "every man, woman and child in Potter County should take a personal interest in this commendable enterprise, not only giving it their moral support, but all the financial aid possible." In one of the more popular benefits, one held at the Bivins opera house on Polk Street, S. M. Curtis and the local drama club performed "Mabel Heath," a favorite old English play. It attracted a large crowd.[11]

Meanwhile, in the summer of 1899, Bush wrote twice to James Hamlin, who led the hospital effort, promising "active and substantial cooperation toward establishing the Sanitarium at Amarillo." Shortly afterward, Bush donated two blocks of prairie land between modern Taylor and Tyler streets north of town and east of Wild Horse Lake, and he promised some financial assistance for building the facility. In response, the editor of the *Amarillo Weekly News*, J. L. Caldwell, wrote that "the Sanitarium is now an assured fact. . . . To the sick and injured it will be an oasis in the desert of human affliction [and] to the health-seeker . . . it will be a haven of rest."[12]

Construction began a few months later, and O. G. Rocquemore, the contractor, erected a two-story red brick building. When completed, it held twenty-five beds but possessed neither running water nor electricity. David Fly became the head physician, and seven Sisters of the Incarnate Word staffed the facility. Named Saint Anthony's Sanitorium, it formally opened with an appropriate ceremony in March, 1901, with nearly half the citizens of Amarillo in attendance. For nearly a decade, the building served as the only hospital in the Panhandle.[13]

About the same time, Bush sold the hotel. Howard P. Canode and his wife, a couple whom Bush and his brother-in-law, Francis T. Simmons, had known in Illinois, purchased the Amarillo Hotel (but not the Annex) in early 1901, paying Bush $17,500 for the building. Bush received only $250 cash but agreed to accept the balance on terms at 7 percent interest for seven years. Although the down payment was small, most people believed that the total price was considerable. Certainly Bush was pleased, for his best previous offer had been $6,000, including the Annex. For his assistance with the sale, Bush agreed to pay Simmons a commission of $1,000, but the commission was to apply toward the purchase of lots in Amarillo.[14]

The Canodes repaired and remodeled the old hotel. They cleaned the place up and installed a steam heating system. Providing "a friendly brand of hospitality, together with a stock of Irish humor," they made the Amarillo Hotel a popular place. When their efforts were rewarded with expanding business, the Canodes soon bought an adjoining lot and made plans for a new building.[15]

Completed in 1910, the splendid new hotel was a steel, concrete, and brick building of five stories. It contained 205 rooms, "all handsomely furnished, bright and cheerful, with everything modern for convenience and comfort." There was an elevator and steam heat, hot and cold water ran in each room, and seventy-five of the rooms contained a bath. It was a "first-class modern hotel" with "luxurious parlors, sitting rooms and other home-like appointments."[16]

Almost immediately after selling to the Canodes, Bush clashed with Henry Sanborn. His old friend first claimed that his sale of the hotel to Bush had not included the furniture, and Sanborn wanted compensation. Then he objected to the sale of the hotel itself, claiming in May, 1901, that the 1898 warranty deed in fact had been merely an agreement that Bush would hold the property in trust until Sanborn could buy it back. Bush, who was in San Francisco at the time, replied by letter that Sanborn's understanding of the 1898 contract was wrong and "that I bought the property." In June, the two men exchanged a second round of strongly worded letters, but for a time there matters stood.[17]

Sometime in the summer, Francis and Hattie Simmons went to Amarillo to select the property agreed upon as their payment for having assisted in the sale of the hotel. Bush offered them a choice: the $1,000 commission could be applied to the purchase of either the remaining lots on the hotel block (priced at $3,500) or block sixty plus four lots in block fifty-three (together priced at $2,500). Bounded by Taylor and Fillmore streets and Fifth and Sixth avenues, block sixty was located near the site of the one-story temporary courthouse the county had built in 1896. The block was to become the focus of another bitter disagreement between Bush and Sanborn, as well as a source of contention between Sanborn and Potter County.[18]

Shortly after returning to Chicago, the Simmonses selected block sixty plus the lots in block fifty-three. Thus, on September 30, 1901, Bush, for $2,500 (less the $1,000 for helping to sell the hotel), deeded the property to his sister, Harriet Simmons. He did not have the deed recorded, however, until July 11, 1902, when he was in Amarillo during his annual visit to the Panhandle.

Meanwhile, the Bush-Sanborn disagreements persisted. Sometime in February, 1902, Sanborn wrote to Elva Bush, suggesting that the two men settle, as Bush stated, "all matters between himself and me." Insisting that he owned the property and believing that little else needed to be done, Bush let the difficulties drift and intensified his efforts to sell his Amarillo holdings—perhaps before Sanborn could embroil him in legal proceedings.[19]

Sanborn continued to press for a settlement. Indeed, through the spring and summer of 1902, he became more aggressive, and eventually he demanded his property back. To that end, in September he went to Chicago to meet with Bush. Sanborn now insisted that the 1898 deal was neither a sale nor a trust, but "simply a mortgage and that he had a right to pay off [the] indebtedness, and retake the property." Bush refused to accept the argument, maintaining, "I bought the property of him, that the conveyance to me was not a mortgage."[20]

Sanborn refused to quit. For several days in Chicago, meeting at the law offices of the Cratty Brothers (attorneys who represented Elva Bush) or at Bush's office, the two men discussed their differences. Sometimes others, including Mrs. Bush and D. J. Carnes

(W. H. Bush's attorney), were present during the talks. Financially, Sanborn was at a considerable disadvantage in dealing with the wealthy Bush, but he nonetheless threatened that, unless Bush sold the property back to him, he would bring suit and "tie the whole matter up in litigation in Texas." Persuaded by his wife and others, Bush finally relented and, "rather than to have any further bother about the matter," agreed to deed back to Sanborn all property he had not sold.

Sanborn's insistence related to a pending sale of the eighteen sections of pasture associated with the 1898 deal. Sanborn had been offered $28,800 for the land and wanted the money to purchase another ranch in the Panhandle and to construct a large home in Amarillo, where he planned to return to live. Thus, once Bush relented, Sanborn hurried from Chicago to Amarillo and on October 13, 1902, sold the eighteen former Frying Pan sections. Four days later, he was back in Chicago to sign a contract with Bush. Although it was a complicated settlement involving commissions, interest payments, fees, liens, purchase money notes, and other considerations, the agreement restored all unsold property from the 1898 settlement to Sanborn. It once again made Bush the mortgage holder on property owned by a man who lived on other people's money.[21]

The agreement, unfortunately, did not end Bush's problems with Sanborn. At the end of the month, with Sanborn back in Chicago, the two men reviewed the agreement, the accounts, and the status of all the properties, both sold and unsold. "The account," noted Bush, "was all gone over by Mr. Sanborn and me and the account found to be correct," including the "statement of the account of the sale of block sixty" to Harriet Simmons. On November 1, 1902, Sanborn paid Bush $4,000 to clear some of his indebtedness. The balance of the $28,800 received in the sale of the pasture lands Sanborn used as down payment on the purchase of a Panhandle ranch and the construction of a magnificent new home in Amarillo.[22]

Over the next several weeks, in letters to Bush, Sanborn continued to complain about one aspect of the settlement after another. He objected to the sale of block sixty, grumbled about having to pay the Simmons' commission, groused about notary fees, and whined that the sale price on the hotel had been too low. In January, 1903, he met with Bush in Chicago. He was persistent, and Bush again compromised, agreeing on January 3 to divide some of the fees with the tenacious Sanborn.[23]

With the Sanborn troubles apparently behind him, Bush turned his attention toward other matters. One was a newly formed library in Amarillo. In 1900, a women's club called J.U.G. (Just Us Girls) had begun meeting weekly at the homes of its members. Some months later, as they initiated various study programs, the women decided that they needed books to ease preparation of the programs and determined to organize a club library. In March, 1902, at a special guest-day meeting, they collected thirty-three books for their "library." Shortly afterward, Margaret Wills, an elementary school teacher and wife of Bush's Amarillo land agent, "donated a set of ninety books which had been given her by William H. Bush to use as she wished." Now the club members, with 123 volumes, agreed to place the collection in a home Ms. Wills owned on Fourth Street, and on October 4, 1902, their little library opened to the public. Through the years, the Bush family continued to add to the library's holdings.[24]

Bush also turned his attention to railroads. The Santa Fe railroad built a roundhouse in the city in 1898, and in 1899 it moved its general offices for the region from Panhandle City to the Amarillo. When the Santa Fe took over operation of the Pecos Valley line about the same time, the city could boast of transcontinental rail service.

In 1901, the Chicago, Rock Island and Mexico Railroad extended its line southwestward into Sherman and Dallam counties, through the site of present-day Dalhart, to the western boundary of Hartley County along the New Mexico border. Bush now hoped to use the railroad to attract farmer-settlers to the Upper Panhandle and thence to his ranch. In a promotional effort that mirrored similar efforts by railroads, he distributed hundreds of circulars advertising Panhandle lands.

More important to Bush was the Choctaw, Oklahoma, and Texas Railroad. According to Potter County Judge J. W. Crudgington, the railroad "through Bush's own efforts . . . was induced to build from Weatherford, Okla., to Amarillo." It ran its line from the east across the Texas Panhandle, and in 1903, its tracks reached Amarillo, giving the city a connection through Oklahoma City and Little Rock, Arkansas, to Memphis, Tennessee.[25]

The Choctaw—which in December, 1903, was purchased by the Chicago, Rock Island and Gulf Railroad—continued west in 1904. It built from Amarillo through Bush's Frying Pan lands along the southern edge of Potter County, but construction halted before it reached the county's western border. Four years later, having resumed construction, the Rock Island, as the railroad was now called, reached Wildorado in Oldham County. Businessman I. A. Allred remembered that, when the first passenger train came through Wildorado on June 15, 1908, "folks from the farms and ranches tuck [*sic*] out an' come to town to see the train go by."[26]

A month later, on July 3, William H. Bush and S. H. Smiser dedicated the townsite of Bush Stop. Located on Frying Pan land along the railroad between Amarillo and Wildorado, the community developed as a typical T-shaped prairie town of the period. That is, the railroad cut through the village, forming the top (crossed) portion of the T, and the main street intersected the railroad. Grain elevators soon stood across the tracks from the business and residential sections of the town. Bush named the north-south streets for relatives, and business associates: Robinson (his sister Clarissa and her husband, F. G. Robinson), Simmons (his sister Hattie and her husband, Francis T. Simmons), Wells (his Chicago secretary, Martha F. Wells), and Wills (his Amarillo land agent, John H. Wills). The east-west streets were numbered, logically, First to Ninth.

Three days after that ceremony, Bush dedicated, on July 6, the townsite of Soncy. It too was located on Frying Pan land along the Rock Island, but it lay six miles closer to Amarillo. Bush again named the streets for relatives and friends. The north-south streets he called Robinson, Simmons, and Smith (his sister Mary and her husband, Frederick E. Smith). The east-west streets he named for Edwin (his brother), Kathryn (his niece), Madeline (stepdaughter of his sister Emma, then about fifteen years old), Rachel (his niece), and Jarvis (unknown).

Two years later, in 1910, the Rock Island, which had purchased the Chicago, Rock Island and Mexico Railroad, completed its line to Tucumcari, New Mexico. Even before completion of the line to Tucumcari, Amarillo had become the railroad and "business center of the Panhandle."[27]

Bush understood the importance of the railroads. In a speech to an Amarillo businessmen's club, he indicated that the city was "the division point of three [trunk] lines." The confluence "makes her the wholesale and distributing center of over forty thousand square miles of Texas territory comprising about fifty counties, and also much of eastern New Mexico." Noting that, to the south, both Lubbock and Plainview were seeking major railroads, he told the group that Amarillo must "keep pace with the rapid development of the country."[28]

To help keep pace, local businessmen and ranchers such as Al Popham, O. H. Nelson, and others organized the Western Stock Yards Corporation. Because the old stock pens were inadequate for the needs of three railroads and the lively traffic in livestock, the corporation in 1905 built new stockyards two miles east of town. They agreed to furnish pens for livestock and to provide services for dipping, vaccinating, branding, and dehorning cattle, and the railroads consented to move their tracks to the new location.[29]

Also to help keep pace, Potter County built a new courthouse. After much discussion concerning the need for a new facility, local citizens, on April 5, 1904, voted to sell fifty thousand dollars' worth of bonds to construct a modern courthouse and new jail. Then followed a bitter debate over location. W. S. Maddrey, an attorney and businessman, and several others offered to provide the county with clear title to block sixty, owned by Bush's sister Harriet Simmons. Henry Sanborn offered to provide the county a choice of two sites: a block between Fillmore and Taylor and First and Second avenues, or the same block sixty that Maddrey's group was agreeing to provide. The county commissioners on July 19 accepted the Maddrey offer, with the understanding that his group would secure the property deed from Simmons.

Sanborn was angry. On July 27, 1904, he filed a lawsuit against William H. Bush, suggesting that Bush had never owned block sixty and consequently had had no legal right to sell the property to Harriet Simmons. Apparently Sanborn believed that block sixty still rightfully belonged to him. This time Bush, backed by Harriet and Francis T. Simmons, who were also named in the suit, refused to compromise with Sanborn, and Potter County District Judge Ira Webster set a trial date for January, 1905.[30]

Meanwhile, the county, on September 1, 1904, secured title to block sixty from Harriet Simmons and issued a call for construction bids. Three weeks later, the commissioners awarded a contract to J. J. Holt and J. M. Stanberry, who proposed to build the courthouse and jail for $48,000 and complete the work within eight months. However, when news of Sanborn's lawsuit became public, some two hundred citizens of Amarillo, led by Warren W. Wetzel, petitioned the county commissioners to reconsider building on block sixty.[31]

Thus, at the beginning of October, the commissioners faced two dilemmas: the petition and the lawsuit. In effect dismissing the petition, they decided to go forward with construction, which began immediately. After much debate over the proper course of action regarding the lawsuit, they determined in December to intervene in the case.

The case, *Sanborn v. Bush*, heard in Potter County District Court No. 47, came to trial in January, 1905. Sanborn's attorneys argued that the warranty deed of February 5, 1898, "was but a mortgage in fact, given by [Sanborn] to secure the payment of the indebtedness to Bush." They requested cancellation of the deed from Bush to Simmons and asked that Sanborn be awarded damages and all costs relating to the lawsuit. Bush's lawyers, joined on February 19 by attorneys representing the county as intervenors, denied Sanborn's claims and insisted that, in the 1898 transaction, Bush had "bought the property of Sanborn."[32]

The jury on February 22, 1905, found in favor of Bush, and it further ordered that Sanborn pay all legal expenses. Sanborn appealed, but a year later lost again before the Texas Court of Civil Appeals.[33]

As the court case proceeded, construction on the courthouse went forward. Although the building project moved slowly and the county experienced some difficulties with its contractors, the three-and-one-half-story courthouse and a two-story jail opened without fanfare in April, 1906. The building was described as "one of the finest courthouses in the Southwest."[34]

When the county courthouse opened, the city was growing rapidly. According to one A. Eberstadt, an Amarillo resident at the time, from 1905 to early 1907, the city "boomed and property values rose." Its population increased from 1,442 in 1900 to nearly 10,000 inhabitants in 1910, as the region attracted both townspeople and farmers. Bush thought the increase in population was easily understandable. "Where lands are cheap and fertile," he stated, "climate delightful and seasons favorable, what is more natural than that the farmer and investor should be attracted" to the area?[35]

Indeed, after 1905 settlers poured into the Panhandle. "Trains," writes Della Tyler Key, "sometimes brought [to Amarillo] as many as two hundred land prospectors." Livery stable operators and land agents met the passengers with hired rigs to carry the land seekers to the prairies and plains for views of the terrain. At the height of the boom, in 1909, the livery operators often used automobiles. They formed "large excursions . . . comprised of dozens of automobiles filled with prospective [settlers and] set out from Amarillo" to places across the Panhandle. To meet the growing demand, McKnight's Transfer and Livery Sales Company "from 1903 to 1928 . . . was never closed day or night."[36]

Bush participated in the promotional activity. Not only did he distribute circulars about the Panhandle, but also he printed business stationery under the heading "William H. Bush Texas Farming Lands" and used it in his letter writing. The stationery indicated that he owned "109,000 acres of very choice agricultural lands in Potter, Randall, Sherman, Moore and Wichita Counties, Texas." The reverse side of his business letters included a map of the Panhandle and South Plains, a comparison of Amarillo temperature and rainfall averages with those of cities across the United States and in Europe, and a listing of businesses needed at selected townsites on or near Frying Pan lands.

To oversee the sale and lease of his Texas landholdings, Bush in late 1906 sent his half-brother James to Amarillo. After his graduation from high school in New York, James had gone to Chicago to live briefly with Edwin and Stella Bush. Afterward, W. H. Bush had financed his education at the University of Illinois at Champaign, from which he graduated in 1906. In Amarillo, James, who was twenty-one years old, first worked in a building with John Wills, but later he established a separate office in one of the Amarillo banks. When his mother arrived from New York in 1907, he moved with her into a home on Frying Pan lands west of Amarillo. Sometime in 1912, they moved to Bush Stop (modern Bushland) where James, who married Maurine Bass about 1915, established a second office to sell town lots and to lease or sell Frying Pan farmland. He also took over management of the ranch's grazing lands, which he leased to area cattle raisers.[37]

J. L. Summers, who, as an agent in the Holland-Wills real estate firm, managed an Amarillo office for Bush's Texas Farming Lands, and James Bush were busy. As Byron Price and Frederick Rathjen have written, "The Panhandle . . . experienced a major land rush during the period" between 1903 and 1917. With crop and land prices advancing "more rapidly than other commodities," pioneer farmers from Illinois, Iowa, Nebraska, and elsewhere in the Midwest arrived to acquire a farmstead. "The number of farms nearly doubled during the . . . period and improved land exceeded two million acres."[38] James Bush and Summers offered farmland for sale at prices ranging from $12.50 to $30 per acre and for lease at from 50 cents to $1.50 per acre, per year.

As these developments occurred in Amarillo, W. H. Bush was active in Chicago. On February 1, 1902, he and Elva celebrated their twenty-fifth wedding anniversary. W. H.'s brother Edwin and his wife Stella hosted a large reception and dinner for the occasion, and many friends and relatives came to the Bush home on North State Street to honor them. Mrs. B. M. Harger of Dubuque, Iowa, sent greetings in the form of a poem calligraphically inscribed on an otherwise plain but elegant greeting card.[39] (That summer, too, James Bush had arrived from New York to live with Edwin and Stella before attending the University of Illinois.)

The next year, in 1903, William H. Bush and Francis T. Simmons dissolved their partnership. They remained close personal friends, but for reasons no longer apparent, they sold off the boot line, and Simmons, who had managed the ladies' kid glove department, established Francis T. Simmons and Company as a separate entity. Bush created William H. Bush and Company and took over the men's wholesale hat business. His brother Edwin continued to manage the office, and Bush turned his attention to his lands in Texas and to the sale of Glidden's various properties.[40]

Then tragedy struck. On May 19, 1906, Elva Bush, who was fifty-four years old, died suddenly. Her husband and her parents, Joseph and Lucinda Glidden, were devastated. W. H. and Elva had been married for more than twenty-nine years, and their relationship had been an intimate, family-oriented one, full of love and quiet pleasures. With no brothers or sisters, Elva had come to enjoy W. H.'s family as her own; she and Hattie Simmons were particularly fond of one another's company. After a memorial service at the Fourth Presbyterian Church, Bush buried her in Graceland Cemetery in Chicago.

Perhaps to ease his sorrow, Bush went to Europe. He had always enjoyed touring in Europe, and this time he took his young half-brother James with him on the summer trip. They were gone nearly three months, visiting England, France, Switzerland, and Italy. Upon their return to the United States, they stopped in Houseville to visit Emma Bush and completed plans for James to go to Amarillo, where he was to oversee the selling and leasing of Frying Pan Ranch lands.

Shortly after returning from Europe, Bush encountered additional tragedy. On October 9, 1906, following a brief illness, Joseph Glidden, who was ninety-three years old, died in DeKalb. Glidden's death was a hard blow, for the two men had developed a firm personal and professional relationship, in which each held a genuine respect and love for the other. For nearly twenty years, Bush had managed many of Glidden's business affairs, especially the major transactions. He and Mrs. Glidden buried the former barbed-wire king in a DeKalb cemetery.[41]

Having lost both his wife and his business partner and father-in-law within just a few months, Bush struggled to deal with his grief and pull his life together. He sold his substantial interest in the Glidden Felt Pad Manufacturing Company, which had not been the financial success that Bush had hoped, and reorganized his wholesale hat business, changing its name to Bush Hat Company, Inc. After relocating to 248 Adams Street (the corner of Market and Adams), the firm restricted itself to wholesaling and retailing hats, caps, straw goods, and gloves.[42]

Turning over additional responsibility for Bush Hat Company to his brother Edwin, W. H. Bush spent the next several months traveling. He went to the Caribbean and spent some time in Jamaica, where he may have lived briefly with a woman companion, but records concerning the affair, if there was one, are cryptic and incomplete. He again journeyed to his boyhood home in Martinsburg and may have returned to Europe once more. On his annual trips to Texas, he stayed in the Panhandle longer than in the past. He visited his sister Clarissa ("Clara," as he called her) and her husband, F. G. Robinson, in Kansas City.

Also in Kansas City, Bush met Ruth Russell Gentry. Ruth, who had been born in Mexico, Missouri, on August 26, 1880, was the daughter of Richard and Susan Emeline (Butler) Gentry of Kansas City. As she possessed the happy faculty of making and keeping friends easily, Bush was immediately attracted to her. An intelligent, lively woman who had graduated from Vassar College in 1902, Ruth took a keen interest in everything around her. She liked to travel, enjoyed art of all kinds, loved books, and was fascinated with the history of China and Chinese culture. Although there was a considerable age difference between them, Ruth and Bush began courting almost from their first meeting, and they were married in Kansas City on October 20, 1908.[43]

Shortly after their marriage, the Bushes went by ship on a long cruise around the world. From California, they crossed the Pacific to China. From there they went to India and then continued on to Europe, where they toured parts of Italy, Switzerland, and France before going to England. They were absent from America for several months, and during the trip Ruth found herself pregnant with their first child—expected, as it turned out, in midsummer, when they were scheduled to be in Paris. The pregnancy complicated the trip, as Ruth often became violently seasick. Aside from the pregnancy-induced seasickness, she enjoyed the exhausting voyage and took pleasure in those times when the couple was on land sightseeing in the countries through which they traveled. Indeed, by the time they reached Europe, Mrs. Bush again was in good health.[44]

About the time the Bushes left Illinois, the city of Chicago began to change its street numbering system. Bush, as a member of the powerful Commercial Club of Chicago, had played a role in establishing the new scheme. Although it was not completely adopted until 1911, the new system made the downtown corner of Madison and State streets the point at which address numbers began. The city designated all streets west of State with the prefix "West" and all streets either south or north of Madison with the corresponding prefix. It assigned 800 numbers to each mile (or 100 numbers to each one-eighth mile). Thus, there were 800 numbers north from Madison to Chicago, which was a mile distant, and another 800 numbers north to North Avenue. As a result, sometime before 1909, the number of the Bush home at 606 changed to 1538 North State Street. About 1911, the city designated North State above Schiller Street as North State Parkway, a road that Lincoln Park officials maintained with special streetlights, lawn care, and sidewalks, making the neighborhood considerably more elegant.[45]

When it was at last fully implemented on April 1, 1911, the modern numbering system created confusion—at least briefly. But not many months passed, wrote J. Seymour Currey, before Chicagoans recognized a "great improvement and convenience" in "the new order of things," and the "changes eventually received the hearty commendations . . . of the people."[46] Although extant records do not reveal how large a role Bush played in creating the new plan, his sense of logic, order, and what he called "good" numbers was evident in the new designations.

His sense of good numbers also was revealed in his telephone listing. Bush, who held shares of stock in a local phone company, had complained in the 1890s about telephone operations, especially about long distance service to DeKalb. Sometimes he could not get through to the Glidden home, and, all too often, when he reached his manufacturing plant in DeKalb, he could not hear the speaker on the other end of the line. Thus, in 1908 or as soon as an updated phone system became available to his home, he got a new telephone. According to his daughter, there were seventy-three residential customers in the new system in Chicago at the time, and he could have selected "74," the next available listing, as his telephone number. Being fond of "good" numbers, however, he chose instead number 123.[47]

Shortly after returning from the world cruise, Mrs. Bush gave birth to a daughter. The beautiful baby girl, born on August 1, 1909, and named Wilhelmina Gentry Bush, was the first of two children born to Ruth and W. H. Strong, healthy, and vigorous, "Billie" (as she was called until she changed her name to Caroline during World War I) must have been a delight to her father, a man nearly sixty years old, who enjoyed the company of children but until now had had none of his own.[48]

Fourteen months later, on November 21, 1910, Mrs. Bush gave birth to a second child. Named Ruth Emeline Bush but called Emeline, she was not as robust as her older sister but was as much a delight to her parents. The girls remained close friends throughout their lives. They attended school in Chicago and spent most of their summers on the Frying Pan Ranch or traveling with their parents before going off to boarding school and college in the East.

With two daughters and a wife who took a lively interest in affairs outside her home, Bush found his life heading in new directions. He and Ruth became members of the Edgewater Golf Club a few miles north of their home, and United Charities of Chicago made him a director. He became more active in Chicago's busy club life and joined several, including the City Club of Chicago.[49]

Bush also joined the Caxton Club of Chicago. Created in 1895, it was a book club whose membership was "primarily centered in the aesthetic aspects of the book." Its constitution stated that "its object shall be the literary study and promotion of the arts pertaining to the production of books," but it soon had evolved into "both a literary club and a printing society." It attracted writers and book lovers, as well as leaders such as the director of the Chicago Historical Society and board chairmen or trustees of the Newberry Library and the Art Institute of Chicago. (Charles Hutchinson, president of the latter for forty-two years, was a friend of Bush's.) More than a book society, the Caxton Club was a dining, printing, literary, historical, and bibliographical society. Average attendance at its monthly meetings about the time Bush began to participate reached fifty-four. According to its historian, its members were "catholic in their interests and that is why the luncheon and dinner meetings [were] invariably remembered as a time of interesting and stimulating conversation."[50]

Not long afterward, Bush joined the Cliff Dwellers, a group whose members were interested in artistic and literary subjects. Mrs. Bush encouraged him to join the club, whose membership included "those professionally engaged in literature, painting, sculpture, architecture, music, or drama, or to lay membership who is a connoisseur and lover of The Fine Arts." Every professional writer in Chicago was expected to belong. Organized in 1907 under the leadership of author Hamlin Garland, the club restricted its membership to 250 males, each of whom paid an initiation fee of fifty dollars and annual dues of forty dollars. The club occupied two floors of Orchestra Hall, but most activities occurred in the "big room" on the top floor of the building, looking out over Lake Michigan. Although membership was restricted to men, women attended as guests in the evening or for dinner. Because they had liquor available during America's Prohibition years, the Cliff Dwellers in the 1920s became one of Chicago's elite social clubs.[51]

By this time, about 1912, Bush had begun to shift his business interests to the Frying Pan Ranch. For one thing, Ruth was far more interested in the ranch than Elva had been. In addition, his brother Edwin was assuming ever greater responsibility for the Bush Hat

Company in Chicago. Moreover, Amarillo and the Panhandle were booming, as additional people moved to the area. Wheat production was attracting farmer-settlers, who were breaking out large tracts of Panhandle grazing land to grow the product. Thus, Bush again turned his attention to the Panhandle, a region that quickly was becoming an empire of wheat.

CHAPTER SEVEN

An Empire of Wheat

During much of the lifetime of William Henry Bush, farming remained a secondary enterprise in the Texas Panhandle. Nonetheless, from the earliest period of Anglo occupation of the region, a few pioneers had tried raising crops. When, in the 1890s, settlers in significant numbers began to claim school lands, farming increased; Bush, hoping to lease his Frying Pan lands to farmer-stockmen who had purchased alternate school sections, began to encourage cultivation of various grain crops. At the turn of the twentieth century, railroads and others advertised the region's farming potential, and a population boom followed after 1905, as farmers swarmed over the area. From the first, wheat was a favorite crop, and by the end of World War I, in 1918, the Panhandle had become an empire of wheat.

Farming the Panhandle was no easy proposition. Breaking the tough prairie sod required great physical strength and special plows with shares strong enough to cut through the thickly matted roots of grass and the sometimes "gummy" soils. The work was difficult and time-consuming. Most farmers tended to break out small areas, get them planted, and then continue to plow up new land as time and weather permitted. Moreover, in the 1890s, drought, grasshoppers, depression, declining agricultural prices, and a shortage of cash all weighed heavily upon pioneer farmer-stockmen. Indeed, "cultivated property," write B. Byron Price and Frederick W. Rathjen, "declined by about 9,000 acres during the decade, as settlers, broken and defeated by the elements, abandoned their claims wholesale."[1]

For those who stayed, living conditions often were as bleak as the natural elements. Pioneer families often lived in tents or in wagon boxes until they had dug a home in the side of a hill or constructed a house dug halfway into the ground with a crude frame structure completed above the dugout portion. Some people built homes from blocks of sod (4 x 12 x 18 inches was the standard size) cut from the earth. They made the roofs of poles, upon which they placed additional sod blocks. Although warm in winter and cool in summer, the dugouts and sod houses were small, dirty, and, after rainfall, often filled with mud. Some people built a flimsy wooden shack and covered it with tarpaper. As soon as possible, the family constructed a frame house.

Pioneer farm families faced an endless round of chores. Men handled the heavy labor of breaking sod and planting, cultivating, and harvesting the major crops. Women labored ceaselessly at household duties of all kinds; among many of the German settlers, their responsibilities included milking the cows, if the place held a few dairy animals. Children took responsibility for certain farm chores, such as tending the cattle, horses, and other livestock.

Water and fuel often were difficult to obtain. There were few trees to use for fuel. In drought years, as in 1892–94, when creeks and playa lakes dried up, pioneers hauled water in barrels from sources many miles away. Eventually, those who stayed drilled wells for water and put up windmills, and they secured fuel, such as coal, from nearby towns.

The homesteaders' social activities were Spartan. There were visits to and from neighbors and events in the nearest town during trips for supplies. With money scarce in the depression of the early 1890s, most pioneer families rarely enjoyed any activities beyond basic social interactions with others.

Early Panhandle farmer-stockmen came from a settled world characterized by levels of comfort and services that did not exist in their new environment. They may have expected to regain their comfortable standard of living quickly, but many were disappointed by the crudity of their new homes and by their failure to recreate rapidly the world they had left behind. As a result, some people gave up and left their homesteads to settle in town or to return to the region from which they had come.[2]

Most people remained. To help themselves through the difficult period of the early 1890s, some pioneer families gathered bones. Early Panhandle settlers, writes Della Tyler Key, "found hundreds of tons of buffalo and cattle bones bleaching on the prairies." The bones, remains of the fantastic buffalo hunts of the middle to late 1870s and "the great cattle loss in the winter of 1885–86," were scattered across the Panhandle. Key indicates that a significant "number of people were able to weather the money panic and drought of the early nineties by gathering these bones." They loaded wagons "with the whitened bones" and hauled them to shipping points along railroads. Sold at eight dollars per ton, the bones "came into use for fertilizers and other purposes."[3]

In the second half of the decade, as the depression ended and the drought broke, conditions improved. New equipment, including better plows and huge steam-powered "traction engines" (tractors), made pioneer farming easier. The state's Four Section Settler Act made it more attractive. Passed in 1895 and amended in 1897, the law allowed a person to purchase one section of agricultural land from the public domain at two dollars per acre and three additional sections of grazing land at one dollar per acre. The act lowered interest rates and extended the payment period for buying the land.

Then, in 1902, state courts declared the "lapse-leasing" system illegal. Under the former system, cattlemen had rented grazing sections from the state for five-year periods and re-leased the land before the contracts expired, blocking settlers' attempts to secure property. After the court's decision in *Ketner v. Rogan*, grazing land leased from the state became available for purchase before it could be leased again. Thus, when large blocks of leases expired after 1902, hundreds of thousands of acres became available to land-hungry farmer-stockmen.[4]

With conditions improving and land more accessible, farming expanded. Because planting and harvesting corn did not require major equipment, it was a favorite crop in the early days of Panhandle farming. Farmer-stockmen also planted such feed crops as hay, sorghum, oats, Johnson grass, Kaffir corn, and millet to provide for their livestock. A few tried winter wheat, and, on some ranches, including the LE and XIT, managers planted small tracts of fruits and vegetables.[5]

On the Frying Pan Ranch, William H. Bush encouraged manager Harry M. Beverley to experiment with fruits and vegetables, particularly grapes and sugar beets. Believing there might be a "satisfactory" market for eggs and poultry, he also tried to interest Beverley in raising chickens on the ranch. Although he was not successful in convincing his manager of the value of such projects, Bush suggested to W. F. McGowan (an Amarillo lawyer and businessman who leased some land along Tecovas Creek downstream from the Frying Pan headquarters) that he try sugar beets. "I have been thinking a little, lately about the beet sugar business," he wrote to McGowan. "I think with a little irrigation you have just the land to do this on."[6]

Bush assisted in other ways, too. "I want to help any body and every body in that section of the country," he wrote to McGowan. Realizing that improvements in the land "will eventually benefit us" at the Frying Pan, he told McGowan, who had written about building a dam along Tecovas Creek, "You can construct this dam." He wished him "every success with your new dam and ditch."[7] By 1910, two dams had been built. In 1995, both were still extant, although the reservoirs behind them were badly silted in and the land near them was unsuited for crops, ruined as pasture, and overgrown in mesquite.

Meanwhile, hoping to attract land buyers and leaseholders, Bush promoted the region. He printed five thousand maps of the Frying Pan Ranch and planned to send "them out all over the country just as soon as I can arrive at the price to put on the different sections." He reasoned that his land in 1895 was worth from one to six dollars per acre. "What I am going to try a little later," he wrote J. H. Wills, his land agent in Amarillo, "is to sell quarters as well as half and whole sections."[8]

Bush wanted Wills, who was also a surveyor, to lay out roads on the Frying Pan in two-mile squares. Under such a scheme, he argued, access to the land would be easier and property lines readily apparent. "My idea in leaving the roads every two miles, square," he wrote, "is to make it so a man can [be] put in every four sections, and can run cattle and other things there, and this will make a splendid deal for him."[9]

To speed the process, Bush hired a new Frying Pan superintendent. Beverley, who wanted to raise cattle, stepped aside, and, sometime before 1897, Thomas A. Curtis became the manager of Bush properties in the Panhandle. Hailing from Henrietta in Clay County, Curtis was a young but experienced cattleman who leased pastures from Bush and concomitantly served as manager of the farm and ranch lands. His mother and other family members soon joined him in Amarillo, where he handled most of the Frying Pan promoting and leasing operations.[10]

Others—railroads, realty companies, town builders, and ranchers—all got into the promotion business. Price and Rathjen write that "some of the more active promoters erected model farms. . . . to demonstrate dryland farming techniques to potential customers." Later the United States Department of Agriculture assisted in developing approaches to Panhandle farming, and it placed a demonstration agent in the area.[11]

The result of all the activities was rapid population expansion. In 1900, 21,284 people lived in the region. Ten years later, the population included 90,000 inhabitants. Many of the new settlers came from Illinois, Iowa, Nebraska, and other midwestern states, but some came from other parts of Texas and from Europe as well.[12]

In anticipation of increased land sales, Bush in 1904 directed that his Frying Pan lands be resurveyed. Many of the original surveyors had used the *vara,* a Spanish measure, rather than the yard, the English measure, when marking off the ranch. The new survey showed that several sections, especially those in the northwestern portions of the ranch, contained more than the standard 640 acres. Some measured out at 660 acres, one at 666, and a few at 680 acres. The survey also revealed that one stretch of land, about a hundred yards wide and five to six miles long in a zigzag pattern, was not recorded. When the survey was completed, Bush quickly secured title to those sections not recorded, and, with the new survey in hand, prepared to sell or lease his agricultural property to prospective farmers.[13]

At the same time, Panhandle agriculture shifted. Ranchers found that maintaining the economic viability of cattle-only operations was difficult on the increasingly expensive land; with land values rising and taxes increasing correspondingly, cattle raising slowly declined. The *Amarillo News* boasted in 1895 that its city was "the largest cattle shipping point in Texas." Three years later, the *Amarillo Weekly News* reported that cattle shipments were "dull and cattle trading exceedingly dull compared with former seasons." Stock-farming ventures, which were favored by many new settlers and promoted by people such as William H. Bush, rose in numbers in the 1890s, but after the turn of the century, they, too, slowly gave way to crop-farming operations, with wheat being one of the primary commercial crops.[14]

As early as 1889, cattleman Charles Goodnight may have harvested the first Panhandle wheat crop. The *Tascosa Pioneer* reported that Goodnight farmed "a hundred acres of wheat in Donley County which looks beautiful now and will be a test of the county, being the first wheat ever sown here." A few years later, a New Yorker inspecting the eastern Panhandle noted that, "on either side of the railroad, as far as the eye could reach, were immense fields of waving grain," including corn, sorghum, Sudan grass, oats, rye, milo, and wheat.[15]

Wheat production increased in the second half of the 1890s and, after the turn of the century and particularly after 1903–4, spread rapidly. In 1909, farmers planted the popular grain on some 82,138 acres in the Panhandle. Most growers sowed winter wheat in the fall and harvested the crop early the next summer. Hard red varieties, such as Turkey, Crimson, and Kharkof (each of which had come from Russia with immigrants to Canada and subsequently reached the Great Plains of the United States), were the favorites until farmers, on the recommendations of specialists, shifted to semihard types. Although some people tried growing it, "spring wheat," according to Garry L. Nall, "did not do well," and most growers stayed with winter varieties.[16]

When both crop yields and crop prices proved exceptional, wheat production expanded. Thousands of people poured into the Texas Panhandle to take up crop farming, with a view to raising the popular and high-priced cereal. With prices averaging about one dollar a bushel and yields in some years reaching an average of fifteen bushels per acre, pioneer farmers broke new land, and the raising of wheat boomed. In 1912, the Santa Fe Railroad shipped from the Panhandle "a total of 2,850 cars containing 2,850,000 bushels" of wheat.[17]

Even greater expansion occurred during World War I, in what some have called "the Great Plow-Up."[18] Wartime demand, writes Nall, increased the price of wheat "from ninety cents per bushel in 1914 to $2.71 three years later." Upon entering the war in 1917, the United States government guaranteed a minimum price of two dollars per bushel, and American farmers all over the southern Great Plains, including Texas, planted wheat. Farmers on the Southern Plains increased their wheat lands by over 13 million acres, "mainly," writes Donald Worster, "by plowing up 11 million acres of native grass."[19]

In the Texas Panhandle during the war, wheat acreage grew rapidly. Farmers plowed new land and "'pressed' [land] into service for wheat" that formerly had supported grain-forage and row crops. With weather mild and rainfall plentiful, crop acreage and production increased each year during the war.[20]

At war's end, Panhandle farmers were planting nearly six hundred thousand acres to the crop, and wheat, representing nearly a quarter of all small grain in cultivation, in 1919 was the region's major farm commodity. When expansion continued into the 1920s, the Panhandle became an empire of wheat, in 1929 producing forty-two million bushels.[21]

On his Frying Pan lands, William H. Bush encouraged wheat production. Settlers who took up school lands west of Amarillo near Soncy and Bush Stop planted wheat, and Bush leased his own alternating sections to wheat growers. In 1912, he instructed his manager and half-brother James Bush to move to Bush Stop and direct efforts to plow up land for wheat. Thousands of acres of former Frying Pan grazing lands became wheat fields, and in 1919 farmers, because of a shortage of railway cars to transport the crop, piled tens of thousands of bushels of wheat on the ground near bulging storage facilities at Soncy and Bush Stop.[22]

W. H. Bush did not devote all his energies to promoting wheat production. He continued, for example, to push railroad construction. "Amarillo," he told a city reporter in 1913, "has a good start on all the rest of the towns of the Panhandle as a railroad center." Pointing out that "Lubbock has had two railroads and is getting another since Amarillo has scored in that particular," he urged that Amarillo "had better not stop right now." He also noted Plainview's "aspirations to build a city." Bush was "glad to hear that the local response to . . . concessions asked" from a group proposing to build a line between Liberal, Kansas, and Amarillo was "prompt." He argued that the proposed rail line "will place Amarillo in the lead for all time, as the Panhandle's principal railroad and distributing center."[23]

Although surveyors made preliminary studies for the proposed line, World War I interrupted building efforts. Not until the mid–1920s did railway interests resume plans for the road, with its construction completed in 1928.[24]

Nonetheless, in 1913 Bush was encouraged by the way Amarillo leaders pursued the railroad. "I have some acquaintance with the steps that have led up to the present status of the railroad situation," he said, indicating that he was "pleased to know . . . that from the experience and success of your local management that the outlook is flattering for the north railroad project." He suggested that "cities, like individuals, are in [a] race . . . and public spirit and foresight of their citizenship are the determining factors of success."[25]

Likewise, Bush promoted the Panhandle State Fair—as it was then called. Begun as a regional undertaking in 1901, the fair struggled through its early years on land west of the city, but in 1906 its leaders, who included Henry Sanborn, abandoned their effort as a financial failure. They sold the grounds to Judge J. W. Crudgington, a local attorney and businessman who with others soon built the city's street railway system. Although they tried reviving the fair as a street carnival and regional exhibition the next year, the effort lasted only one season.[26]

In 1913, R. B. Masterson, one of the earliest settlers in the area, led efforts to reestablish the fair. Now located at Glenwood Park, which had been established about 1908 as an amusement park with a merry-go-round and other attractions, the fairgrounds included horse and cow barns, hog and sheep sheds, and various exhibit buildings. Now that Sanborn, who had died in 1912, was out of the fair's promotional efforts, Bush quickly became an enthusiastic supporter of, and, as the *Amarillo Daily News* reported, "a liberal contributor" to, the new endeavor.[27]

Bush in 1914 provided large but unspecified funds to the fair to support the "Boys' and Girls' Kaffir and Milo Maize Club of Potter and Randall Counties." The money went for prizes for young people with ribbon-winning entries, and, according to the local paper, Bush "expressed himself as being greatly pleased with the showing presented." In a conversation with a representative of the *Amarillo Daily News*, he said, "This is a great country. . . . Production this year has been nothing short of astonishing, and I am glad to note that the young people of the Panhandle . . . are awaking to the importance of the right kind of farming."[28]

Despite enthusiastic support, the fair lasted only five years. The *Amarillo Daily News* reported that, when American participation in World War I "interrupted pleasure activities," the fair's leaders discontinued the annual event in 1918. The current popular Tri-State Fair began in 1923.[29]

Support of the fair suggests that Bush's interests in the Panhandle were expanding. Indeed, they were. In 1912, Bush started construction of a large home on the eastern edge of the Frying Pan Ranch. Located on a hill just west of the city, the house was among the first in Amarillo to be wired for electricity. As the home was too far from town, however, electric power was not available for about eight years. Completed in 1914, the attractive and comfortable stone dwelling was situated with a grand view of the surrounding country, which fell gently away from the house. A long, curving roadway led up to the home, and in subsequent years Mrs. Bush oversaw the planting of trees and shrubs to enhance the drive, yard, and bordering lawn.[30] In the 1920s, according to the *Amarillo Daily News*, the magnificent home became the scene each summer "of the season's outstanding social events in Amarillo."[31]

Bush built a large garage and a barnlike structure near the home and made other improvements. The garage held two cars and included a place for a buggy, as well as a room for a chauffeur. He sunk a well, erected a windmill, and nearby constructed a water tower high enough to provide pressure for running water to reach the second-floor bathroom in the house. A short distance away, he provided a house for a resident who cared for the Bush property in the family's absence.[32]

Mrs. Bush encouraged her husband to establish a shallow, concrete-lined pond behind the house that could be used as a swimming area for their daughters, and she asked him to erect a low rock wall to provide a boundary at a point where the land sloped away from the house. Mrs. Bush took a lively interest in the ranch and wanted a comfortable home near Amarillo for those times when she brought her girls to the Panhandle.[33]

Caroline and Emeline came to Amarillo for the first time in 1914. "I was almost five," Caroline remembered. After three nights and two days on the train with their mother and a maid, the girls arrived at the Santa Fe station about five o'clock in the morning. Two Harvey girls, waitresses hired by the Santa Fe's incomparable Harvey House restaurant chain, said Caroline, were "starched and ready to serve breakfast to us." After eating, they waited for a carriage and a cart to take them and their luggage "out to the ranch house." When the vehicles arrived, Caroline recalled, "Mother didn't think that the carriage was suitable [for] my rather delicate younger sister, herself, me and a maid." Instead, the driver transported them "to the old Amarillo Hotel, where Mother and the maid were absolutely scandalized to see the number of drunks lying in armchairs in the halls."[34]

With a new home in the area, the Bushes got involved in the development of a country club for Amarillo. Located on a tract of 170 acres on the west side of the city about a mile south of the Bush home and on land that once had been part of the Frying Pan Ranch, the Amarillo Country Club included a golf course and handball and tennis courts. It also included a large clubhouse with shower facilities; not long afterward, its members established a dining area. Charles Fisk led the movement between 1910 and 1913 to create the country club, and W. H. Bush was among the original group of one hundred people who bought a $100 share in the corporation.[35]

Mrs. Bush insisted that the country club establish a mixed-foursome golf program. Although it "scandalized" many of Amarillo's male golf enthusiasts, the new but optional playing format became popular on the club's rolling fairways that wound through a twisting draw at the upper end of the west fork of Amarillo Creek. The Bushes, with their guests, played the course on a regular basis during the weeks when they were at their Panhandle summer home, and, after the dining room opened, they used its facilities from time to time.[36]

During the early stages of the country club's development, Bush laid out the town of Cliffside. Located on Frying Pan pastures along the Fort Worth and Denver Railroad about five miles northwest of Amarillo, Cliffside is directly north of the old site of Ragtown, the original tent community from which Amarillo grew. Bush dedicated Cliffside as a townsite on August 5, 1915, with three north-south streets (Clinton, State, and Fulton) and six east-west streets numbered One to Six. The place never developed as a farming community.[37]

Farther west, however, the tiny farming village of Bush Stop showed some growth. Located on Frying Pan lands along the Rock Island Railroad about fourteen miles from Amarillo, it attracted farmers, businessmen, and townspeople. Believing that the name of the town "was [not] elegant enough to represent the family," Mrs. Bush determined to change it "to something more suitable." She went to the train station, where she persuaded the station master to repaint the east and west walls of the depot with the name "Bushland"; when no one objected, the new name stuck. Local residents in 1917 organized a Baptist church in the community, and before long Bushland grew into a "lively little town." In terms of numbers of residents, it reached a peak in the late 1950s; but by 1995 its population had slipped back to 130 inhabitants.[38]

As Amarillo grew in the 1910s, Bush turned to the promotion of dairy farming. Having grown up amid dairy farms in upstate New York and having seen them prosper in Illinois, he wanted people in the Panhandle to try milk cows. "It is my judgment," he told a representative of the *Amarillo Daily News* in 1914, "that . . . our greatest development will be found in connection with the dairy business." His experience with "producing dairy products," he continued, "forces me to the conclusion that we [should put] cows into every farm scheme where profits, maximum profits, are sought." Noting that cows stay "through thick and thin, and all kinds of weather," he hoped "that action may be taken to install . . . dairy cows in varying numbers on every farm throughout this section."[39]

To encourage dairy farming in the area, Bush in 1916 placed a small herd of Guernsey milch cows on the Frying Pan Ranch. He hired a local farmer to tend the animals, milk them, and sell the product to local dairies. The *Amarillo Daily News* reported that "so strongly is he in favor of it and to demonstrate his faith . . . he is willing to cut his land up into small dairy farms and sell it to dairy farmers at terms to suit the purchaser." Bush, the paper indicated, "says the country is coming to that sooner or later and it is the best thing for the country."[40]

After Bush established his small herd of Guernseys on the ranch, Mrs. Bush insisted that he record the Frying Pan cattle brand. Although the family had been using it on its livestock since 1881, the brand officially had been reported as the "Pan Handle" in Oldham, Potter, and Randall counties. Thus, on September 15, 1916, Bush recorded the Frying Pan brand at the Potter County courthouse, and afterward he used it on his milk cows. In 1995, Bush's heirs, who had reestablished a beef operation in the 1970s, continued to use the brand on its herds of Frying Pan cattle.[41]

As these developments occurred in Amarillo, William H. Bush maintained a busy round of activities in Chicago. The Bush Hat Company, of which he was still president and treasurer, remained profitable. With his brother Edwin, who was now a junior partner in the firm, he moved its location to 217 West Monroe Street. Because Francis T. Simmons had retired and moved to California, the Bush Hat Company took over some of the Simmons company clients, but Edwin and William continued to concentrate on hats, caps, and gloves. Bush also located the "home office" for his Texas Farming Lands operation at the Monroe Street address.[42]

Although he retained most of the investment property he owned on the North Side, when opportunities appeared, Bush sold many of his real estate holdings on Chicago's southern and western sides. He also began to sell farm property that he owned, some of it in partnership with Edwin, in rural areas outside of Chicago. Income from these sales he reinvested in business, public utility, and banking stocks. The latter included stocks of the First National Bank of DeKalb, the National Bank of Commerce in Amarillo, and at least three in Chicago: Globe National Bank, First Union Trust and Savings Bank, and First National Bank.

Bush also took a more active role in the Chicago Historical Society. Elected one of its governing annual members in 1910, he regularly attended its meetings. He was one of eighteen members who, on April 13, 1913, represented the society at the dedication of the Stephen A. Douglas Monument. Located near Lake Michigan on the eastern end of 35th Street, the monument is a tribute to one of Chicago's most famous public citizens of the mid-nineteenth century. Bush and other members who attended the dedication met at the society headquarters, boarded automobiles for the short trip, and drove to the site on Chicago's South Side. After a round of dedicatory speeches and the monument's unveiling, they joined other celebrities in attendance at a reception for those people involved in the dedication. In the evening, a large audience filled the historical society's lecture hall to hear Col. Clark E. Carr deliver an oration on Douglas.[43]

Shortly after the Douglas Monument dedication, Bush bought an automobile, a large Packard limousine. A magnificent touring sedan, it contained lounge seats in the front that were separated by little doors from the rear portion. In the back were a spacious seat that held three people comfortably and two smaller "jump seats." An aisle allowed the Bush girls to walk to the front and "get in daddy's lap" on the passenger side. Splendid isinglass curtains covered the windows.

Long running boards, as they were called, existed on either side of the automobile, each holding two spare tires. At the rear of the car was, by Bush's design, "a specially contrived suitcase trunk" that held several suitcases wrapped in protective material to keep out any dust the vehicle might stir up on the dirt and gravel roads of the time.[44]

Although keenly interested in automobiles, Bush never drove the Packard. Nor did he drive any of his subsequent motor vehicles, including his favorite "big green Cadillac," which he purchased in the early 1920s. Nearly sixty-four years of age in 1913, he believed that he was too old to drive. He hired a chauffeur, which proved just as well, for it was difficult to change the flat tires that occurred so frequently with early autos on the rough roads characteristic of the period. On a thirty-mile trip along Sheridan Road from Chicago to Lake Forest one Sunday afternoon, the car had three flat tires: one on the outbound trip and two while returning. Bush and his driver normally needed thirty minutes to change a flat tire on the big automobile.[45]

When the vehicle was not in use, the driver parked it in the stable behind the Bush home. Although he had sold the horses and removed the carriages from the stable, Bush had not removed the hay, straw, and manure from the building, and his chauffeur drove the Packard onto the dried mixture on the floor. No one objected until a couple of years later, when Bush bought bicycles for his daughters. At that moment, about 1915, Mrs. Bush demanded that the old, decaying manure be hauled away, so that Caroline and Emeline might have a clean place to keep their new bikes. It was done, of course.[46]

Upon Ruth's influence, the Bushes took a lively interest in the Art Institute of Chicago. In the 1890s, Bush had joined the institute as its first life member, and in 1909 he had become a governing member. After 1914, however, Mrs. Bush was more active in the organization than W. H., who nonetheless supported the institute and encouraged his wife's involvement there. Although she dabbled in painting, Mrs. Bush was "not terribly good at it." Still, she attended educational sessions and took painting lessons at the institute. She also engaged in a variety of other activities and became one of the institution's more spirited members.[47]

Located in a large building along Michigan Avenue at Adams Street in the heart of the city, the Art Institute of Chicago had been created in 1879 as an academy of fine arts. Under the leadership of

Martin Ryerson and Charles L. Hutchinson, businessmen who had made themselves collectors of art, the institute grew to become one of the finest art museums in the nation. About 1921, according to records at the institute, Bush—who knew Hutchinson, a banker who headed the institute for some forty years—"originated the idea of a Life Membership Fund to be used as a permanent endowment of the Art Institute." He "was active in soliciting Life Members, provided many marketing and solicitation suggestions to the Art Institute, and had many (quite modern) ideas for 'circular letters' to draw people to become members." He became a governing life member in 1928, and in 1930, when Mrs. Bush became a governing member, the Life Membership Fund contained more than one million dollars.[48]

Meanwhile, on October 22, 1914, his sixty-fifth birthday, William Henry Bush retired from the clothing business. Handing over all responsibilities for the Bush Hat Company to Edwin, who operated the firm until his death in 1923, W. H. turned his attention elsewhere, particularly to his real estate operations. In effect sharing an office with his brother, Bush for about two years kept the headquarters of Bush Farming Lands at 217 West Monroe. Sometime before 1917, however, Bush moved into the First National Bank Building at 38 South Dearborn, where he occupied an office (number 1446) on the fourteenth floor. He also changed the heading on his stationery to read "Texas Dairy-Farming Lands," perhaps reflecting his interest in promoting milk cows in the Panhandle.[49]

Bush continued to go to his office nearly every day. Sometimes he walked the two miles from his home near North Avenue to his downtown office, but usually he rode a "Clark Street car," as he called the transit vehicles. If his streetcar was full, as it often was, even at age seventy he was not above riding on the rear step and hanging onto the guide rail, much to Mrs. Bush's consternation. He encouraged his faithful secretary, Martha F. Wells, who also may have been from Martinsburg, to retire, but she insisted that, as she was ten years younger than Bush, she would retire when he did. Wells, who had begun working for Bush in 1888, stayed with him for several more years.[50]

Although retired from the wholesale clothing business, Bush maintained his other interests. He directed Arthur J. Dalies, Bush's Chicago real estate agent and a friend, to concentrate all building properties on the Near North Side by selling, when the price was advantageous, his other landholdings in Chicago. He began to spend more time during daily lunch hours at the Chicago Club, where upon occasion he was invited to sit at the "millionaires' table," a place dominated by the city's wealthy elite. Perhaps under their influence, or maybe on his own, he switched his political allegiance to the Republican party; according to a clipping in the Bush Collection at the Panhandle-Plains Historical Museum, however, he was politically "independent, believing that the best man should win."[51]

The Bush home on North State Parkway continued to be an active place. After his wife Stella died in 1912, Edwin came for dinner each Sunday. Each week he was accompanied by his younger daughter, Marguerite, born in 1905, and sometimes his older daughter Rachel came along. Before their move to California, Hattie and Francis Simmons continued to visit the Bushes regularly. The Bush girls enjoyed the company of their uncle Francis, for he was an amateur magician and a wonderful storyteller—attributes that made him popular "at stuffy dinner parties."[52]

When Caroline started school in 1916, Bush walked most weekdays with his daughter the half-mile down State Street to Division, where she was enrolled in the Boys Latin School. Caroline was one of four girls in her class of twenty-nine students at the private institution. She remained there through second grade, after which she, and later Emeline, attended the University School for Girls on Lake Shore Drive. Meanwhile, upon bidding his daughter good-bye at the school, Bush boarded a streetcar for his downtown office.[53]

In retirement, Bush began to spend more time traveling with his family. "Taking his recreation late in life to make up for the hard work of his younger years," writes one observer, Bush and his family began a regular pattern of vacations. Part of each summer they spent at the Frying Pan Ranch, with Mrs. Bush, perhaps a maid, and the girls arriving after school was out in May and staying until the first of August. The family spent some time nearly every year at a resort area along the southeastern Atlantic coast, going to a different spot each time. One year, 1923, the Bushes spent the Easter season at Hot Springs, Virginia, a resort area nestled in a western valley beyond the Blue Ridge Mountains. They also went to Missouri, where, in Kansas City, they spent time with Clara and her husband Frank Robinson, as well as with Mrs. Bush's relatives. In California, they visited old friends from Chicago and such relatives as Francis and Hattie Simmons and Frederic and Mary Smith, who lived in Pasadena. In the 1920s, they also began a series of trips to Europe.[54]

Sometimes the family took touring vacations through parts of the United States. In 1923, for example, Bush brought a chauffeur with him from Chicago to the Panhandle, and from Amarillo the family, with the driver, went in a large touring car on a trip to New Mexico. At Mrs. Bush's insistence, family members visited the growing art colonies at Santa Fe and Taos, and they shopped at, or at least viewed, the old market in Santa Fe. From there the Bushes traveled along twisting gravel roads through the Rocky Mountains to Utah, where they spent a few days during September at the Utah Hotel in Salt Lake City.[55]

The touring vacations to California and elsewhere, the spring breaks along the Atlantic Coast, and the summers in the Texas Panhandle helped to forge strong bonds in the Bush family. During such times together, the girls listened to their father's stories about the Chicago fire, about his experiences with cowboys and outlaws at Old Tascosa, and about ranch life in the early Panhandle. Not one given to hyperbole, Bush seldom exaggerated, and usually the girls had to coax their father to elicit a story about his early life. But the long vacation trips, with their quiet yarns and their shared experiences, unified the Bush family to an extent that might not have occurred, had they spent a greater portion of their time in Chicago, each engaged in separate activities with friends and away from the family.

Upon returning home to Chicago from Amarillo each August, the family rested briefly before getting the girls ready for school. When they had the children prepared for another year at the University School for Girls, W. H. and Mrs. Bush attended to other matters. Ruth again picked up some of her activities at the Art Institute, and Bush, who in 1919 was nearing his seventieth birthday, resumed his regular routine at his downtown office.

Although he had retired from the hat and glove business in 1914, William Henry Bush continued to lead a busy life. Freed from the daily pressures involved in running a large clothing enterprise, he had turned more and more to activities in which his entire family could participate. As new events occurred in the Panhandle's growing wheat industry, however, Bush's attention again was drawn away from Chicago and toward Amarillo and his Texas farmlands.

CHAPTER EIGHT

From Chicago to Amarillo

In retirement in the 1920s, William Henry Bush devoted more and more energy to activities associated with his property in the Texas Panhandle. The discovery of oil and natural gas in the region, the growing attractiveness of wheat as a paying proposition, and the leasing of Frying Pan Ranch lands dominated his Texas business interests. With a large, comfortable home on the western edge of a booming Panhandle city, Bush, although not forsaking his Illinois interests, turned much of his attention from Chicago to Amarillo.

It made sense for him to do so. Bush in 1920 owned some 110,000 acres of land in the Panhandle of Texas, and two years earlier the Hapgood Drilling Company of Oklahoma had struck natural gas in Potter County north of the Canadian River. The well's huge output, fifteen million cubic feet of gas per day, opened a new and exciting era in the Panhandle.[1]

Bush got involved. Because the Frying Pan Ranch lay just south of the discovery well, he reasoned that if the large gas field extended below the Canadian, he and his family were in a good position to benefit financially from the development of gas and oil reserves in Potter County. When news of the December, 1918, gas strike reached him in Chicago, Bush, who since 1914 had been interested in Panhandle oil exploration, went to Amarillo. In February, 1919, he met with M. C. Nobles, Lee Bivins, R. B. Masterson (on whose ranch the well had been drilled), and others associated with the discovery, and he indicated that he was "greatly interested in the development of the oil fields around Amarillo."[2]

Little came from the meeting, but early in the summer Bush was back in Amarillo. He not only attended to affairs associated with his farm and grazing leases but also inquired of gas and oil field developments. Then, he and James, with James' wife Maurine, journeyed to Burkburnet and Ranger to examine at first hand the oil explorations that were underway in those towns. Traveling by automobile, they struggled along poor dirt trails and through muddy sections of the roads they followed. Frequent flat tires complicated the trip, and on one occasion a front tire blew out in the middle of a water-filled stretch of road at an arroyo crossing.

The Bushes went first to Burkburnet and the Wichita Falls area before turning south toward Ranger, where they spent several days. Ranger was in the middle of a gigantic boom in 1919. As a man who sought order and harmony in life, Bush was dismayed and disturbed by Ranger's exploding population of mostly men and its enormous number of irregularly placed oil derricks. He desired no such wild and unrestrained growth for Amarillo.

After inspecting the oilfields and their associated boom towns, the Bushes drove west through Abilene and then to Lubbock before heading north toward home. Bush returned with a better, although still not a clear, understanding of the impact that oil development in the Panhandle might have on Amarillo and his Frying Pan Ranch.[3]

Bush continued to gather information on the Panhandle's gas explorations. He met with Amarillo business leaders, inspected the work on Masterson's ranch, and consulted with geologists about gas and oil prospects for his own property. In 1919, however, neither gas and oil companies nor wildcatters showed much interest in securing leases to drill wells on Frying Pan lands.

Consequently, Bush turned to other matters. In the summer, his family went by train to southern California, where his sisters Mary and Hattie lived. James and Maurine Bush, with their three-year-old son William Sydney Bush (born in 1916), also went, but they traveled by automobile and made an extended vacation of the trip. All of them gathered with Mary and Hattie and their families at Mary's large home (Hattie later inherited it) in Pasadena. As other Bushes were there as well, the event became a large family gathering.[4]

In the meantime, each year near the first of May, Bush went to

Amarillo. When the school year ended in Chicago a few weeks later, Mrs. Bush, the girls, and a maid followed him. The family stayed in the Panhandle until the first of August (by which time—even after there was electricity for fans at their Frying Pan home—the heat was severe) and then returned to Illinois.

Before his family arrived in Amarillo each spring, Bush attended to his grazing leases. Up for renewal on the first of May, the leases were annual contracts in which Bush provided a house, a windmill, and a water tank, plus barbed-wire fencing and posts. By 1920, he had developed a regular pattern. Upon getting to the Panhandle, he inspected the fence lines to make sure that tumbleweeds (mainly Russian thistle) had been removed or burned off. He did not want rolling tumbleweeds to pile along the barbed wire where, over the years, they might collect enough drifting dirt and dust to bury the fences, a phenomenon that had become common since the beginning of the Great Plow-Up. To make sure that his land was not overgrazed, he also inspected the condition of the pastures, inquired of the annual rainfall amounts, and checked on the size of the cattle and remuda herds. Believing that sheep cropped the sparse grass too close to the ground, Bush refused to lease to men who wanted to raise sheep and wool. If everything was satisfactory, he and his tenant might renew the agreement for a year.[5]

Bush followed much the same practice with his farm leases, which were up for renewal after the wheat harvest (usually between June 20 and July 10), or about the first of August each year. He inspected the fence lines and consulted with the leaseholder. Then he looked after the farmstead and fields. Again, if he found everything satisfactory, he renewed the lease for a year.[6]

Most of his tenants stayed with Bush for long stretches, re-leasing the land each May or August. The farmers who grew wheat and other grains and the dairy operators usually returned about one-third of the cash receipts to Bush and kept the other two-thirds for themselves. Bush leased the grazing land to ranchers at different prices each year, depending upon the annual rainfall and the availability of good water, as well as upon the market for beef cattle. In the early 1920s, the price was normally about six cents per acre per year.

In 1921, after he had inspected the leases, Bush and his family, rather than staying in Amarillo for the summer, went to Europe. The trip, his first across the Atlantic in some years, was memorable. Not only did it occur while Europe was still recovering from the devastating effects of World War I, but also Caroline celebrated her twelfth birthday during the tour, and ten-year-old Emeline kept a diary in which she recorded some of her youthful impressions of the trip.

Crossing the Atlantic, which took about seven days, was particularly memorable, at least to the girls. During the trip Bush reserved in the ship's dining area two tables. The Bushes ate breakfast and lunch together at one table, but in the evening W. H. and Mrs. Bush asked another couple to join them, and the girls sat at the adjoining table. The first night Bush ordered wine for the adults and a split of sauterne, a little bottle of sweet French wine, for Caroline and Emeline. He instructed the waiter to pour only half the sauterne for his daughters and to save the rest for the next evening, repeating the procedure with a new bottle two nights later. The girls, as a result, divided just a tiny portion of the drink, but in the process they tasted the popular, but in the United States forbidden, beverage with their parents and their adult guests.

The Bushes stopped in Great Britain, where they spent several days at the home of Mrs. Bush's sister, who lived in Edinburgh. From England they crossed the channel in rough water in a dreadful channel boat; during the crossing, Mrs. Bush and Caroline became terribly seasick. "Oh, I was sick," remembered Caroline. In France, Bush chartered a large touring car and hired a driver, and the family for more than a month traveled through France and Switzerland. They visited several battlefields of World War I, including some in which trenches and dugouts still remained from the war. In one of the dugouts, they saw a piano upon which the crown prince of Germany had played while he visited the troops. They also crossed fields in which they found remaining from the war at least three unexploded land mines.[7]

They visited as well the usual places that long had been popular among American tourists in Europe. They stayed in Paris for a time and stopped at some of the finest old European resorts. Bush noted that tourism from the United States was "about 50 percent more than usual." With France still recovering from the war's devastation, however, Bush indicated that "conditions . . . [were] far from good."[8]

Shortly after returning from Europe to Chicago, Bush went by train to Amarillo. News had reached him that, on May 2, 1921, Gulf Production Company had struck oil at a well in Carson County, and he wanted to confirm the discovery. When he arrived in the Panhandle, he learned that the well, located south of the Canadian River, produced only 175 barrels per day. But he also learned that the same company had found oil in a second well on the Dial Ranch north of the Canadian, in Hutchinson County. Although production in the second well was only 135 barrels per day, drilling companies, when Bush arrived in late October, were making plans to test the oil potential of the land between the two discovery wells. This area a few years later became known as the Borger Field and proved to be rich in oil.[9]

Meanwhile, although drilling companies made a few minor oil strikes, geologists, noting the abundance of granite located near most of the test wells, believed that large quantities of oil and gas did not exist in the Panhandle. Such pessimism may have discouraged pipeline development in the region, but it did not keep independent drillers from prospecting.[10] Bush, encouraged by all the news of continued oil and gas exploration, willingly signed leases to operators, including the Amarillo Gas Company, who wanted to test his land for oil and gas deposits.[11]

Believing that the development of oil and gas in the Panhandle could have a positive effect on the growth of Amarillo, Bush talked about the city's development. In a speech on November 1, 1921, to the Lions Club at its biweekly meeting in the Amarillo Hotel, he said that "with a fine spirit of cooperation[Amarillo] is destined to be a big city, and will be a center of much importance."[12]

As a result, Bush wanted regional diversification. Recalling the lingering devastation he had seen recently in Europe, he urged Lions Club members not to neglect industrial development. "Manufacturing enterprises," he said, "should be encouraged to come [to Amarillo] and use the gas from the extensive fields in this vicinity." Manufacturing "will add to the expansion and stability of the community."

With prices for beef cattle and wheat dropping in the aftermath of World War I, Bush also called for agricultural diversification. As he had in a similar speech two years earlier, he suggested that area farmers try dairying. "I am delighted that Amarillo has a cheese factory and a good creamery," he said. Now the city should join other "farming communities in real consideration of the worth of dairying, as a money making item on the farm."

Because "Amarillo is destined to be a great city," Bush declared, I "believe that all future additions [to the community] should be laid out under the directions of capable landscape people." He wanted the city to build a "belt line" railroad that would encircle "Amarillo to a distance of from five to ten miles out." Such a railroad "would extend the limits of the city and make for numerous desirable features." The belt line would ease transportation, lessen congestion, and allow "home making possibilities under which savings would be possible." In effect, he wanted the city to be prepared for the growth that he anticipated as a result of oil and gas development in the Panhandle.

Finally, perhaps in jest but demonstrating his knowledge of Texas history, Bush suggested that "Northwest Texas should be a separate state." He called attention to provisions in the 1845 agreement of annexation that allowed Texas to subdivide into five states, and he made note of subsequent efforts by various Texas legislators to divide the state. However, the *Amarillo Daily News* representative who reported the Bush speech did not explain what benefits Bush saw in separate statehood for the Panhandle.[13]

Although little effort was made to follow Bush's prescriptions for the city's future, growth and development in Amarillo and the Panhandle, spurred by oil and gas discoveries, moved forward. The Panhandle Pipeline Company, in the fall of 1920, write Price and Rathjen, "had constructed a conduit through which gas from the Panhandle Field flowed to Amarillo," and the Panhandle Gas Company then made "the product available to local customers." The county paved a section of highway, which passed near the Bush home, through Amarillo in 1921, and two years later the American Smelting and Refining Company, to take advantage of the large quantities of gas available, located a smelter in northwest Amarillo near the site of the original stockyards. By 1924, several oil companies had established headquarters in the city, and their oil and gas rigs were at work north and east of Amarillo.[14]

Much of the material used in paving Amarillo streets came from gravel deposits located on the Jack Hall Ranch northwest of the city on former school land that once had been part of Frying Pan Ranch pastures. Jack Hall, who for a time served as a Potter County commissioner, had purchased his ranch in 1914; for several years, he and Mrs. Hall were the Bushes' nearest neighbors. Although the Halls had no children, Caroline and Emeline Bush, in the early 1920s, enjoyed riding horses across the prairie to a gate on the fence between their property and the Hall Ranch, a little more than a mile away. Mrs. Hall, "a straight-laced woman who always dressed in black," made delicious Scottish scones that she served to the girls, much to their delight. The Bushes saw the Halls often.[15]

Even as he watched oil and gas developments in Amarillo, Bush became interested in the development of a library in Martinsburg, New York, his birthplace. Local citizens had founded a library there as early as 1807, and in 1835 it contained "a good selection of 200 volumes." But, according to the 1995 librarian Dawn Manzer, "no records can be found of any library from then until 1912," when Ms. M. Anstice Harris, later dean of Elmira College, and others helped Alice Whitaker start a book club. Over the next few years, the "library" moved from place to place in town, and in 1918, a Mr. Fuller provided a "small brick building" for the library.[16]

When the building proved inadequate a few years later, Harris, who was in Chicago on college business, sought assistance from Bush. Harris "had a long interview with [Bush]" in February, 1924, at his First National Bank Building office. She found that not only was Bush "very aware of the formation of the library," but also he "did not like the idea of it having to move around town so often." Before she had left the office, Bush told her that he was "going to give you the money to buy a house for the library."[17]

Bush agreed to provide up to $1,500 for the purchase of the Violetta C. Hazen home for the library. He hoped that the money would be sufficient to buy the house, to make any necessary repairs on it, and to secure a vacant lot between the house and the main road (now Route 26) through town. If the Hazen home was unavailable, he suggested that perhaps "it will be possible to purchase our old home, or the Griffiths' house, just opposite." Bush wanted no mention of his name, he wrote, no "*publicity*—at least no publicity until after the building is secured."[18]

When negotiations for the Hazen property began to drift, Bush increased his offer to $1,800. As the higher amount was not at first accepted, the library committee sought to purchase another home. Bush, in fact, had wired $100 to attorney George Reed of Lowville,

New York, to close the purchase of a house called the Pelo place in April, when M. Anstice Harris convinced the Hazen family to accept a smaller offer. A long delay followed, as the library people, acting on Bush's recommendation, attempted to secure from the local Catholic church the vacant lot west of the house, so that the library might front the main road through town. When the lot was secured a year later, Violetta Hazen deeded the property, at Bush's request, to Martha F. Wells, his secretary, and on September 30, 1925, Bush and Wells turned the house over to the Martinsburg library association.[19]

Bush paid for both the vacant lot and the new library building. Until his death, he also paid the librarian's salary. In addition, he and the Martinsburg Home Bureau assumed the cost of extensive repairs and improvements in the Hazen house. Local contractors installed a new heating system, removed partitions, built bookshelves, and in general turned the old house into a comfortable little library. In the deed, Bush provided that "the property *can never be mortgaged.*" He reasoned that "ten or even forty years from now the Library Association may have an entirely different lot of people to manage it, and some ... person in the same might want to put a mortgage on it, and in time the property might be lost." For his help, the library association named the building the William H. Bush Free Library.[20]

Library personnel held a formal opening for the library on September 3, 1925. Bush was unable to attend the opening, but in October, with his sister Hattie, his brother James, and his secretary Martha, he visited Martinsburg. Several people in the area who had grown up with W. H. and Hattie attended a reception for Bush at the library. Pleased with "what had been accomplished," Bush purchased for library use a book plate bearing a picture of his mother. Later, writes Dawn Manzer, "he sent formal portraits of all the presidents of the United States. He also gave freely for books and magazines and provided quite a sum of money to improve the building grounds and library."[21] In his will, he left a percentage of income from a trust to continue maintenance of the library. In the 1980s, the sum became sufficient to build an entirely new structure.

As the library remodeled its new building during the summer of 1925, Bush and his family went to Europe. They sailed from New York on the *Belgiumland* at the end of June and arrived in Europe a week later. They visited many of the countries of northern and western Europe, including Belgium, Holland, Norway, Sweden, Denmark, Germany, Switzerland, and France. Absent from home for more than three months, Bush indicated that we "were well all the time we were gone." They returned from France on board the *Columbus*. It was, wrote Bush, "a very calm, beautiful voyage, and the best service I have ever seen and the most beautiful boat I have ever crossed on."[22]

About the time they returned from Europe, W. H. and Ruth Bush joined the Shoreacres Golf Club, located at Lake Bluff, several miles north of Chicago and near Lake Michigan. Bush apparently did not play golf there, for the deep ravines of the course made conditions too difficult for him—he was seventy-six years old—to walk the steep fairways. But he and Mrs. Bush enjoyed the club's many social activities, and they arranged to have dinner at Shoreacres when they were at the club.[23]

The Bushes also joined the Casino Club. Located at Delaware Place near the lake on Chicago's North Side, its elegant interior had been designed by Rue Carpenter, one of the country's trendsetting decorators during the early twentieth century. On spring evenings, Chicago's elite walked in evening clothes to dinner parties or dances at the club. The gilded youth of Chicago's North Side also patronized the place, and, according to Finis Farr, "during the winter social season, with music a mild version of jazz, the Casino was the favored place for debutante dances."[24]

Mrs. Bush, who enjoyed activities at the Casino Club, maintained a busy round of engagements. According to records at the Art Institute, she was "active in charitable, historical, and art endeavors." She had worked with the Canteen of the Red Cross in Chicago during World War I, for example, and there she had helped to provide doughnuts and coffee to terrified eighteen-year-old soldiers (most of whom had come from the West) leaning from windows of very slowly moving troop trains on tracks of the Michigan Central. She served as a volunteer at the North Side Center of Infant Welfare. She was a founding member of the American Friends of China at the University of Chicago and a board member of the school's International House.[25]

As a member of the International House board, Mrs. Bush became interested in the Chinese graduate students—four women and fourteen men—attending the University of Chicago in the mid-1920s. From time to time, she would have two or more of them for Sunday dinner, although never men and women together, for it was socially incorrect for them to meet each other in such a way.

One day, to W. H.'s total consternation, Mrs. Bush agreed to have a Chinese wedding in her home, and she talked her reluctant husband into serving with her as proxies for the parents who would not be present. Although details of the affair are unavailable, apparently she had received a letter written entirely in Chinese from the parents of a young man (the Bushes called him "William") whom the parents had determined would never be happy as the husband of a Chinese girl to whom he had been pledged in marriage at the age of two. After having the letter translated for her by a Chinese physician (also a practitioner of traditional Chinese healing methods), Mrs. Bush learned that the parents, through matchmakers in China, had examined "the pedigrees" of the available Chinese women at the university, had chosen a woman whom the Bushes called "Dorothy," and had made suitable arrangements with her parents in China. The parents wanted the wedding to proceed before two more years of graduate school had passed. Thereupon, Mrs. Bush completed arrangements for the event, and Dorothy, who was not sure which of the Chinese graduate students would be her husband, spent the last night before her wedding at the Bush home. Then, on a warm Sunday afternoon, a very nervous Bush did his part to ensure a successful marriage and stood in for the absent young couple's parents.[26]

As he sweated through his role in the Chinese wedding, Bush also struggled with the City of Amarillo over the construction of water lines on his farm property. With Bush's willing consent, the city, in need of additional water sources for its expanding population, in early 1926 had drilled several wells on Bush-owned land southwest of Amarillo. Problems developed, however, when the city contracted for the extension of water lines from the wells. James Bush, who managed Bush properties from an office on East Fifth Street in Amarillo, and W. H. believed that they had received assurances from city commissioners that Amarillo would build "a hard-surfaced, or well-improved highway alongside the pipeline" across five sections of their land. The Bushes also wanted "water privileges for tenants on the Bush land," and they "wanted to tap the main line and use water for irrigating tracts" of their farm property. When the city indicated that it would not build the road, the Bushes countered by not granting right-of-way privileges.[27]

By denying right-of-way privileges, the Bushes held up pipeline construction for Amarillo's new water system. James Bush told a *Globe* reporter in June, 1926, that "he had not denied the city right-of-way, and that the city might cross his land 'under terms of an understanding I had with the commission several weeks ago.'" Insisting that "I am not denying them the right to cross my land," James indicated that "I'm ready to do my part when they do what they promised." The commissioners responded that they had made no such "agreement with [James] Bush" and that, "when approached several weeks ago, he told us we were at liberty to cross his land."[28]

The delay was short-lived. When they understood that the city could not build roads outside the city limits, W. H. and James signed the right-of-way agreements and dropped their requests to tap into the main line. Construction started immediately, and, before long, Amarillo's new water system was in operation.[29]

As Bush negotiated with the Amarillo commissioners over the proposed water line, the United States Government, through its Bureau of Mines, became interested in developing natural gas reserves on Bush's land. Bureau personnel had determined that helium—a light, nonflammable gaseous element—existed in the southern portions of the large Panhandle gas field that stretched north across the Canadian River; and they wanted to develop its potential, particularly from a source called the "Cliffside structure," or Bush Dome, on the ranch a few miles north and west of Amarillo. They reasoned that helium, which had multiple uses and was at the time considered essential, was a military asset, and it was particularly important for use in army and navy dirigibles and other lighter-than-air ships.[30]

Accordingly, Bureau of Mines officials, beginning in 1926, sought leasing and drilling rights to the Cliffside gas field. They negotiated with Bush and the Amarillo Oil Company (formerly the Amarillo Gas Company), which held leases to some of Bush's property, and by 1927 the bureau had secured "an operating contract for gas, with option (to purchase gas rights), covering 20,000 acres of land on the Cliffside structure." Afterward, in 1929, Bush leased additional drilling rights to the bureau, and when it exercised its option to purchase gas rights and signed other leasing contracts, the government controlled about fifty thousand acres (about fifty-five percent of which belonged to Bush) of the richest known helium reserves in the world.[31]

The Bureau of Mines also wanted a facility to extract helium from the natural gas taken at the Cliffside field. It sent a representative to Amarillo to inspect various sites, and he met with Harve H. Haines, vice-president and general manager of the Amarillo Board of City Development, which had received several site proposals, including one from Bush. When the inspections were complete, the bureau, in late 1927, chose the Bush proposal, an eighteen-acre site along the Rock Island Railroad near Soncy, about seven miles west of Amarillo. Bush donated the site to the bureau.[32]

The bureau began constructing a pipeline from the Cliffside gas field in July 1928 and the next month broke ground for the helium plant. A year later, in April, 1929, personnel at the plant placed the facility in regular production. In 1929, the plant contained eight major buildings "together with their appurtenances, including roadways; water-cooling pond; water wells and tower; gas holders; water, steam, gas, electric and waste lines." The six-inch welded steel pipeline that connected the Cliffside wells to the plant crossed several sections of Bush property.[33]

By the end of 1929, Amarillo had become known as the "Helium Capital of the World." The facility at Soncy, suggested Roy Roddy, was "the only helium [extracting] plant in America," turning out "practically the entire supply of the world." The four helium-bearing gas wells in the Cliffside field, wrote Andrew Stewart, produced "a total open-flow capacity of about 30,000,000 cubic feet of gas per day."[34]

Bush did not earn a substantial income from the gas leases and helium contracts. He received only the price of "sour" (that is, nonburnable) gas from the Bureau of Mines. There were no royalties, and he had donated the eighteen-acre site for the helium plant.

Amarillo benefited. The helium plant, under the supervision of C. W. Seibel, employed nearly five hundred people, many of them highly trained scientists and technicians who came to Amarillo from a helium plant the government had closed near Fort Worth. Other people worked on the well-drilling rigs or constructed the pipeline. Over the next several years, private companies in Amarillo contracted to sell and transport helium, to build tube trailers, and to test helium containers. Local railroads and truck lines also participated in the business of transporting helium from Amarillo to other parts of the United States.

During negotiations over the helium leases, Bush began changing his bookkeeping system from ledger to double-entry. Herbert S. Bush, a cousin who may have been an accountant for Marshall Field and Company, introduced Bush to the double-entry procedure in 1928. W. H., who was "incredibly able to accept new ideas," immediately recognized the benefits of a method in which both the debit and credit sides of a business transaction were recorded. Although the change was expensive and time-consuming, he adopted the practical and efficient scheme in his business accounts, a decision that eased recordkeeping for his many real estate transactions and greatly benefited his estate.[35]

As he approached eighty years of age, Bush continued a vigorous round of activities. He had become a governing life member of the Art Institute of Chicago; and he and Mrs. Bush, who was forty-nine, maintained a busy schedule of social activities, which included plans for another trip to Europe with their girls in 1929. Mrs. Bush became active in the Chicago Historical Society; and Bush, as he had done at the Art Institute, started a life membership program at the society, buying the first life membership in the name of his daughter Caroline. In 1930, Bush bought a membership in the Martinsburg (New York) Golf Club, half a continent away, but he probably did not intend to play the course.

Bush's daughters, in the meantime, were off to school in the East. Caroline in 1925 attended the Shipley School, a college preparatory institution at Bryn Mawr near Philadelphia, before enrolling in Vassar College. Later she took classes at the MIT Architecture School. Emeline, who was a gifted artist, attended Miss Porter's School in Connecticut before enrolling at Sarah Lawrence College in Bronxville, New York, in 1928, the very year the women's school opened for classes.[36]

By 1928, Bush had begun to provide large sums of money to charitable organizations. The Art Institute of Chicago, the Chicago Historical Society, and the Fourth Presbyterian Church, where he continued to be a trustee, received significant annual gifts. He also gave money to the Red Cross, the United Charities (of which he was a director), the Glenwood School for Boys, the Park Ridge School for Girls, the Kirkland Mission, and the Presbyterian Hospital in Chicago. The William H. Bush Free Library received annual donations; and in 1929, in Lowville, New York, to whose weekly paper he still subscribed, he gave, in the name of his mother, a substantial gift to the Johnson Home for Children.[37]

In the summer of 1930, during their annual visit to the Panhandle, the Bushes hosted a grand party for all their farm and ranch tenants and their families. It was primarily a social gathering, but the Bushes were concerned also about the financial status of their tenants. Cattle prices were very low, and wheat prices, in the face of huge bumper crops in 1929 and 1930, were low enough that it was more economical for the tenants to burn wheat in their heating stoves than to sell their crops and buy fuel. The Bushes, accordingly, used the large gathering in part to rally their tenants and offer them moral support.[38]

In early 1931, after visiting an old friend who was suffering from a serious case of influenza, Bush became sick. The illness, according to his secretary, became debilitating, and he spent most of his time in bed, feeling well enough over the next few weeks to go to his office only a few times. Without recovering, he went with Mrs. Bush by train to Kansas City near the end of March to attend the funeral of their brother-in-law, Frank Robinson, Clara's husband. Upon returning to Chicago, he entered a hospital, but when the infection entered his mastoid process, his condition grew worse, and physicians at Chicago's Presbyterian Hospital were unable either to operate or to treat the illness effectively. His health continued to decline, and on Wednesday, April 8, 1931, Bush died in Chicago, at the age of eighty-one.[39]

On Saturday afternoon, April 11, at the Fourth Presbyterian Church, Mrs. Bush and her daughters, accompanied by James Bush and many friends, attended funeral services for Bush. Shortly afterward, they buried him on a woody spot of ground in Graceland Cemetery in Chicago.

William Henry Bush was a remarkable and complex individual with varied interests and activities. He had little formal education, but he became a man of letters who enjoyed serious literature. A powerful and well-connected Chicago businessman, he was also a Texas rancher and successful wheat grower who, in addition, raised dairy cows. A practical man who was conservative with his money, he nonetheless acted as a willing philanthropist, and on occasion he might slip his young nephews a twenty-dollar gold piece. He could be firm and unyielding at times (as he was with the Hurlbuts over unpaid grazing leases), but more often he showed compassion and understanding—perhaps expected of a leader in his Presbyterian church. A person who enjoyed quiet evenings at home with a good book, he also was a world traveler who crossed the Atlantic Ocean some twenty-seven times. Unassuming and unpretentious, he nonetheless was always well dressed and carefully groomed. Although a hesitant storyteller, he was a prolific correspondent, sometimes drafting up to twelve letters a day.

In many ways, Bush was representative of the well-to-do entrepreneurs of his day. Through a combination of good fortune, careful money management, and timely marriage, he acquired the means to establish a clothing firm; through intense application and hard work, he built it into one of the Chicago's largest and most successful wholesale hat and glove operations. He reinvested his income in a variety of enterprises, and, like other wealthy Chicagoans (the XIT syndicate, for example), he entered the booming western land and cattle industry at a time when it was attracting large sums of eastern and foreign capital. He traveled often to New York, London, and Paris, and he enrolled his children in preparatory boarding schools in the East and subsequently in eastern colleges.

After his father died, Bush reluctantly became head of his family; over the next forty years, he kept it in touch and together. Indeed, his extended but close-knit family looked to him for direction, for leadership, and for financial support—at least in their younger years. Likewise, his immediate family, consisting of his wife Ruth and his daughters Caroline and Emeline, remained close, supportive, and friendly.

Bush did not always get his way. He could not convince Harry Beverley, his ranch manager in the early 1890s, to diversify Frying Pan operations, and Bush's plans for developing fruit and vegetable ventures foundered. His experiment with eucalyptus and fruit trees did not succeed, and the Tecovas Spring ranch house crumbled away after the 1890s. Likewise, his efforts to diversify Panhandle agriculture with dairy farming, although undertaken as much for personal financial reasons as for the agricultural good health of the region, had little effect. Except for the helium and natural gas fields, his Frying Pan land was too far west of the large underground pools for him to benefit from the great Panhandle oil boom of the mid–1920s. In Illinois, perhaps his biggest setback related to his hat manufacturing plant in DeKalb. It did not succeed as he had planned, and, after a decade of difficulty, he sold it, accepting the loss as a frustrating experience.

Although Bush usually got along well with others, his one great interpersonal disappointment was his split with Henry Sanborn. The two men had been friends and business partners for nearly twenty years when they clashed over issues related to money, loans, and a new courthouse for Potter County. After their differences were decided in court, the men had little to do with one another.

Like other men of his day, Bush was not without his prejudices. For unexplained reasons, he did not entirely trust the Jewish merchants and men of wealth with whom he traded; and, believing that it was too parsimonious, he only reluctantly engaged the Catholic church in real estate ventures. Except as employees of the social clubs to which he belonged, Bush had little contact with Chicago's African-American residents, but in the 1890s he willingly hired large numbers of the city's rapidly growing immigrant population.

Much of the good work Bush performed went unnoticed. An unobtrusive man, he was uncomfortable talking about his accomplishments. Nor was he particularly interested in public recognition for his work. In fact, most of the time he shunned publicity. He even remained quiet about, or at least did not emphasize, his extensive philanthropy. Because the records remain hidden in his unpublished letters, for example, his important role in securing Northern Illinois University for DeKalb is not mentioned in histories of the institution.

One can also look to histories of the Frying Pan Ranch to see how Bush's achievements have gone unrecognized. Some studies of the early Frying Pan, for example, describe the ranch as an experiment by Joseph Glidden and Henry Sanborn to prove the effectiveness of barbed wire and suggest that Bush's leadership in the enterprise began only after the ranch failed. The truth is that Bush was part of the venture from the first and that Glidden had sold his share of the barbed-wire company at least five years before he and Sanborn acquired the ranch. Moreover, Bush, although he gave up cattle raising, bought out Sanborn's interest in the ranch and, during some of the worst months of the depression in the 1890s, secured it, free of all debt.

Clearly, Bush was both an enterprising Chicago capitalist and a pioneer builder of Amarillo. In many ways his life was, to borrow a phrase from Charles Dickens, "a tale of two cities." He was, said Frank R. Jamison of the Amarillo Lions Club, "a resident of Amarillo who stays in Chicago."[40] Bush enjoyed remarkable success in both cities, and the record shows that, in both places, he was a stable and dependable leader. In Chicago, Bush remained in the clothing business for forty-five years, from his first arrival in the city in 1869 until his retirement in 1914. In Amarillo, he stayed with the Frying Pan Ranch for fifty years, from his first visit to the Panhandle in 1881 until his death in 1931. He was, reported the *Amarillo Daily News*, "a tireless civic worker in Chicago, just as he was a builder in the Panhandle."[41]

As he built his fortune in Chicago, Bush established a reputation as a cautious risk-taker and a practical businessman who was quiet, hardworking, and intensely loyal to his friends and associates. His secretary, Martha Wells, for example, remained with Bush for forty-three years, from 1888 to his death in 1931. Like other prominent leaders of his city, he made business deals over lunch at the Chicago Club, used his contacts to widen financial opportunities, and when possible drew his friends and relatives into his own successful business ventures.

As a civic leader, his interests were catholic. Through membership, attendance, and financial contributions, Bush supported both scholarly and artistic organizations and political and social clubs. He encouraged the preservation and expansion of Lincoln Park, the renumbering of Chicago's street system, and the continued development of the Art Institute. He delighted in dinners at the Casino and other clubs, but he also found pleasure at home, where he collected and read a large number and wide range of books, enjoying them for their content as well as their design and physical beauty.

"Chicago," writes a city chronicler, "has much to boast about, but perhaps its greatest asset is . . . its unassuming leaders—men like William Henry Bush." They do their own work, "then turn to the needs of Chicago and finding some good they may perform . . . , perform it without making any fuss about the matter."[42]

In Amarillo, cattle ranching, wheat growing, and farm and grazing leases occupied most of Bush's time. After he built a home in the city, Bush spent the summers with his family in the Panhandle, where he joined local businessmen's organizations and participated in their important activities. He was, said a contemporary, "probably the greatest benefactor Amarillo ever had."[43] Through his efforts, the city got its first high-quality hotel. He helped to convince at least two railroads to extend their lines to Amarillo, and he provided both land and money for the construction of the region's first hospital. He promoted the area's agricultural development and encouraged many settlers to take up farms in the Panhandle. After engineers discovered on and near his property the world's largest helium reserves known at the time, his work with the U.S. Bureau of Mines helped prompt the government to establish near Amarillo what became the country's largest helium extracting plant.

One of the Panhandle's most active boosters, Bush consistently engaged in enterprises crucial to the region's growth and prosperity. He was, suggested a prominent local attorney, "a man whose vision of the future of this city and the Panhandle was greater than that of any [person] I ever knew."[44] For half a century, from 1881 to 1931, William Henry Bush played a key role in promoting the economic development of Amarillo and in building the larger Panhandle of Texas.

Epilogue

Although his wealth was substantial, the legacy of William Henry Bush amounted to more than real estate and bank accounts. Bush came to admire the Texas Panhandle's enormous, open stretches and the wild emptiness that characterized much of the early Frying Pan Ranch. His daughters, who visited the ranch for only a couple months each summer, inherited his love of the wide, sweeping panoramas of the Llano Estacado and the rugged, rolling vistas of the Canadian River breaks. Through them, Bush's grandchildren—two of whom were living on the ranch permanently in 1995—also discovered a transcendent beauty in the expansive Panhandle landscape and a shared attachment to the arid southwestern environment.

By the end of the 1920s, Bush at last had begun to worry about conservation and the changing condition of his Texas range lands. Bush's daughters, largely through Mrs. Bush's influence, learned to appreciate the emerging concern for conservation, and they passed ideas about careful land management and preservation of the environment to their children. Considering the exploitive era in which Bush lived, his grandchildren, to a much greater degree than Bush, sought to conserve and manage the land well, since they, too, hoped to pass the Frying Pan Ranch and the Bush legacy on to their children and grandchildren.

The Bush legacy included an estate with a value estimated in 1931 at several million dollars.[1] Rapidly declining land prices during the Great Depression of the 1930s, however, drastically diminished its practical worth. Nonetheless, when W. H. died in 1931, he left a will that contained detailed instructions as to how his property and the money from his estate should be dispersed. In a broad sense, the will provided one-third of the land and estate for Mrs. Bush; one-third for Caroline and Emeline; and one-third for the William H. Bush Trust, commonly known as Trust B.

The will designated Mrs. Bush, James A. Bush, and Arthur J. Dalies of Chicago as trustees. It further provided that initial funds from Trust B were to go to several relatives; to such associates as his secretary, Martha F. Wells; and to various charities, including the Glenwood Manual Training School, the Park Ridge School for Girls, the Chicago Children's Hospital, the Chicago Historical Society, and the William H. Bush Free Library in Martinsburg, New York.

After such bequests had been paid, the will directed that future income from Trust B was to be dispersed in quarterly payments to relatives and selected charities. The charities included the Art Institute of Chicago; the McCormick Presbyterian Theological Seminary in Chicago; and the cemetery, the Whitaker Falls park, and the Bush library in Martinsburg.[2]

Because land and property in Amarillo and Chicago represented a significant portion of the Bush estate, the trustees, after the will had been probated and they had paid inheritance taxes, distributed the land. By lot (drawing), in 1935 they divided twenty-five pieces of North Side real estate in Chicago and the more than 110,000 acres of the Frying Pan Ranch, which for the most part remained scattered in 640-acre blocks (sections) in its original checkerboard fashion, into three units representing Mrs. Bush's share, Caroline and Emeline's share, and Trust B's share. From time to time, as land values improved, trustees sold portions of the trust properties, and through farm and grazing leases, they continued to manage the Frying Pan lands remaining under their control.

Through careful management and wise investments, the Bush Trust by 1994 had grown to over $18 million. Income from the trust provided for permanent, named endowments that keep the Bush legacy viable and significant. They include the William H. Bush Permanent Endowment Fund (for student scholarships and faculty compensation) at McCormick Presbyterian Theological Seminary, and the William H. Bush Special Life Membership Fund at the Art Institute of Chicago, an endowment Bush had started in the 1920s.

In addition, the Bush will provided money for the William H. Bush Endowment Fund and the Kathryn Simmons Blankenhorn (his niece) Memorial Endowment Fund at Park Ridge School for Girls.

Income from the funds was to be used for the maintenance and improvement of the school's buildings and grounds. The will also established unnamed endowments at the Glenwood Manual Training School and for the Martinsburg cemetery, Whitaker Falls Park, and the William H. Bush Free Library, which was to use its endowment to construct a new fireproof building.

In the late 1970s, directors of the Bush library, in desperate need of a modern facility, moved to erect a new building. With funds from the Bush estate having accumulated to an amount that made construction possible, they hired architects and secured contractors. Workmen removed the former building—the old Hazen house—and in 1979 began construction of a one-story, 3,750-square-foot building that, as Bush had instructed, fronted the main road through Martinsburg. The attractive red-brick library opened on July 26, 1980, and its directors changed its name to the William H. Bush Memorial Library.[3]

Meanwhile, Ruth Bush, after her husband's death, continued her active life. In Chicago, she moved into an apartment on Lake Shore Drive and became more involved with the Chicago Historical Society. According to notes in the society's reference files, as a "Colonial Dame," she collected items for one of its museum rooms, and in 1936 the society named her an honorary life member. In July, 1931, shortly after W. H.'s death, she gave twenty-six thousand dollars to the Trust Fund of the Art Institute of Chicago; in 1951, the institute made her an honorary governing member. The next year it elected her deceased husband a benefactor. In Amarillo, she took the leading role in administering Frying Pan lands, and, under her initiative, the ranch "became a model of good management." She also contributed liberally to the Boys Ranch, a home for "boys needing a second chance," at Old Tascosa near Amarillo.[4]

To commemorate Bush's "pioneer work and his faith in the future of the Panhandle," Mrs. Bush collected first-edition books on the early Southwest. From among the large number of books that she and W. H. had owned, she pulled together books and materials on the history of the region, added others written before 1890, and in 1941 presented the collection to the Amarillo Public Library. Over the years, the Bush family continued to add to the collection's contents; in 1979, the Bush Collection, as it was called, consisted "of more than 800 items of books, drawings, narratives, private papers, etc." It included "overland journeys, early narratives, early biographies, Indian captivities, outlaws, government reports, . . . fur trade, western trails, Texas rangers and sheriffs, Texas as a sovereign state, and other early publications." It was an important asset to the library, for both its reading and research offerings and its material worth. With publication dates as early as 1807, many of the books are rare and valuable.[5]

As she put together the Bush Collection, Mrs. Bush's daughters married: Emeline to Francis "Tim" O'Brien in 1936 (a wedding that was described as the "social event" of the season in Chicago) and Caroline to Frederick L. Emeny in 1940. After World War II, the O'Briens moved with their two children from Chicago to Amarillo to look after the Bush interests, and they lived in the Bush home. O'Brien practiced law in Amarillo, and in 1946, although he lost the election, he "was the first Republican in the Panhandle to run for a Congressional seat." In the early 1950s, he was director of the United States foreign operations administration office in Montevideo, Uruguay.[6]

The Emenys lived in Cleveland, Ohio, where Frederick Emeny was a banker. With their three children, writes Donna Flenniken, the Emenys "traveled often to Texas to visit the ranch." As she became "more involved with responsibilities" in the Panhandle, Caroline determined to build a house in Texas and at her husband's suggestion selected a site on the western edge of the ranch "at the top of a bluff overlooking a breathtaking view of canyons and river breaks." After the home was completed in 1970, the family, just as Caroline's had done when she was a child, spent part of each year at the ranch.[7]

In the 1970s, one of Emeline's daughters, Gwendolyn "Wendy" Bush O'Brien Marsh, and her husband Stanley Marsh 3; and one of Caroline's daughters, Mary T. Emeny, and her husband Hunter Ingalls; lived on the now divided ranch. Just as Bush had done, they continued to lease farm and range lands and share profits with their tenants. They reestablished "medium-sized cattle operations" on their property, writes Donna Flenniken, and their farmers produced "wheat, grain sorghum, sugar beets, pinto beans, and seed maize."[8] Concerned with modern land-use problems and ecological questions, they attempted to develop a "holistic" approach to farm and ranch management and sought ways to conserve the ranch environment and preserve it for the future.

In the early 1990s, Bush relatives maintained an elusive but powerful bond to Bush and to one another. Income they shared from the Bush estate, the century-old Frying Pan Ranch, and Bush's continuing legacy all contributed to the bond. In early August, 1994, many of them gathered in Amarillo, having come to the Panhandle from scattered parts of the United States. They toured the Frying Pan Ranch and its "offspring," the Dripping Springs Ranch (created by the division of Bush property); visited the former Bush home (now owned by Wendy and Stanley Marsh) in Amarillo for a Texas-style barbecue; and enjoyed a ranch-style chuckwagon breakfast at Tecovas Spring. Those few who had known Bush shared their experiences, and everyone, most of whom had not met previously, celebrated his memory. The gathering represented the first time that such a large number of Bush relatives had come together at the ranch.

In 1995, Bush heirs and the Bush estate still owned nearly one hundred thousand acres of land that in 1881 had been enclosed within Joseph Glidden and Henry Sanborn's original "#9 Galvanized wire" fence. Some of the original fence, in fact, remained in use. Tecovas Spring, reduced by heavy irrigation from underground water formations that fed it, was little more than a trickle. The first adobe ranch house was gone, but the little stone milk house survived. A historical marker confirmed the isolated but attractively rugged spot as the site of the original Frying Pan Ranch headquarters—the place where William Henry Bush in 1881 had begun helping others in the region build an empire in the Panhandle of Texas.

Notes

ABBREVIATIONS

ASNG	*Amarillo Sunday News and Globe*
BET	Bush-Emeny Trust, Amarillo, Texas
BL	Bush Letters, William H. Bush Collection, Amarillo Public Library, Amarillo, Texas
BOBC	Bush-O'Brien Collection, Archives, Panhandle-Plains Historical Museum, Canyon, Texas
Golden Anniv. Ed.	Golden Anniversary Edition
SC	Southwest Collection, Texas Tech University, Lubbock, Texas
WHB	William H. Bush
WHB Library	William H. Bush Memorial Library, Martinsburg, N.Y.

PREFACE

1. H. A. Nobles, "Incidents in the Life of a Pioneer Merchant," *ASNG*, Golden Anniv. Ed., Aug. 14, 1938, sec. B, p. 30.

CHAPTER ONE

1. Lloyd Lewis and Henry Justin Smith, *Chicago: The History of Its Reputation* (New York: Harcourt, Brace, 1929), 123. See also *The Great Chicago Fire* (New York: Chicago Historical Society, 1958), 1–5.
2. Lewis and Smith, *Chicago*, 130. See also Caroline Bush Emeny (WHB's daughter), interview by Paul H. Carlson, Aug. 7, 1994 (transcript in SC); William Cronon, *Nature's Metropolis: Chicago and the Great West* (New York: Norton, 1991), 345–46; Finis Farr, *Chicago: A*

Personal History of America's Most American City (New Rochelle, N.Y.: Arlington House, 1973), 100–109; Donna Flenniken, "Barbed Wire and the Frying Pan Ranch," *Accent West* 19 (Feb. 1991): 18; Bessie Louise Pierce, *A History of Chicago* (New York: Knopf, 1957), 3:3–6.

3. See "Bush, William Henry," *The National Cyclopaedia of American Biography* (New York: James T. White and Co., 1927), B:424. "The First and Present Library and Founder" (n.p., n.d.), typescript in Historical Files, William H. Bush Trust Properties, Amarillo, Tex. Book clipping, n.d., in William H. Bush Collection, Archives, Panhandle-Plains Historical Museum, Canyon, Tex.
4. David Hackett Fischer, *Albion's Seed: Four British Folkways in America* (New York: Oxford Univ. Press, 1989), 23, 25, 27–28, 31–35; "Bush, William Henry," *National Cyclopaedia of American Biography*, B:424.
5. Charles Edward Banks, *Topographical Dictionary of 2,885 English Emigrants to New England, 1620–1650*, ed. and indexed by Elijah Ellsworth Brownell (Baltimore, Md.: Genealogical Publishing Co., 1981), 52.
6. "First and Present Library and Founder."
7. Ibid.; WHB to William Stevens, Lowville, N.Y., Dec. 12, 1892, in BL.
8. Franklin B. Hough, *History of Lewis County, New York, with Illustrations and Biographical Sketches of Some of Its Prominent Men and Pioneers* (Syracuse, N.Y.: D. Mason and Co., 1883), 515.
9. Ibid.; "First and Present Library and Founder"; Franklin B. Hough, *A History of Lewis County, in the State of New York, from the Beginning of its Settlement to the Present Time* (Albany: Munsell and Rowland, 1860), 214.
10. "First and Present Library and Founder."
11. G. Byron Bowen, ed., *History of Lewis County, New York, 1880–1965* (Lowville, N.Y.: Board of Legislators of Lewis County, 1970), 372, 384, 390; Hough, *A History of Lewis County, in the State of New York*, 180, 186.
12. Advertisement in Historical Files, WHB Library; D. G. Beers, *Atlas of Lewis Co., New York, from Actual Surveys by and under the Direction of D. G. Beers* (Philadelphia: Pomeroy, Whitman and Co., 1875), 57; "First and Present Library and Founder"; Dawn Manzer, "Library Named for Benefactor," *Journal and Republican* (Lowville, N.Y.), May 27, 1987.
13. Chalkley J. Hambleton to Ruth G. Bush, Nov. 17, 1948, in Historical Files, William H. Bush Trust Properties, Amarillo.
14. "First and Present Library and Founder." The dates for the children's births and deaths are also noted on headstones at the Bush family plot in the Martinsburg Cemetery, Martinsburg, N.Y.

15. Ibid.
16. Ibid. First quotation from Emeny, interview by Carlson, Aug. 7, 1994; second quotation from clipping in Historical Files, BET; Albert Nelson Marquis, ed., *The Book of Chicagoans: A Biographical Dictionary of Leading Living Men and Women of the City of Chicago* (Chicago: A. N. Marquis, 1917), n.p.
17. "First and Present Library and Founder."
18. Ibid. Quotation in *Whetstone Gulf State Park* (Alexandria Bay, N.Y.: Office of Parks, Recreation and Historic Preservation, State of New York, n.d.), n.p.
19. Bowen, *History of Lewis County*, 377.
20. Emeny, interview by Carlson, Aug. 7, 1994; Flenniken, "Barbed Wire and the Frying Pan Ranch," 18.
21. Herm Ortlieb, manager of Whitaker Park, interview by Paul H. Carlson, Oct. 13, 1994 (notes in possession of author); Bowen, *History of Lewis County*, 377.
22. "First and Present Library and Founder." M. Anstice Harris to Arthur J. Dalies, July 8, 1931, in Bowen, *History of Lewis County*, 392–95. Book clipping, n.d., in William H. Bush Collection, Archives, Panhandle-Plains Historical Museum, Canyon, Tex. Flenniken, "Barbed Wire and the Frying Pan Ranch," 18.
23. M. Anstice Harris to the People of Martinsburg, n.d. [ca. 1947?], in Bowen, *History of Lewis County*, 393.
24. Book clipping, n.d., and newspaper clipping, "Rites to be Held Tomorrow for Wm. Henry Bush," n.d., in William H. Bush, Reference Files, Chicago Historical Society. Seth T. Miller to Anyone Whom It May Concern, Aug. 29, 1868, in BOBC.
25. Book clipping, n.d., in William H. Bush Collection, Archives, Panhandle-Plains Historical Museum, Canyon, Tex. "First and Present Library and Founder."
26. Aurelia R. King (later WHB's neighbor) to friends and family (Jule), Oct. 21, 1871, in *Great Chicago Fire*, 21–25.
27. Emeny, interview by Carlson, Aug. 7, 1994; Flenniken, "Barbed Wire and the Frying Pan Ranch," 18; Lewis and Smith, *Chicago*, 76–77, 130; *Great Chicago Fire*, 2.
28. King to friends and family (Jule), Oct. 21, 1871, in *Great Chicago Fire*, 24.
29. WHB to Charles S. Kirk, June 7, 1894, in BL.
30. WHB to Laura V. Hamner, Sept. 13, 1922, in Historical Files, BET; Caroline Bush Emeny, interview by Mrs. Clyde W. Warwick, n.d, transcript in Mrs. Clyde W. Warwick, *The Randall County Story* (Hereford, Tex.: Pioneer Book Publishers, 1969), 30.

31. "First and Present Library and Founder." Book clipping, n.d., in William H. Bush Collection, Archives, Panhandle-Plains Historical Museum, Canyon, Tex.
32. Caroline Bush Emeny, telephone interview by Paul H. Carlson, June 29, 1994 (notes in possession of author).
33. Cronon, *Nature's Metropolis*, 346–47.
34. WHB to Emma Bush (his stepmother), Nov. 26, 1894, in BL.
35. The secondary literature on the subject is extensive. See Walter Prescott Webb, *The Great Plains* (Boston: Ginn & Co., 1931), 294–311; Joseph M. McFadden, "From Invention to Monopoly: The History of the Consolidation of the Barbed Wire Industry, 1873–1899" (Ph.D. diss., Northern Illinois Univ., DeKalb, 1968), 24–46; Henry D. and Frances T. McCallum, *Wire That Fenced the West*, 25–43. See also WHB to Hamner, Sept. 13, 1922, in Historical Files, BET. Joseph F. Glidden patented an ineffective barbed wire on May 24, 1874, and he received a third patent in 1875.
36. Webb, *Great Plains*, 309; McFadden, "From Invention to Monopoly," 31–32, 43.
37. "Glidden, Joseph Farwell," *National Cyclopaedia of American Biography* (1933), 23:350–51; McFadden, "From Invention to Monopoly," 24–25; WHB to William Stevens, Lowville, N.Y., Dec. 12, 1892, in BL.
38. Pierce, *A History of Chicago*, 3:184, n. 104; WHB to Seth T. Miller, Constableville, N.Y., Aug. 24, 1894, in BL.
39. WHB to Henry B. Sanborn, Sept. 25, 1893; WHB to E. T. Lyon, Omaha, Neb., Jan. 3, 1894; WHB to Mr. Prendergast, Hastings, Mich., Mar. 30, 1894; all in BL.
40. See WHB to H. M. Beverley, superintendent of Frying Pan Ranch, Sept. 22, 1892, in BL.
41. Pierce, *History of Chicago*, 3:483, 3:495. Book clipping, n.d., in William H. Bush Collection, Archives, Panhandle-Plains Historical Museum, Canyon, Tex. Emmett Dedman, *A History of the Chicago Club* (Chicago: Chicago Club, 1960), 159. Quotation in Robert Shackleton, *The Book of Chicago* (Philadelphia: Penn Publishing, 1920), 110. Emeny, interview by Carlson, Aug. 7, 1994.
42. WHB to John Peter Altgeld, Mar. 19, 1894, in BL. Kenny J. Williams, *In the City of Men: Another Story of Chicago* (Nashville, Tenn.: Townsend Press, 1974), 142. Book clipping, n.d., in William H. Bush Collection, Archives, Panhandle-Plains Historical Museum, Canyon, Tex. Stanley Marsh 3, "The Bush Memorial Collection," in Clara T. Hammond, comp., *Amarillo* (Austin: Best Printing Co., 1974), 299–300. Lewis and Smith, *Chicago*, 143.
43. Emeny, interview by Carlson, Aug. 7, 1994.

CHAPTER TWO

1. *Texas Almanac and State Industrial Guide, 1990–1991* (Dallas: A. H. Belo Corp., 1989), 235–36.
2. Edna Kahlbau, "Ghostly Plazas Once Rang with Songs of Shepherds," *ASNG*, Aug. 14, 1938, sec. C, p. 4; Paul H. Carlson, *Texas Woollybacks: The Range Sheep and Goat Industry* (College Station: Texas A&M Univ. Press, 1982), 86–100.
3. William F. Cummins, *Report on the Geography, Topography, and Geology of the Llano Estacado or Staked Plains*, 3rd Annual Report of the Geological Survey of Texas (Austin: State Printing Office, 1891), 148–51.
4. Mrs. Albert Bivins and Cora Green, interview by Mrs. L. E. Moyer, accompanied by C. Boone McClure, Jan. 20, 1958, transcript in Wendy and Stanley Marsh 3, Records, Toad Hall, Amarillo.
5. B. Byron Price and Frederick W. Rathjen, *The Golden Spread: An Illustrated History of Amarillo and the Texas Panhandle* (Northridge, Calif.: Windsor Publications, 1986), 52.
6. Emeny, interview by Carlson, Aug. 7, 1994. For a good discussion of early Anglo occupation of the Panhandle, see Frederick W. Rathjen, *The Texas Panhandle Frontier* (Austin: Univ. of Texas Press, 1973), 228–49.
7. Seymour V. Connor, "Early Land Speculation in West Texas," *Southwestern Social Science Quarterly* 42 (Mar. 1962): 360.
8. McFadden, "From Invention to Monopoly," 34–35; John Arnot, "Horses and the Frying Pan," *ASNG*, Golden Anniv. Ed., Aug. 14, 1938, sec. E, p. 27; B. B. Paddock, ed., *A Twentieth-Century History and Biographical Record of North and West Texas* (New York: Leois Publishing Co., 1906), 1:302–307; WHB to Hamner, Sept. 13, 1922, in Historical Files, BET.
9. For a brief discussion of how myth and folklore may have played a role in the scramble to invest in western lands and cattle, see Webb, *Great Plains*, 233–35. The number of books on western ranches is large. Two of the best are David J. Murrah, *The Pitchfork Land and Cattle Company: The First Century* (Lubbock: Texas Tech Univ. Press, 1983) and William M. Pearce, *The Matador Land and Cattle Company* (Norman: Univ. of Oklahoma Press, 1964). The best recent history of the western cattle industry is Terry G. Jordan, *North American Cattle-Ranching Frontiers: Origins, Diffusion, and Differentiation* (Albuquerque: Univ. of New Mexico Press, 1993). A good older study is Ernest Osgood, *The Day of the Cattleman* (Minneapolis: Univ. of Minnesota Press, 1929).
10. Webb, *Great Plains*, 234. See also James Cox, *Historical and Biographical Record of the Cattle Industry and the Cattlemen of Texas and Adjacent*

Territory (St. Louis, Mo.: Woodward and Tiernan Printing Co., 1895), 139.

11. Arnot, "Horses and the Frying Pan," sec. E, p. 27; H. Allen Anderson, "Frying Pan Ranch," Reference Files, SC; Ernest C. Shearer, "The History of Potter County, Texas" (Master's thesis, Univ. of Colorado, Boulder, 1933), 68; WHB to Hamner, Sept. 13, 1922; Dick Breen, "Sanborn, Civic Builder," *ASNG*, Golden Anniv. Ed., Aug. 14, 1938, sec. G–1, p. 4.
12. WHB to Hamner, Sept. 13, 1922.
13. Most secondary studies spell the name Wetsel or Wetsell, but Bush wrote "Wetzel" in his many letters to the man, and Price and Rathjen, in *Golden Spread* (74, 168), also use "Wetzel."
14. Daisey Currie, "The Story of Her Life as Told to Me by Her: The Life Story of Mrs. W. W. Wetsel," 1, transcript in Interview Files, Archives, Panhandle-Plains Historical Museum, Canyon, Tex.; Laura V. Hamner, *Short Grass and Longhorns* (Norman: Univ. of Oklahoma Press, 1965), 211.
15. WHB to Hamner, Sept. 13, 1922.
16. "Bush Thinks Amarillo Outlook is Promising," *Amarillo Daily News*, Jan. 25, 1913; "Found Only 5 Tents," *ASNG*, Golden Anniv. Ed., Aug. 14, 1938, sec. F, p. 11.
17. WHB to Hamner, Sept. 13, 1922.
18. Ibid.; Arnot, "Horses and the Frying Pan," sec. E, p. 27; John L. McCarty, *Maverick Town: The Story of Old Tascosa* (Norman: Univ. of Oklahoma Press, 1946), 159–60.
19. Hamner, *Short Grass and Longhorns*, 211–12; Currie, "Life Story of Mrs. W. W. Wetsel," 1; Bivins and Green, interview by Moyer, Jan. 20, 1958.
20. Hamner, *Short Grass and Longhorns*, 210.
21. Brothers C. T. and A. F. Moss of Llano County, on Apr. 7, 1887, recorded a Bar O brand, which is sometimes referred to as the "Frying Pan," but J. F. Glidden and Sanborn had been using their Panhandle or Frying Pan brand for several years before that. See "By Their Brands Ye Shall Know Them," *ASNG*, Golden Anniv. Ed., Aug. 14, 1938, sec. E, pp. 3–4.
22. Emeny, interview by Carlson, Aug. 7, 1994.
23. WHB to Hamner, Sept. 13, 1922; Hamner, *Short Grass and Longhorns*, 210.
24. Hamner, *Short Grass and Longhorns*, 210–11.
25. See, e.g., WHB to C. W. Gillespie, Bowie, Texas, Oct. 26, 1893, in BL.
26. Currie, "Life Story of Mrs. W. W. Wetsel," 1–2.

27. Ibid., 2.
28. Ibid., 3–5.
29. Ibid., 4.
30. Hamner, *Short Grass and Longhorns*, 212.
31. See Robert E. Zeigler, "The Cowboy Strike of 1883: Its Causes and Meaning," *West Texas Historical Association Year Book* 47 (1971): 32–46; Charles B. McClure, "A History of Randall County and the T-Anchor Ranch" (Master's thesis, Univ. of Texas at Austin, 1930), 61–67; Della Tyler Key, *In the Cattle Country: History of Potter County, 1887–1966* (Wichita Falls, Tex.: Nortex, 1966), 27.
32. Currie, "Life Story of Mrs. W. W. Wetsel," 2.
33. Ibid., 2–3.
34. Ibid., 3–4.
35. WHB to Hamner, Sept. 13, 1922.
36. Currie, "Life Story of Mrs. W. W. Wetsel," 5; Hamner, *Short Grass and Longhorns*, 213.
37. Currie, "Life Story of Mrs. W. W. Wetsel," 5.
38. Arnot, "Horses and the Frying Pan," sec. E, p. 27.
39. J. Evetts Haley, "The Grass Lease Fight and Attempted Impeachment of the First Panhandle Judge," *Southwestern Historical Quarterly* 38 (July 1934): 1–27; *Fort Worth Gazette*, Dec. 24, 1885; *State v Goodnight*, 11 S. W. 119 (S. C. of Texas 1888); C. L. Douglas, *Cattle Kings of Texas* (1939; reprinted Austin: State House Press, 1989), 283–85; Key, *In the Cattle Country*, 27.
40. Sanborn to P. L. Moen, president, Washburn and Moen Manufacturing Co., Dec. 30, 1886, in *Light 'n Hitch: A Collection of Historical Writing Depicting Life on the High Plains*, ed. Laura V. Hamner (Dallas: American Guild Press, 1958), 335–36.
41. Judge Newton P. Willis, "Biographical Sketch of Frank Willis, Sr., 1840–1894," *Panhandle-Plains Historical Review* 3 (1930): 18–21.
42. Sanborn to P. L. Moen, president, Washburn and Moen Co., Dec. 30, 1886, in Hamner, *Light 'n Hitch*, 335. See also Price and Rathjen, *Golden Spread*, 60.
43. Key, *In the Cattle Country*, 28.
44. Price and Rathjen, *Golden Spread*, 59.
45. Quote in Ray Allen Billington and Martin Ridge, *Westward Expansion: A History of the American Frontier*, 626; Key, *In the Cattle Country*, 28. For descriptions of the blizzards, see newspaper clippings, Morgue Files, Texas Sheep and Goat Raisers Association, Records, SC; and David J. Murrah, *C. C. Slaughter: Rancher, Banker, Baptist* (Austin: Univ. of Texas Press, 1981), 57–58 and 150, n. 5.

46. See Connor, "Early Land Speculation in West Texas," 361.
47. Key, *In the Cattle Country*, 29.
48. *Tascosa (Tex.) Pioneer*, Aug. 27, 1887; *Texas Almanac, 1990–91*, 55; Price and Rathjen, *Golden Spread*, 59.

CHAPTER THREE

1. Sanborn to P. L. Moen, president, Washburn and Moen Co., Dec. 30, 1886, in Hamner, *Light 'n Hitch*, 335–37; Audra M. Spray, "H. B. Sanborn," in *Texas Panhandle Forefathers*, comp. Barbara C. Spray (Dallas: National Sharegraphics, 1983), 111–13; Price and Rathjen, *Golden Spread*, 68–69.
2. *Tascosa (Tex.) Pioneer*, May 28, 1887; Richard C. Overton, *Gulf to Rockies: The Heritage of the Fort Worth and Denver — Colorado and Southern Railways, 1861–1898* (Austin: Univ. of Texas Press, 1953), 167–69, 171–72; Ruth Sallie Boaz, "A History of Amarillo, Texas" (Master's thesis, Univ. of Texas at Austin, 1950), 112.
3. Arthur S. Cornahan, "Sketch of Amarillo," in *Charter of the City of Amarillo: Commission-Manager Government, Adopted Nov. 16, 1913* (Amarillo, Tex.: City of Amarillo, Nov., 1931), 7; John McCarty, "Jess Jenkins, Ragtown Owner," *ASNG*, Golden Anniv. Ed., Aug. 14, 1938, sec. D, p. 27.
4. WHB to Beverley, Sept. 22 and Nov. 5, 1892, in BL.
5. Key, *In the Cattle Country*, 37.
6. *Tascosa (Tex.) Pioneer*, Aug. 13, 1887; Price and Rathjen, *Golden Spread*, 68–69; Key, *In the Cattle Country*, 40–41.
7. *Tascosa (Tex.) Pioneer*, Aug. 27, 1887.
8. Currie, "Life Story of Mrs. W. W. Wetsel," 3–5; *Tascosa (Tex.) Pioneer*, Aug. 20, 1887; Key, *In the Cattle Country*, 41–42.
9. Price and Rathjen, *Golden Spread*, 69.
10. Bivins and Green, interview by Moyer, Jan. 20, 1958.
11. Price and Rathjen, *Golden Spread*, 69; John McCarty, "Jim England," *ASNG*, Golden Anniv. Ed., Aug. 14, 1938, sec. F, p. 14.
12. See Currie, "Life Story of Mrs. W. W. Wetsel," 5–6; Bivins and Green, interview by Moyer, Jan. 20, 1958; Arnot, "Horses and the Frying Pan," sec. E, p. 27.
13. Lester Fields Sheffy, *The Francklyn Land and Cattle Company: A Panhandle Enterprise, 1882–1957* (Austin: Univ. of Texas Press, 1963), 236, 240–44.
14. *Amarillo (Tex.) Champion*, May 17, 1888.
15. Key, *In the Cattle Country*, 50; *Amarillo (Tex.) Champion*, May 17, 1888;

Boaz, "A History of Amarillo, Texas," 47–48; Bivins and Green, interview by Moyer, Jan. 20, 1958.

16. *Amarillo Champion*, May 17, 1888.
17. Key, *In the Cattle Country*, 50; Price and Rathjen, *Golden Spread*, 69; Cox, *Historical and Biographical Record*, 697.
18. Duncan Kersey, "Going Back to the Wild and Woolly Days in Amarillo with City's First Native," *ASNG*, Nov. 27, 1927, sec. 2, p. 1.
19. Bivins and Green, interview by Moyer, Jan. 20, 1958; Key, *In the Cattle Country*, 50; Kersey, "Going Back to the Wild," sec. 2., p.1.
20. Cited in Key, *In the Cattle Country*, 50; "Judge Turner Tells Realtors of Days When City Hall Had Only One Hotel," *Amarillo Daily News*, Nov. 28, 1926.
21. Price and Rathjen, *Golden Spread*, 69. See also Emily Kelly, "Pioneer Erected First Tent in Present City," *ASNG*, Golden Anniv. Ed., Aug. 14, 1938, G–3.
22. Cited in Key, *In the Cattle Country*, 77.
23. *Tascosa (Tex.) Pioneer*, Sept. 8, 1888.
24. Key, *In the Cattle Country*, 79; Emeny, interview by Carlson, Aug. 7, 1994.
25. Quotes in Key, *In the Cattle Country*, 78; Price and Rathjen, *Golden Spread*, 70–71; "Hotel Amarillo," *Amarillo Daily News*, Oct. 6, 1915.
26. Price and Rathjen, *Golden Spread*, 70; "Judge Turner Tells Realtors of Days When City Hall Had Only One Hotel."
27. Bivins and Green, interview by Moyer, Jan. 20, 1958.
28. Price and Rathjen, *Golden Spread*, 70–72, 76.
29. Quote in Bivins and Green, interview by Moyer, Jan. 20, 1958.
30. WHB to Warren W. Wetzel, Mar. 23, 1894, in BL.
31. Ibid. WHB to Judge J. C. Sherwin, Denver, Colo., Mar. 24, 1893, in BL. See also Key, *In the Cattle Country*, 36, 106, 156.
32. See T. Lindsay Baker, "Windmills of the Panhandle Plains," *Panhandle-Plains Historical Review* 53 (1980): 71–110.
33. Bivins and Green, interview by Moyer, Jan. 20, 1958.
34. Ibid.; Key, *In the Cattle Country*, 102–103.
35. "Holland and Wills General Land Agents," *Amarillo Weekly News*, Dec. 2, 1898.
36. *Evening News*, May 22, 1901; Price and Rathjen, *Golden Spread*, 81; Kersey, "Going Back to the Wild," sec. 2, p. 1.
37. *Amarillo Champion*, May 17, 1888.
38. Ibid.
39. See, e.g., WHB to Beverley, May 30, 1894, in BL.
40. WHB to Beverley, Sept. 22, 1892, in BL; Cox, *Historical and Biograph-*

ical Record, 320; Key, *In the Cattle Country*, 74; Price and Rathjen, *Golden Spread*, 74.

41. WHB to J. F. Glidden, Nov. 26, 1894, in BL; Sanborn to P. L. Moen, president, Washburn and Moen Manufacturing Co., Dec. 30, 1886, in Hamner, *Light 'n Hitch*, 335–36.
42. Bivins and Green, interview by Moyer, Jan. 20, 1958; Arnot, "Horses and the Frying Pan," sec. E, p. 27.

CHAPTER FOUR

1. Lee WHB to Beverley, Sept. 22, 1892, in BL. Arnot, "Horses and the Frying Pan," sec. E, p. 27; Cox, *Historical and Biographical Record*, 563.
2. Bivins and Green, interview by Moyer, Jan. 20, 1958; J. M. Winchester, "Drift Walkers," *ASNG*, Golden Anniv. Ed., Aug. 14, 1938, sec. B, p. 14.
3. Bivins and Green, interview by Moyer, Jan. 20, 1958.
4. Ibid. See also Hamner, *Short Grass and Longhorns*, 212.
5. Cited in Sister M. Aloysius DuBronz, "History of the Frying Pan Ranch," 41, typescript in John McCarty Papers, Amarillo Public Library, Amarillo, Tex.
6. Bivins and Green, interview by Moyer, Jan. 20, 1958.
7. Roy Riddle, "When the City Was Rough and the Gunman Ready," *ASNG*, Golden Anniv. Ed., Aug. 14, 1938, sec. B, p. 16.
8. Ibid.
9. Bivins and Green, interview by Moyer, Jan. 20, 1958; WHB to Beverley, Sept. 27, 1892, in BL.
10. Key, *In the Cattle Country*, 69.
11. Cited in ibid. Records for December show similar numbers.
12. Ibid.; "Potter County Officers," *Amarillo Weekly News*, Nov. 25, 1898.
13. Bivins and Green, interview by Moyer, Jan. 20, 1958.
14. Ibid.
15. Ibid. See also Price and Rathjen, *Golden Spread*, 59.
16. Ibid.
17. WHB to Beverley, Sept. 22, 1892, in BL.
18. Ibid.
19. WHB to Beverley, Oct. 10, 1892; WHB to John Warner, Oct. 27, 1892; and WHB to S. C. Lott, Oct. 29, 1892; all in BL.
20. WHB to James Holland and J. H. Wills of Amarillo, Nov. 5, 1892; WHB to H. B. Sanborn, Dec. 12, 1892; WHB to R. E. Montgomery, Land Agent, Fort Worth and Denver Railroad, Jan. 10, 1893; WHB to B. E. Hoppin, Chicago, Mar. 17, 1894; all in BL. *Amarillo Champion*, Aug. 20, 1892; Key, *In the Cattle Country*, 141.

21. WHB to Hoppin, Mar. 17, 1894, in BL.
22. WHB to J. M. Cooper, Tax Collector, Randall County, Tex., Dec. 27, 1892; and WHB to Sanborn (in Houston), Dec. 29, 1892; both in BL.
23. WHB to Beverley, Oct. 10, Oct. 27, Nov. 5, and Nov. 11, 1892, all in BL.
24. WHB to Beverley, Nov. 5, 1892, in BL.
25. WHB to George H. Bowen, Leavenworth, Kans., Dec. 2, 1892, in BL.
26. WHB to Beverley, Dec. 8, 1892, in BL.
27. McCarty, *Maverick Town*, 250; Bivins and Green, interview by Moyer, Jan. 20, 1958; Key, *In the Cattle Country*, 285.
28. WHB to W. F. McGowan, Mar. 22, 1893, in BL.
29. Ibid.
30. WHB to Beverley, Mar. 22 and Apr. 3, 1893, both in BL.
31. Ibid.
32. WHB to General Superintendent, St. Louis and San Francisco Railway, Apr. 6, 1893; WHB to McGowan, Apr. 6, 1893; both in BL.
33. WHB to McGowan, Apr. 6, 1893; WHB to James Holland and J. H. Wills, June 14, 1893; both in BL.
34. Lewis and Smith, *Chicago*, 208. WHB to A. H. Butler, May 10, 1893; WHB to James Hobbs, Mar. 14, 1894; both in BL. See also Pierce, *History of Chicago*, 3:197.
35. WHB to Sanborn, Sept. 25, 1893, in BL; Cox, *Historical and Biographical Record*, 502.
36. WHB to Sanborn, Oct. 17, 1893, in BL.
37. WHB to Sanborn, and WHB to Isaac L. Ellwood, both Oct. 30, 1893, in BL.
38. WHB to Sanborn, Oct. 30, 1893, in BL.
39. Arnot, "Horses and the Frying Pan," sec. E, p. 27.
40. Ibid.
41. Ibid.
42. Ibid.
43. WHB to Beverley, Dec. 21, 1893, in BL.
44. WHB to James Holland and J. H. Wills, Jan. 24 and Feb. 1, 1894, both in BL.
45. WHB to Beverley, Feb. 17, 1894; WHB to Sanborn, Mar. 16, 1894; WHB to Hoppin, Mar. 17, 1894; all in BL.
46. WHB to Sanborn, Mar. 16, 1894, in BL.
47. WHB to Sanborn, May 2, 1894, in BL.
48. WHB to Sanborn, Sept. 8, 1894, in BL.
49. WHB to W. W. Wetzel, Sept. 22 and Oct. 12, 1894, both in BL.

50. WHB to Isaac L. Ellwood, Oct. 16, 1894; WHB to Sanborn, Oct. 16, 1894; both in BL.
51. Arnot, "Horses and the Frying Pan," sec. E, p. 27; Journal Book #1, p. 261, Dec. 5, 1894, Isaac L. Ellwood, Estate Papers (C133.2A), in SC; WHB to C. B. Bush, Earlville, Iowa, Nov. 26, 1894, in BL; Hamner, *Short Grass and Longhorns*, 215.
52. WHB to C. B. Bush, Nov. 26, 1894, in BL; R. C. Hopping, "The Ellwoods: Barbed Wire and Ranches," *Museum Journal* 6 (1962): 15.
53. WHB to J. F. Glidden, Nov. 26, 1894, in BL; Journal Book #1, p. 261, Dec. 5, 1894, in Isaac L. Ellwood, Estate Papers (C133.2A), in SC.
54. WHB to J. F. Glidden, Nov. 26, 1894, in BL; Sanborn to R. C. Walker, Austin, Tex., May 24, 1904, in Henry B. Sanborn Collection, Archives, Panhandle-Plains Historical Museum, Canyon, Tex.; Arnot, "Horses and the Frying Pan," sec. E, p. 27.
55. WHB to Emma Bush, Nov. 26, 1894, in BL. See also Kersey, "Going Back to the Wild," sec. 2, p. 1.

CHAPTER FIVE

1. WHB to Miles Willis, Sept. 26, 1892; WHB to Andrew Peterson, Jan. 11, 1893; WHB to E. B. Woolworth, Apr. 3, 1893; WHB to G. W. McLester and Co., Apr. 6, 1893; WHB to Henry L. Turner and Co., May 2, 1893; WHB to Brockhausen, Fischer and Co., May 2, 1893; WHB to William Mulvery, May 17, 1893; all in BL.
2. WHB to J. F. Glidden, Jan. 17, 1893, in BL.
3. WHB to J. A. McDole, Elva Station, Ill., Apr. 6, 1893; WHB to James C. Talmage, Denver, Colo., May 2, 1893; both in BL.
4. WHB to S. C. Lott, DeKalb, Ill., Oct. 29, 1892; WHB to Joel D. Harvey, Nov. 10, 1892; WHB to Isaac L. Ellwood, Apr. 12, 1893; all in BL.
5. WHB to Beverley, Oct. 10, 1892; WHB to J. F. Glidden, Jan. 17, 1893; WHB to Beverley, Apr. 17, 1893; all in BL.
6. WHB to W. R. Caldwell, Manitowish, Wisc., June 14, 1894; WHB to S. T. Miller, Aug. 24, 1894; WHB to Isaac L. Ellwood, Oct. 31, 1894; all in BL.
7. WHB to Isaac L. Ellwood, Oct. 31, 1894, in BL.
8. WHB to H. Van Pelt, Chicago, Mar. 30, 1893; WHB to W. L. Ellwood, DeKalb, Apr. 12, 1893; WHB to Chase E. Glidden, Fredonia, N.Y., Apr. 20 and May 23, 1893; WHB to Will Glidden, DeKalb, May 15, 1893; WHB to D. W. Voorheas, chairman, Finance Committee, Feb. 17, 1894; all in BL.

9. WHB to Chase E. Glidden, May 23, 1893; WHB to Will Glidden, May 15, 1893; both in BL.
10. Lewis and Smith, *Chicago*, 181; Pierce, *History of Chicago*, 3:503.
11. WHB to Mr. Prendergast, Mar. 30, 1894, in BL; Pierce, *History of Chicago*, 3:183–84 and p. 184, n. 104.
12. WHB to Voorheas, Feb. 17, 1894, in BL. On tariff schedules see Karl Everett Ashburn, "Tariffs and Wool Duties Since 1867," *Sheep and Goat Raisers' Magazine* 10 (Nov. 1929): 104–106; Carlson, *Texas Woollybacks*, 141–43.
13. WHB to D. W. Voorheas, Feb. 17, 1894, in BL; Ashburn, "Tariffs and Wool Duties Since 1867," 104–106.
14. WHB to C. B. Bush, Earlville, Iowa, Jan. 13, 1894; WHB to Charles Bush, Feb. 3, 1894; both in BL.
15. WHB to Charles Bush, Feb. 12, 1894; WHB to C. B. Bush, Apr. 6, 1894; WHB to Mrs. Augusta Bush, Apr. 10, 1894; all in BL.
16. WHB to C. B. Bush, July 23, 1894; WHB to Miller Bros., Earlville, Iowa, July 6, 1894; both in BL.
17. WHB to C. B. Bush, July 23, 1894; WHB to Col. Rogers, Orchard Lake, Mich., July 24 and Aug. 29, 1894; all in BL.
18. WHB to Mrs. J. F. Glidden, Aug. 6, 1894; WHB to Mrs. James Bush, May 23, 1894; both in BL.
19. WHB to E. J. Wood, Plainfield, Ill., July 30, 1894, in BL.
20. WHB to S. T. Miller, Constableville, N.Y., Aug. 24, 1894, in BL.
21. Emeny, interview by Carlson, Aug. 7, 1994; Shackleton, *Book of Chicago*, 204; Susan E. Hirsch and Robert I. Goler, *A City Comes of Age: Chicago in the 1890s* (Chicago: Chicago Historical Society, 1990), 100–101.
22. Barbara Kerst, Anne Bush, and Roger Williams, Jr., interview by Paul H. Carlson, Aug. 5, 1994 (notes in possession of author); Emeny, interview by Carlson, Aug. 7, 1994.
23. Hirsch and Goler, *A City Comes of Age*, 54–55, 57. See also Pierce, *History of Chicago*, 3:183–84.
24. Hirsch and Goler, *A City Comes of Age*, 55–56.
25. WHB to Emma Bush, Nov. 26, 1894, in BL; Shackleton, *Book of Chicago*, 329, 331; Hirsch and Goler, *A City Comes of Age*, 32.
26. Emeny, interview by Carlson, Aug. 7, 1994. David Bush, a grandson of WHB's cousin Herbert, telephone interview by Paul H. Carlson, Dec. 3, 1994 (notes in possession of author).
27. Emeny, interview by Carlson, Aug. 7, 1994. For a general description of homes in the Bush neighborhood, see Shackleton, *Book of Chicago*, 328–31.
28. WHB to Mrs. James Bush, Dec. 19, 1893; WHB to J. McCulloch, Willow Springs, Ill., June 12, 1894; both in BL.

29. WHB to Mary E. Weber, Brookline, Mass., Dec. 10, 1894; Feb. 14, 1895; Mar. 22, 1895; and Apr. 16, 1895; all in BL.
30. WHB to Mr. Hurlbut, Brownwood, Tex., Nov. 26, 1894, in BL.
31. WHB to H. R. Morrow, Amarillo, Jan. 8, 1894; and WHB to M. B. Sylvester, Martinsburg, N.Y., Jan. 17, 1895; both in BL.
32. WHB to Mrs. James (Emma) Bush, Nov. 26, 1894, in BL.
33. Ibid.; Hamner, *Short Grass and Longhorns*, 215.
34. WHB to J. F. Glidden, Nov. 26, 1894, and WHB to Seth Miller, Dallas, Jan. 17, 1895, both in BL; Key, *In the Cattle Country*, 203–204.
35. WHB to C. B. Bush, Dec. 28, 1894, in BL.
36. "William Henry Bush," in Department of Development, Records, Art Institute of Chicago. WHB to Emma C. Bush (his sister), Jan. 22, 1895, in BL.
37. WHB to W. B. Thom, Apr. 1, 1895; WHB to H. B. Sanborn, Apr. 8, 1895; both in BL.
38. WHB to Thom, Mar. 16 and 21, 1895; WHB to Mary Weber, Apr. 16, 1895; WHB to Charles B. Bush, July 31, 1895; WHB to Mary K. Bush, Paris, France, Aug. 28, 1895; all in BL.
39. WHB to Mary K. Bush, Aug. 28, 1895, in BL.
40. Ibid.
41. WHB to Sanborn, Mar. 2, 1895; WHB to Thom, Mar. 16, 1895; both in BL.
42. WHB to Mary Weber, Mar. 22, 1895, in BL.
43. WHB to O. D. Wetherall, Apr. 11, 1895, in BL.
44. WHB to Sen. D. D. Hunt, Springfield, Ill., Jan. 12 and 17, 1894; both in BL.
45. WHB to Clinton Rosette, Springfield, Ill., Apr. 22, 1895; WHB to Isaac L. Ellwood, May 9, 1895; WHB to Ed Williams, Port Lydon, N.Y., Aug. 7, 1895; WHB to C. P. Treat, Aug. 27, 1895; all in BL.
46. WHB to John Peter Altgeld, Governor of Illinois, Mar. 19, 1894, in BL.
47. WHB to C. B. Bush, Aug. 7, 1895, in BL.
48. Ibid. David Bush, telephone interview by Carlson, Dec. 3, 1994.
49. WHB to Holland and Wills, Amarillo, Jan. 25, 1894, in BL.
50. WHB to Beverley, Dec. 11, 1894; WHB to Sanborn, Dec. 12, 1894; both in BL.
51. WHB to Charles N. Whitman, Denver, Colo., Apr. 16, Apr. 22, and May 1, 1895; WHB to Isaac L. Ellwood, May 9 and Aug. 27, 1895; all in BL.
52. WHB to Warren Wetzel, May 1, 1895; WHB to Whitman, May 1, 1895; WHB to Beverley, Feb. 22, Apr. 12, and May 2, 1895; all in BL.

53. WHB to Isaac L. Ellwood, May 9, 1895; WHB to Sanborn, Aug. 2, 1895; both in BL.
54. Emeny, interview by Carlson, Aug. 7, 1994. WHB to Isaac L. Ellwood, May 9, 1895; WHB to Sanborn, Aug. 2, 1895; both in BL.

CHAPTER SIX

1. See Price and Rathjen, *Golden Spread*, 74; Key, *In the Cattle Country*, 85–89; Fred Post, "A Major Change in Government of City," *ASNG*, Golden Anniv. Ed., Aug. 14, 1938, sec. B, p. 15.
2. Key, *In the Cattle Country*, 89; Kersey, "Going Back to the Wild," sec. 2, p. 1.
3. Cox, *Historical and Biographical Record*, 697; *Amarillo News*, May 4, 1895; Key, *In the Cattle Country*, 103; Price and Rathjen, *Golden Spread*, 74.
4. WHB to Carnes and Dunton (attorneys), Sycamore, Ill., Apr. 8, 1895, in BL; "The New Land Law," *Amarillo News*, May 4, 1895; Kersey, "Going Back to the Wild," sec. 2, pp. 1, 5; Price and Rathjen, *Golden Spread*, 74–75; Key, *In the Cattle Country*, 161–62.
5. Price and Rathjen, *Golden Spread*, 75.
6. WHB to Emma Bush, Nov. 26, 1894; and WHB to J. F. Glidden, Nov. 26, 1894, both in BL; Key, *In the Cattle Country*, 204–206.
7. WHB, deposition in *Sanborn v Bush*, Jan.—Feb. 1905, Potter County District Court No. 47, Case No. 431 (File Box 41) (hereafter, cited as WHB, deposition in *Sanborn v Bush*, 1905); Key, *In the Cattle Country*, 204–205; "Hotel Victor in Battle Over Site of City," *ASNG*, Golden Anniv. Ed., Aug. 14, 1938, sec. G–3, p. 21.
8. *Amarillo Northwest*, Feb. 21, 1891; "Hotel Victor in Battle Over Site of City," sec. G–3, p. 21.; quoted in Key, *In the Cattle Country*, 71, 78; Cummins, *Report on the Llano Estacado*, 149.
9. *Amarillo Weekly News*, May 6, 1898.
10. *Evening News* (Amarillo), June 23, 1899; "Angel of Mercy," *ASNG*, Golden Anniv. Ed., Aug. 14, 1938, sec. G–3, p. 6; Price and Rathjen, *Golden Spread*, 78.
11. Emeny, interview by Carlson, Aug. 7, 1994; *Amarillo Weekly News*, Aug. 26, 1899.
12. *Amarillo Weekly News*, Aug. 26, 1899; *Evening News* (Amarillo), Aug. 21, 1899.
13. "Angel of Mercy," sec. G–3, p. 6; Herbert Timmons and Carolyn Timmons, "Plains Catholics,"*ASNG*, Golden Anniv. Ed., Aug. 14, 1938,

sec. G–3, p. 2; Price and Rathjen, *Golden Spread*, 78; Key, *In the Cattle Country*, 174.

14. "Hotel Amarillo"; "Amarillo Goes on Booming," *Amarillo Daily News*, Aug. 13, 1929; "Hotel Victor in Battle Over Site of City," sec. G–3, p. 21; Key, *In the Cattle Country*, 171, 205, 208; WHB, deposition in *Sanborn v Bush*, 1905.
15. Key, *In the Cattle Country*, 171.
16. "Hotel Amarillo"; Key, *In the Cattle Country*, 171; Price and Rathjen, *Golden Spread*, 76.
17. WHB, deposition in *Sanborn v Bush*, 1905.
18. Price and Rathjen, *Golden Spread*, 74; Key, *In the Cattle Country*, 203.
19. WHB, deposition in *Sanborn v Bush*, 1905.
20. Ibid.
21. See *Sanborn v Bush*, 91 S. W. 883 (C. A. of Tex. 1906).
22. Ibid.; Paddock, *Twentieth-Century History*, 306.
23. See Sanborn to WHB, May 25, Aug. 6, Aug. 11, and Aug. 30, 1903, all in Henry B. Sanborn Collection, Archives, Panhandle-Plains Historical Museum, Canyon.
24. Key, *In the Cattle Country*, 230–31; Stanley Marsh 3, "Bush Memorial Collection," 299–300.
25. "W. H. Bush, Known as Benefactor of City, Succumbs in Chicago," *Amarillo Daily News*, Apr. 10, 1931. See also "Here You Are, More Good News," *Evening News* (Amarillo), June 11, 1901.
26. *ASNG*, Golden Anniv. Ed., Aug. 14, 1938, sec. B, p. 14. U.S. Interstate Commerce Commission, *Decisions of the Interstate Commerce Commission of the United States*, vol. 24: Valuation Reports, Jan.—Mar., 1929 (Washington, D.C.: U.S. Government Printing Office, 1929), 1066–67.
27. "W. H. Bush, Known as Benefactor of City," *Amarillo Daily News*, Apr. 10, 1931; Price and Rathjen, *Golden Spread*, 75.
28. "Bush Thinks Amarillo Outlook is Promising," *Amarillo Daily News*, Jan. 25, 1913.
29. Key, *In the Cattle Country*, 174–75.
30. See Sanborn's petition to Judge Ira Webster, July 27, 1904, in *Sanborn v Bush*, Jan.—Feb. 1905, Potter County District Court No. 47, Case No. 431 (File Box 41).
31. Key, *In the Cattle Country*, 204.
32. *Sanborn v Bush*, Jan.—Feb. 1905, Potter County District Court No. 47, Case No. 431 (File Box 41).
33. Ibid. *Sanborn v Bush*, 1906; Key, *In the Cattle Country*, 209.
34. Key, *In the Cattle Country*, 210; Kersey, "Going Back to the Wild and Woolly Days," sec. 2, p. 1.

35. First quotation from "$100,000 for Amarillo," *ASNG*, Golden Anniv. Ed., Aug. 14, 1938, sec. B, p. 14; second quotation from "Mrs. Emma A. Bush, Mother of Prominent Amarilloan, Is Dead," *Amarillo Daily News*, Jan. 25, 1913; Price and Rathjen, *Golden Spread*, 76.
36. Key, *In the Cattle Country*, 175.
37. "Mrs. Emma A. Bush," *ASNG*, Nov. 24, 1935.
38. Price and Rathjen, *Golden Spread*, 63.
39. See newspaper clippings and greeting card in Historical Files, WHB Library.
40. "Bush, William Henry," *National Cyclopaedia of American Biography* (1927) B:424; Emeny, interview by Carlson, Aug. 7, 1994.
41. "Glidden, Joseph Farwell," *Dictionary of American Biography* (1931) 7:331.
42. Edwin S. Bush to WHB, Oct. 16, 1906, in William H. Bush Collection, Archives, Panhandle-Plains Historical Museum, Canyon, Tex.; "Bush, William Henry," *National Cyclopaedia of American Biography* (1927), B:424.
43. Emeny, interview by Carlson, Aug. 7, 1994; William Henry Bush file, Archives, Chicago Historical Society, Chicago.
44. Emeny, interview by Carlson, Aug. 7, 1994.
45. Ibid.; newspaper clipping, Oct. 22, 1909, in Historical Files, WHB Library; J. Seymour Currey, *Chicago: Its History and Its Builders, A Century of Marvelous Growth* (Chicago: A. J. Clarke, 1912), 3:299–300.
46. Currey, *Chicago: Its History*, 3:300.
47. Emeny, interview by Carlson, Aug. 7, 1994; WHB to E. J. McKenzie, Detroit, Apr. 2, 1894, in BL. For WHB's complaints about telephone service, see WHB to A. W. Fiske, DeKalb, Ill., Feb. 23, 1895, in BL.
48. Bush family Christmas card, 1912, in Historical Files, WHB Library.
49. Marquis, *Book of Chicagoans*, n.p.
50. Norman L. Cram, "The Caxton Club of Chicago: Three Generations of Bibliophiles," *Book Club of California Quarterly News-Letter* 21, no. 2 (Spring, 1953): 35–45; Edward T. Hill, "The Cliff Dwellers of Chicago," (Master's thesis, De Paul Univ., 1953), 7–11; Marquis, *Book of Chicagoans*, n.p.
51. Hill, "Cliff Dwellers of Chicago," 7–11; Shackleton, *Book of Chicago*, 111; Farr, *Chicago: A Personal History*, 324; Lewis and Smith, *Chicago*, 327; Marquis, *Book of Chicagoans*, n.p.

CHAPTER SEVEN

1. Price and Rathjen, *Golden Spread*, 62–63.
2. L. F. Sheffy, "The Experimental Stage of Settlement in the Panhandle of Texas," *Panhandle-Plains Historical Review* 3 (1930): 87.

3. Key, *In the Cattle Country*, 74. See also Ralph Smith, "West Texas Bone Business," *West Texas Historical Association Year Book* 55 (1979): 111–34; *Tascosa (Tex.) Pioneer*, Oct. 18, 1886; McClure, "History of Randall County," 112–13; "Some Memories of W. S. Mabry," *Panhandle-Plains Historical Review* 11 (1938): 39–40.
4. See Donald Abbe, Paul H. Carlson, and David J. Murrah, *Lubbock and the South Plains: An Illustrated History* (Chatsworth, Calif.: Windsor Publications, 1989), 34–35; "The New Land Law," *Amarillo News*, May 4, 1895.
5. Sheffy, "Experimental Stage of Settlement," 89; Price and Rathjen, *Golden Spread*, 62.
6. WHB to W. F. McGowan, Apr. 1, 1895, in BL.
7. Ibid.
8. WHB to J. W. Wills, Feb. 23, 1895, in BL.
9. Ibid.
10. Key, *In the Cattle Country*, 146, 179.
11. Price and Rathjen, *Golden Spread*, 64; Garry L. Nall, "Panhandle Farming in the 'Golden Era' of American Agriculture," *Panhandle-Plains Historical Review* 46 (1973): 69–75.
12. Price and Rathjen, *Golden Spread*, 63.
13. Emeny, interview by Carlson, Aug. 7, 1994.
14. *Amarillo News*, May 4, 1895; *Amarillo Weekly News*, May 6, 1898; Marvin A. Patrick, "A Survey of Land Colonization Companies in Texas," (Master's thesis, Univ. of Texas at Austin, 1925), 37–39; David B. Gracy II, "A Preliminary Survey of Land Colonization in the Panhandle-Plains of Texas," *Museum Journal* 11 (1969): 56–58; Sheffy, "Experimental Stage of Settlement," 80–81, 88–89, 93–94, 102.
15. First quotation from *Tascosa (Tex.) Pioneer*, Nov. 10, 1888; second quotation cited in Sheffy, "Experimental Stage of Settlement," 92.
16. Nall, "Panhandle Farming," 85; *Amarillo News*, Feb. 2, 1895.
17. Nall, "Panhandle Farming," 85; "Syndicate to Buy Land Near Hereford," *Amarillo Daily News*, May 14, 1912.
18. See, e.g., Donald Worster, *Under Western Skies: Nature and History in the American West* (New York: Oxford Univ. Press, 1992), 98–99.
19. First quotation is from Garry L. Nall, "Specialization and Expansion: Panhandle Farming in the 1920s," *Panhandle-Plains Historical Review* 47 (1974): 47; second quotation is from Worster, *Under Western Skies*, 99. See also "Wheat Acreage Shows Increase," *Amarillo Daily News*, Dec. 1, 1914.
20. Quotation in "Wheat Acreage Shows Increase," *Amarillo Daily News*,

Dec. 1, 1914. See also "Bush Likes Dairy Cows," *Amarillo Daily News*, Sept. 29, 1914; *Amarillo Daily News*, Apr. 29 and Oct. 17, 1919.

21. Nall, "Specialization and Expansion," 47, 56–57; Sheffy, "Experimental Stage of Settlement," p. 92, n. 25. According to F. A. Swenson, chief clerk of the Santa Fe railway, with headquarters in Amarillo, the Panhandle in 1919 held "at least 1,250,000 acres of wheat." See W. W. Wright, "The Panhandle of Texas," *Amarillo Daily News*, May 9, 1919.
22. Bush Family Scrapbook and Album, n.p., in possession of William S. Bush, Jr., Houston, Tex. See also Nall, "Specialization and Expansion," 57; "A Prosperous County," *Amarillo Daily News*, Apr. 29, 1919.
23. "Bush Thinks Amarillo Outlook Is Promising," *Amarillo Daily News*, Jan. 25, 1913.
24. Key, *In the Cattle Country*, 164.
25. "Bush Thinks Amarillo Outlook is Promising," *Amarillo Daily News*, Jan. 25, 1913.
26. "Present Institution Formed Six Years Ago," *Amarillo Daily News*, Sept. 8, 1929.
27. "Bush Likes Dairy Farming," *Amarillo Daily News*, Sept. 29, 1914. See also "Incidents in the Life of a Pioneer Merchant," *ASNG*, Golden Anniv. Ed., Aug. 14, 1938, sec. B, p. 30.
28. "Bush Likes Dairy Farming," *Amarillo Daily News*, Sept. 29, 1914.
29. "Present Institution Formed Six Years Ago," *Amarillo Daily News*, Sept. 8, 1929.
30. Emeny, interview by Carlson, Aug. 7, 1994.
31. "W. H. Bush, Known as Benefactor of City," *Amarillo Daily News*, Apr. 10, 1931.
32. Emeny, interview by Carlson, Aug. 7, 1994.
33. Ibid.
34. Cited in Flenniken, "Barbed Wire," 19.
35. Emeny, interview by Carlson, Aug. 7, 1994; "Railroad Administration Will Take Steps to Move Enormous Wheat Crop," *Amarillo Daily News*, Jan. 28, 1913, and Oct. 21, 1924.
36. Emeny, interview by Carlson, Aug. 7, 1994.
37. Key, *In the Cattle Country*, 296.
38. Cited in Flenniken, "Barbed Wire," 19. See also Key, *In the Cattle Country*, 295.
39. "Bush Likes Dairy Farming," *Amarillo Daily News*, Sept. 29, 1914.
40. "William Bush Is Here on Short Visit," *Amarillo Daily News*, Feb. 18, 1919.
41. Emeny, interview by Carlson, Aug. 7, 1994; "By Their Brands Ye Shall Know Them," sec. E, p. 41; Flenniken, "Barbed Wire," 23.
42. Roger Williams, Jr. (grandson of Edwin Bush), telephone interview

by Paul H. Carlson, Jan. 19, 1995 (notes in possession of author); "Bush, William Henry," *National Cyclopaedia of American Biography* (1927), B:424.

43. Paul M. Angle, *The Chicago Historical Society, 1856–1956: An Unconventional Chronicle* (New York: Rand McNally, 1956), 178–80; Shackleton, *Book of Chicago*, 126.
44. Emeny, interview by Carlson, Aug. 7, 1994.
45. Ibid.
46. Ibid.
47. Ibid.; Roger Williams, Jr., telephone interview by Carlson, Jan. 19, 1994; "William Henry Bush," Department of Development, Records, Art Institute of Chicago.
48. "William Henry Bush," and WHB to Art Institute of Chicago, Jan. 6, 1925, both in Department of Development, Records, Art Institute of Chicago.
49. Emeny, interview by Carlson, Aug. 7, 1994; Roger Williams, Jr., telephone interview by Carlson, Jan. 19, 1995. WHB to M. Anstice Harris, Elmira, N.Y., Mar. 5, 1924; and Dora W. Stiles, Martinsburg, N.Y., to Martha F. Wells, July 13, 1950; both in Historical Files, WHB Library. "Bush, William Henry," mimeographed clipping, 1925, in Historical Files, BET.
50. Emeny, interview by Carlson, Aug. 7, 1994. Martha F. Wells to Mrs. Pitcher, Oct. 11, 1940; Stiles to Wells, July 13, 1950; and WHB to Harris, Apr. 25, 1924; all in Historical Files, WHB Library. "Bush, William Henry," mimeographed clipping, 1925, in Historical Files, BET.
51. Book clipping, n.d., in William H. Bush Collection, Archives, Panhandle-Plains Historical Museum, Canyon, Tex. "Bush, William Henry," *National Cyclopaedia of American Biography* (1927), B:424. "Bush, William Henry," mimeographed clipping, 1925, in Historical Files, BET.
52. Emeny, interview by Carlson, Aug. 7, 1994.
53. Emeny, telephone interview by Carlson, Jan. 20, 1995.
54. Book clipping, n.d., in William H. Bush Collection, Archives, Panhandle-Plains Historical Museum, Canyon, Tex. Emeny, interview by Carlson, Aug. 7, 1994. Bush family photographs, in Historical Files, WHB Library. "The First and Present Library and Founder," typescript in Historical Files, William H. Bush Trust Properties, Amarillo.
55. Bush family photographs, in Historical Files, WHB Library.

CHAPTER EIGHT

1. W. W. Wright, "The Panhandle of Texas," *Amarillo Daily News*, May 9, 1919; Price and Rathjen, *Golden Spread*, 87; N. D. Bartlett, "Discovery of the Panhandle Oil and Gas Fields," *Panhandle-Plains Historical Review* 12 (1939): 48–54; "Helium Highlights Amarillo in International Picture," *ASNG*, Golden Anniv. Ed., Aug. 14, 1938, sec. G–3, p. 1.
2. "William Henry Bush Here on Short Visit," *Amarillo Daily News*, Feb. 18, 1919; WHB to R. S. Rule, Amarillo, Aug. 24, 1914, in Henry B. Sanborn Collection, Archives, Panhandle-Plains Historical Museum, Canyon, Tex.
3. Bush Family Scrapbook and Photograph Album.
4. Ibid.
5. Emeny, interview by Carlson, Aug. 7, 1994.
6. Ibid.
7. Ibid.; Emeline Bush, Diary, 1921, in BOBC.
8. "Bush Tells of Bad Conditions through Europe," *Amarillo Daily News*, Nov. 2, 1921.
9. Price and Rathjen, *Golden Spread*, 87; Key, *In the Cattle Country*, 263.
10. Price and Rathjen, *Golden Spread*, 87.
11. "New Helium Field in Amarillo Shifts Scene of U.S. Operations," *Amarillo Daily News*, Aug. 28, 1928, and "Purchase of Helium Tract Made Public," *Amarillo Daily News*, July 17, 1929. Key, *In the Cattle Country*, 258.
12. "Bush Tells of Bad Conditions through Europe," *Amarillo Daily News*, Nov. 2, 1921.
13. Ibid.
14. Price and Rathjen, *Golden Spread*, 89; Key, *In the Cattle Country*, 259–60.
15. "Scotland to High Plains," *ASNG*, Golden Anniv. Ed., Aug. 14, 1938, sec. 2, p. 22. Emeny, interview by Carlson, Aug. 7, 1994.
16. Dawn Manzer, "Library Is Started in 1807," *Journal and Republican* (Lowville, N.Y.), May 20, 1987.
17. Ibid. See also WHB to Alice Whitaker and M. A. Harris, Martinsburg, N.Y., Feb. 25, 1924, in Historical Files, WHB Library.
18. WHB to Whitaker and Harris, Feb. 25, 1924; WHB to Harris, Feb. 29, 1924; both in Historical Files, WHB Library. Manzer, "Library Is Started," *Journal and Republican* (Lowville, N.Y.), May 20, 1987.
19. WHB to Harris, Apr. 14, 1924; WHB to George S. Reed, Lowville, N.Y., Apr. 22, 1924; WHB to Harris, Apr. 25, 1924; Reed to Harris, Apr. 25, 1924; WHB to Board of Trustees, Martinsburg Public Li-

brary, Mar. 3, 1925; WHB to Harris, Sept. 30, 1925; all in Historical Files, WHB Library. "Many Present at Library Opening," *Journal and Republican* (Lowville, N.Y.), Sept. 3, 1925, and May 20, 1987.

20. WHB to Harris, Apr. 14, 1924, and Mar. 26, 1925; WHB to Reed, Apr. 22, 1924; all in Historical Files, WHB Library. Manzer, "Many Present at Library Opening," *Journal and Republican* (Lowville, N.Y.), Sept. 3, 1925; "Martinsburg Dream Comes True," *Journal and Republican*, Aug. 6, 1980; and Manzer, "Library Is Started in 1807," May 20, 1987.
21. Manzer, "Library Named for Benefactor," *Journal and Republican*, (Lowville, N.Y.), May 27, 1987. M. Anstice Harris to Martinsburg, N.Y., n.d., in Historical Files, WHB Library. "William H. Bush, James Bush," newspaper clipping, n.d. (from *Journal and Republican*), in Historical Files, WHB Library.
22. WHB to Harris, June 8, 1925, and Sept. 30, 1925, both in Historical Files, WHB Library.
23. Emeny, interview by Carlson, Aug. 7, 1994. "Bush, William Henry," *National Cyclopaedia of American Biography* (1927), B:424.
24. Farr, *Chicago: A Personal History*, 344, 367. Emeny, interview by Carlson, Aug. 7, 1994. "Bush, William Henry," *National Cyclopaedia of American Biography* (1927), B:424.
25. "William Henry Bush," Department of Development, Records, Art Institute of Chicago.
26. Emeny, interview by Carlson, Aug. 7, 1994.
27. "Jim Bush Ready to Give Water Rights if City Keeps Pledge," *ASNG*, June 25, 1926.
28. Ibid.
29. "First Water at Word Site Soft as That Taken From Bush Wells," *Amarillo Daily News*, Oct. 23, 1929.
30. Roy Roddy, "Texas Helium for War or Peace," *Texas Digest*, June 28, 1941, pp. 12–13; "New Helium Field in Amarillo Shifts Scene of U.S. Operations," *Amarillo Daily News*, Aug. 28, 1928; Andrew Stewart, "About Helium," U.S. Bureau of Mines, mimeographed report (I.C. 6745), 1923, pp. 31–32. See also C. W. Seibel, "The Development of Helium Production as Now Carried on at Amarillo, Texas, by the U.S. Bureau of Mines, Department of the Interior," *Panhandle-Plains Historical Review* 9 (1936): 43–51; and C. C. Anderson, "Helium from a Scientific Curiosity to Large Scale Production," *Panhandle-Plains Historical Review* 12 (1939): 24–47.
31. Stewart, "About Helium," 31; "Purchase of Helium Tract Made Public," *Amarillo Daily News*, July 17, 1929.
32. Stewart, "About Helium," 31; "Helium Plant Proposals Are To Be

Gone Into," *Amarillo Daily News*, Aug. 29, 1927; "Purchase of Helium Tract Made Public," *Amarillo Daily News*, July 17, 1929; "Helium Plant," *ASNG*, Feb. 17, 1929.

33. Stewart, "About Helium," 31; C. W. Seibel, "The Government's New Helium Plant at Amarillo, Texas," *Chemical and Metallurgical Engineering* 37 (Sept. 1930): 550–52.
34. First quotation from U.S. Department of the Interior, Bureau of Mines, "Helium Capitol of the World—Amarillo," in Hammond, *Amarillo*, 157–59; second quotation in Roddy, "Texas Helium for War or Peace," 12; third quotation in Stewart, "About Helium," 31.
35. Emeny, interview by Carlson, Aug. 7, 1994.
36. Ibid.; WHB to Harris, Sept. 30, 1925, in Historical Files, WHB Library.
37. Newspaper clipping, in Historical Files, WHB Library. Book clipping, in William H. Bush Collection, Panhandle-Plains Historical Museum, Canyon, Tex.
38. Emeny, interview by Carlson, Aug. 7, 1994; Nall, "Specialization and Expansion," 67; "Rep. White of Borger Shows How Panhandle Farms Bring Fortune," *Amarillo Daily News*, Aug. 2, 1929; "Wonder District Men Back From Showing Exhibit at Alva," *Amarillo Daily News*, Oct. 17, 1929; Price and Rathjen, *Golden Spread*, 90, 93, 97.
39. Emeny, interview by Carlson, Aug. 7, 1994; "Pioneered in Panhandle of Texas in 1881," *Amarillo Globe*, Apr. 9, 1931; "W. H. Bush, Known as Benefactor of City," *Amarillo Daily News*, Apr. 10, 1931; Wells to Pitcher, Oct. 11, 1940, in Historical Files, WHB Library.
40. "Bush Tells of Bad Conditions through Europe," *Amarillo Daily News*, Nov. 2, 1921.
41. "W. H. Bush, Known as Benefactor of City," *Amarillo Daily News*, Apr. 10, 1931.
42. Book clipping, n.d., in William H. Bush Collection, Archives, Panhandle-Plains Historical Museum, Canyon, Tex.
43. "W. H. Bush, Known as Benefactor of City," *Amarillo Daily News*, Apr. 10, 1931.
44. Ibid.

EPILOGUE

1. "W. H. Bush, Known as Benefactor of City," *Amarillo Daily News*, Apr. 10, 1931.
2. WHB, Last Will and Testament, Nov. 8, 1930, photocopy in Historical Files, BET.
3. "Martinsburg Dream Comes True," *Journal and Republican* (Lowville,

N.Y.), Aug. 6, 1980; Dawn Manzer, "New Library is Constructed," *Journal and Republican*, June 10; Manzer, "New Library Dedicated," *Journal and Republican*, June 17, 1987.

4. William Henry Bush File, Archives, Chicago Historical Society. Emeny, interview by Carlson, Aug. 7, 1994. "William Henry Bush," Department of Development, Records, Art Institute of Chicago.
5. William Neal Howard, comp., *Bibliography of the Bush/FitzSimon/-McCarty Southwest Collection*, ed. Mary Kay Holmes Snell (Amarillo: Amarillo Public Library, 1974), i. See also Stanley Marsh 3, "Bush Memorial Collection," 299–300; "History of Plains Recorded in Bush Collection's Books," *Amarillo Globe-Times*, Mar. 11, 1969; "History Is Traced in Bush Collection," *Amarillo Globe-Times*, Jan. 11, 1971.
6. "Notes," BOBC; "William Henry Bush," Department of Development, Records, Art Institute of Chicago.
7. Flenniken, "Barbed Wire," 19–20; Emeny, interview by Carlson, Aug. 7, 1994.
8. Flenniken, "Barbed Wire," 23.

Bibliography

A. MANUSCRIPT MATERIALS

Bush Family Scrapbook and Photograph Album. In possession of William S. Bush, Jr., Houston.

Bush-O'Brien Collection. Archives. Panhandle-Plains Historical Museum, Canyon, Tex.

Bush, William H. Collection. Amarillo Public Library, Amarillo, Tex. Includes Bush Letters.

———. Collection. Archives. Panhandle-Plains Historical Museum, Canyon, Tex.

———. Historical Files. William H. Bush Trust Properties, Amarillo, Tex.

———. Reference File. Chicago Historical Society, Chicago.

Department of Development. Records. Art Institute of Chicago, Chicago.

Ellwood, Isaac L. Estate Papers. Southwest Collection. Texas Tech University, Lubbock.

Frying Pan Ranch. Reference File. Southwest Collection. Texas Tech University, Lubbock.

Historical Files. Bush-Emeny Trust, Amarillo, Tex.

Historical Files. William H. Bush Memorial Library, Martinsburg, N.Y.

Interview Files. Archives. Panhandle-Plains Historical Museum, Canyon, Tex.

McCarty, John L. Collection. Amarillo Public Library, Amarillo, Tex.

Marsh, Wendy Bush O'Brien, and Stanley Marsh 3. Records. Toad Hall, Amarillo, Tex.

Sanborn, Henry B. Collection. Archives. Panhandle-Plains Historical Museum, Canyon, Tex.

Sanborn v. Bush (February 1905). Potter County District Court No. 47. Case No. 431 (File Box 41). County Courthouse, Amarillo, Tex.

Southwestern Sheep and Goat Raisers' Association. Morgue Files, Records. Southwest Collection. Texas Tech University, Lubbock.

Vandale, Earl. Collection. Center for American History. University of Texas, Austin.

B. INTERVIEWS

Bivins, Mrs. Albert, and Cora Green. Interview by Mrs. L. E. Moyer, accompanied by C. Boone McClure. January 20, 1958. Transcript in Wendy Bush O'Brien Marsh and Stanley Marsh 3, Records, Toad Hall, Amarillo.

Bush, David. A grandson of W. H. Bush's cousin Herbert. Telephone interview by Paul H. Carlson. December 3, 1994. Notes in possession of author.

Emeny, Caroline Bush. Interview by Paul H. Carlson. August 7, 1994. Transcript in Southwest Collection, Texas Tech University, Lubbock.

Emeny, Caroline Bush. Telephone interview by Paul H. Carlson. June 29, 1994. Notes in possession of author.

Kerst, Barbara; Anne Bush; and Roger Williams, Jr. Interview by Paul H. Carlson. August 5, 1994. Notes in possession of author.

Ortlieb, Herm. Manager of Whitaker Park. Interview by Paul H. Carlson. October 13, 1994. Notes in possession of author.

Williams, Roger, Jr. Grandson of Edwin Bush. Telephone interview by Paul H. Carlson. January 19, 1995. Notes in possession of author.

C. NEWSPAPERS

Amarillo Champion. 1887–88, 1892.

Amarillo Daily News. 1912–35.

Amarillo Globe. 1931.

Amarillo Globe-Times. 1969, 1971.

Amarillo News. 1895.

Amarillo Sunday News and Globe. 1935–38.

Amarillo Weekly News. 1898–1900.

Chicago Tribune. 1931.

Fort Worth Gazette. 1885.

Evening News (Amarillo). 1899–1901.

Journal and Republican (Lowville, N.Y.). 1924–25, 1980, 1987.

Tascosa (Tex.) Pioneer. 1886–88.

D. GOVERNMENT DOCUMENTS

Charter of the City of Amarillo: Commission-Manager Government, Adopted November 13, 1913. Amarillo, Tex.: City of Amarillo, November, 1931.

Cummins, William F. *Report on the Geography, Topography, and Geology of the*

Llano Estacado or Staked Plains. 3rd Annual Report of the Geological Survey of Texas. Austin: State Printing Office, 1891.

Sanborn v Bush 91 S. W. 883 (C. A. of Tex. 1906).

State v Goodnight 11 S. W. 119 (S. C. of Tex. 1888).

Stewart, Andrew. "About Helium." United States Department of the Interior, Bureau of Mines. Mimeographed report (IC 6745), 1933. Copy in John L. McCarty Collection, Amarillo Public Library, Amarillo, Tex.

U.S. Interstate Commerce Commission. *Decisions of the Interstate Commerce Commission of the United States*. Vol. 24: Valuation Reports, Jan.–Mar., 1929. Washington, D.C.: U.S. Government Printing Office, 1929.

Whetstone Gulf State Park. Alexandria Bay, N.Y.: Office of Parks, Recreation and Historic Preservation, State of New York, n.d.

E. THESES AND DISSERTATIONS

Boaz, Sallie Ruth. "A History of Amarillo, Texas." Master's thesis, University of Texas at Austin, 1950.

Dolman, Wilson Elbert. "The Public Lands of Western Texas, 1870–1900: The Conflict of Public and Private Interests." Ph.D. diss., University of Texas at Austin, 1974.

Evans, Samuel Lee. "Texas Agriculture, 1880–1930." Ph.D. diss., University of Texas at Austin, 1960.

Hill, Edward T. "The Cliff Dwellers of Chicago." Master's thesis, De Paul University, Chicago, 1953.

McCarty, John Lawton. "The History of Tascosa, Texas." Master's thesis, West Texas State Teachers College, Canyon, 1945.

McClure, Charles B. "A History of Randall County and the T-Anchor Ranch." Master's thesis, University of Texas at Austin, 1930.

McFadden, Joseph M. "From Invention to Monopoly: The History of the Consolidation of the Barbed Wire Industry, 1873–1899." Ph.D. diss., Northern Illinois University, DeKalb, 1968.

Patrick, Marvin A. "A Survey of Colonization Companies in Texas." Master's thesis, University of Texas at Austin, 1925.

Phillips, Francis. "The Development of Agriculture in the Panhandle-Plains Region of Texas to 1920." Master's thesis, West Texas State Teachers College, Canyon, 1946.

Pope, Billy N. "The Freighter and Railroader in the Economic Pattern of Panhandle History." Master's thesis, West Texas State Teachers College, Canyon, 1956.

Shearer, Ernest C. "The History of Potter County, Texas." Master's thesis, University of Colorado, Boulder, 1933.

BOOKS

Abbe, Donald; Paul H. Carlson; and David J. Murrah. *Lubbock and the South Plains: An Illustrated History*. Chatsworth, Calif.: Windsor Publications, 1989.

Adams, William. *Business Directory of Lewis County, N.Y. With Map. 1895–1896*. Lowville, N.Y.: William Adams, n.d.

Angle, Paul M. *The Chicago Historical Society, 1856–1956: An Unconventional Chronicle*. New York: Rand McNally, 1956.

Banks, Charles Edward. *Topographical Dictionary of 2,885 English Emigrants to New England, 1620–1650*. Edited and indexed by Elijah Ellsworth Brownell. Baltimore, Md.: Genealogical Publishing Co., 1981.

Beers, D. G. *Atlas of Lewis Co., New York, from Actual Surveys by and under the Direction of D. G. Beers*. Philadelphia: Pomeroy, Whitman and Co., 1875.

Billington, Ray Allen, and Martin Ridge. *Westward Expansion: A History of the American Frontier*. 5th ed. New York: Macmillan, 1982.

Blodgett, Jan. *Land of Bright Promise: Advertising the Texas Panhandle and South Plains, 1870–1917*. Austin: University of Texas Press, 1988.

Bowen, G. Byron, ed. *History of Lewis County, New York, 1880–1965*. Lowville, N.Y.: Board of Legislators of Lewis County, 1970.

Carlson, Paul H. *Texas Woollybacks: The Range Sheep and Goat Industry*. College Station: Texas A&M University Press, 1982.

Cox, James. *Historical and Biographical Record of the Cattle Industry and the Cattlemen of Texas and Adjacent Territory*. St. Louis, Mo.: Woodward and Tiernan Printing Co., 1895.

Cromie, Paul. *The Great Chicago Fire*. New York: McGraw-Hill, 1958.

Cronon, William. *Nature's Metropolis: Chicago and the Great West*. New York: Norton, 1991. Currey, J. Seymour. *Chicago: Its History and Its Builders, A Century of Marvelous Growth*. 5 vols. Chicago: A. J. Clarke, 1912.

Dedman, Emmett. *A History of the Chicago Club*. Chicago: Chicago Club, 1960.

Douglas, C. L. *Cattle Kings of Texas*. 1939 reprint. Austin: State House Press, 1989.

Farr, Finis. *Chicago: A Personal History of America's Most American City*. New Rochelle, N.Y.: Arlington House, 1973.

Fischer, David Hackett. *Albion's Seed: Four British Folkways in America*. New York: Oxford University Press, 1989.

Gentry, Richard. *The Gentry Family in America, 1876–1909*. New York: Printed for author by Grafton Press, 1909.

Glidden Barb Wire Pocket Compendium. Houston: Sanborn and Warner, 1885.

The Great Chicago Fire. With an introduction and notes by Paul M. Angle. Chicago: Chicago Historical Society, 1971.

Haley, J. Evetts. *Charles Goodnight: Cowman and Plainsman*. Norman: University of Oklahoma Press, 1949.

———. *The XIT Ranch of Texas and the Early Days of the Llano Estacado*. Norman: University of Oklahoma Press, 1929.

Hammond, Clara T., comp. *Amarillo*. Austin: Best Printing Co., 1974.

Hamner, Laura V. *Short Grass and Longhorns*. Norman: University of Oklahoma Press, 1965.

———, ed. *Light 'n Hitch: A Collection of Historical Writing Depicting Life on the High Plains*. Dallas: American Guild Press, 1958.

Hirsch, Susan E., and Robert I. Goler. *A City Comes of Age: Chicago in the 1890s*. Foreword by Sam Bass Warner, Jr. Chicago: Chicago Historical Society, 1990.

Howard, William Neal, comp. *Bibliography of the Bush/FitzSimon/McCarty Southwest Collection*. Edited by Mary Kay Holmes Snell. Amarillo: Amarillo Public Library, 1974.

Hough, Franklin B. *A History of Lewis County, in the State of New York, from the Beginning of Its Settlement to the Present Time*. Albany: Munsell and Rowland, 1860.

———. *History of Lewis County, New York, With Illustrations and Biographical Sketches of Some of Its Prominent Men and Pioneers*. Syracuse, N.Y.: D. Mason and Co., 1883.

Jewell, Frank. *Annotated Bibliography of Chicago History*. Chicago: Chicago Historical Society, 1979.

Johnson, Allen, and Dumas Malone, eds. *Dictionary of American Biography*. 20 vols. New York: Charles Scribner's Sons, 1931.

Johnson, F. W., and Eugene C. Barker. *A History of Texas and Texans*. Chicago: American Historical Society, 1914.

Kelton, Steve. *Renderbrook: A Century Under the Spade Brand*. Fort Worth: Texas Christian University Press, 1989.

Key, Della Tyler. *In the Cattle Country: History of Potter County*. Wichita Falls, Tex.: Nortex, 1966.

Kogan, Herman, and Robert Cromie. *The Great Fire: Chicago, 1871*. New York: G. P. Putnam's Sons, 1971.

Lewis, Lloyd, and Henry Justin Smith. *Chicago: The History of Its Reputation*. New York: Harcourt, Brace, 1929.

Lowe, David, ed. *The Great Chicago Fire*. New York: Dover, 1979.

McCallum, Henry D., and Frances T. McCallum. *The Wire That Fenced the West*. Norman: University of Oklahoma Press, 1965.

McCarty, John L. *Maverick Town: The Story of Old Tascosa*. Norman: University of Oklahoma Press, 1946.

Marquis, Albert Nelson, ed. *The Book of Chicagoans: A Biographical Dictionary of Leading Living Men and Women of the City of Chicago*. Chicago: A. N. Marquis, 1917.

Murrah, David J. *C. C. Slaughter: Rancher, Banker, Baptist*. Austin: University of Texas Press, 1981.

The National Cyclopaedia of American Biography. Annual volumes. New York: James T. White and Co., 1927, 1933.

Overton, Richard C. *Gulf to Rockies: The Heritage of the Fort Worth and Denver—Colorado and Southern Railways, 1861–1989*. Austin: University of Texas Press, 1953.

Paddock, Ed B., ed. *A Twentieth-Century History and Biographical Record of North and West Texas*. 2 vols. New York: Leois Publishing Co., 1906.

Pierce, Bessie Louise. *A History of Chicago*. 3 vols. New York: Knopf, 1957.

Price, B. Byron, and Frederick W. Rathjen. *The Golden Spread: An Illustrated History of Amarillo and the Texas Panhandle*. Northridge, Calif.: Windsor Publications, 1986.

Porter, Millie Jones. *Memory Cups of Panhandle Pioneers*. Clarendon, Tex.: Clarendon Press, 1945.

Rathjen, Frederick W. *The Texas Panhandle Frontier*. Austin: University of Texas Press, 1973.

Shackleton, Robert. *The Book of Chicago*. Philadelphia: Penn Publishing, 1920.

Sheffy, Lester Fields. *The Francklyn Land and Cattle Company: A Panhandle Enterprise, 1882–1957*. Austin: University of Texas Press, 1963.

Spray, Barbara C., comp. *Texas Panhandle Forefathers*. Dallas: National Sharegraphics, 1983.

Stanley, F. *Story of the Texas Panhandle Railroads*. Borger, Tex.: Hess Publishing, 1976.

———. *The Texas Panhandle: From Cattlemen to Feed Lots, 1880–1970*. Borger, Tex.: Jim Hess Printers, 1971.

Texas Almanac and State Industrial Guide, 1990–1991. Dallas: A. H. Belo Corporation, 1989.

Thorp, Howard J. *The Pardner of the Wind*. Caldwell, Idaho: Caxton Printer, 1945.

Warwick, Mrs. Clyde W. *The Randall County Story*. Hereford, Tex.: Pioneer Book Publishers, 1969.

Weaver, Bobby, ed. *Panhandle Petroleum*. Canyon, Tex.: Panhandle-Plains Historical Society, 1982.
Webb, Walter Prescott. *The Great Plains*. Boston: Ginn and Co., 1931.
Williams, Kenny J. *In the City of Men: Another Story of Chicago*. Nashville, Tenn.: Townsend Press, 1974.
Worster, Donald. *Under Western Skies: Nature and History in the American West*. New York: Oxford University Press, 1992.

ARTICLES

Anderson, C. C. "Helium from a Scientific Curiosity to Large Scale Production." *Panhandle-Plains Historical Review* 12 (1939): 24–47.
Archambeau, Ernest R. "The First Federal Census in the Panhandle, 1880." *Panhandle-Plains Historical Review* 23 (1950): 23–103.
Ashburn, Karl Everett. "Tariffs and Wool Duties Since 1867." *Sheep and Goat Raisers' Magazine* 10 (Nov. 1929): 104–106.
Baker, T. Lindsay. "Turbine-Type Windmills of the Great Plains and Midwest." *Agricultural History* 54 (Jan. 1980): 38–51.
———. "Windmills of the Panhandle Plains." *Panhandle-Plains Historical Review* 53 (1980): 71–110.
Bartlett, N. D. "Discovery of the Panhandle Oil and Gas Fields." *Panhandle-Plains Historical Review* 12 (1939): 48–54.
Carlson, Paul H. "Panhandle Pastores: Early Sheepherding in the Texas Panhandle." *Panhandle-Plains Historical Review* 53 (1980): 1–16.
Connor, Seymour V. "Early Land Speculation in West Texas." *Southwestern Social Science Quarterly* 42 (Mar. 1962): 354–62.
———. "Early Ranching Operations in the Panhandle: A Report on the Agricultural Schedules of the 1880 Census." *Panhandle-Plains Historical Review* 27 (1954): 47–69.
Cram, Norman L. "The Caxton Club of Chicago: Three Generations of Bibliophiles." *Book Club of California Quarterly News-Letter* 21, no. 2 (Spring, 1955): 35–45.
Crane, R. C. "The Press in the Development of West Texas." *West Texas Historical Association Year Book* 24 (Oct. 1948): 64–70.
Crudgington, John W. "Old Town Amarillo." *Panhandle-Plains Historical Review* 30 (1957): 79–113.
Dolman, Wilson E., III. "Conflicts Over Land: The Settler and the Rancher in West Texas." *West Texas Historical Association Year Book* 50 (1974): 61–75.
Flenniken, Donna. "Barbed Wire and the Frying Pan Ranch." *Accent West* 19 (Feb. 1991): 18–20, 22–25, 27–29.

Gracy, David B., II. "A Preliminary Survey of Land Colonization in the Panhandle-Plains of Texas." *Museum Journal* 11 (1969): 53–79.

Haley, J. Evetts. "The Grass Lease Fight and Attempted Impeachment of the First Panhandle Judge." *Southwestern Historical Quarterly* 38 (July 1934): 1–27.

Hopping, R. C. "The Ellwoods: Barbed Wire and Ranches." *Museum Journal* 6 (1962): 1–81.

Kinchen, Oscar A. "Pioneers of No Man's Land." *West Texas Historical Association Year Book* 18 (1942): 22–26.

McFadden, Joseph M. "Monopoly in Barbed Wire: The Formation of the American Steel and Wire Company." *Business History Review* 52 (1978): 465–89.

Nall, Garry L. "Panhandle Farming in the 'Golden Era' of American Agriculture." *Panhandle-Plains Historical Review* 46 (1973): 68–93.

———. "Specialization and Expansion: Panhandle Farming in the 1920s." *Panhandle-Plains Historical Review* 47 (1974): 46–67.

"The Panhandle Country and Its Metropolis." *Texas Magazine* 2 (July 1910): 50–55.

Parker, G. A. F. "Incipient Trade and Religion in Amarillo in the Late Eighties." *Panhandle-Plains Historical Review* 2 (1929): 137–44.

Roddy, Roy. "Texas Helium for War or Peace." *Texas Digest*, June 28, 1941, pp. 12–13.

Seibel, C. W. "The Development of Helium Production as Now Carried On at Amarillo, Texas, by the U.S. Bureau of Mines, Department of the Interior." *Panhandle-Plains Historical Review* 9 (1936): 43–51.

———. "The Government's New Helium Plant." *Chemical and Metallurgical Engineering* 37 (Sept. 1930): 550–52.

Sheers, Margaret. "The LX Ranch of Texas." *Panhandle-Plains Historical Review* 6 (1933): 45–57.

Sheffy, L. F. "The Experimental Stage of Settlement in the Panhandle of Texas." *Panhandle-Plains Historical Review* 3 (1930): 78–103.

Smith, Ralph. "West Texas Bone Business." *West Texas Historical Association Year Book* 55 (1979): 111–34.

"Some Memories of W. S. Mabry." *Panhandle-Plains Historical Review* 11 (1938): 31–51.

Storm, J. G. "Wonderful Growth of Amarillo." *Texas Magazine* 4 (Aug. 1911): 68–73.

Willis, Judge Newton P. "Biographical Sketch of Frank Willis, Sr., 1840–1894." *Panhandle-Plains Historical Review* 3 (1930): 18–21.

Zeigler, Robert E. "The Cowboy Strike of 1883: Its Causes and Meaning." *West Texas Historical Association Year Book* 47 (1971): 32–46.

Index